A Father Gone Too Soon

Clifford Ley Herbert Hinton 1921-1957

Judith Anne Atkinson

J Atkinson
May 2024

A Father Gone Too Soon

Clifford Ley Herbert Hinton 1921-1957

Is the first book in the series

Sharing Family History

written and published by

Judith Anne Atkinson

2023.

For my sisters Susan and Deborah

in memory of our parents Dorothy and Clifford

Cover Photo:

Clifford with daughters Susan, Deborah, and Judy

taken in Preston, Ontario

Christmas 1954

Many aspects of the cover photo interest me and prompt my memories: hardwood floors and area rugs; my dad's slippers; his soft Viyella shirt and khaki pants; the well used green hassock he sits on; our organza dresses and MaryJane shoes worn with sensible socks; mom's Santa and reindeer ornaments on the mantel; the bookshelves on either side of the bricked fireplace where dad would often light a wood fire; and on the bottom shelf, the set of the encyclopedias I learned to search for my school assignments. I always felt that my dad considered himself a very lucky man, to have a beautiful wife and such lovely daughters. *See* **Pg 173**

Contents

Foreword:	Author's Introduction	1
British Roots in England and Wales (up to 1921)		3
Emigration to Toronto, Ontario, Canada (1922-25)		19
Growing Up in Oshawa, Ontario (1926-41)		31
World War II Years (1941-45)		71
Returning to Oshawa, Family, Friends, and Family		87
Marriage and Starting a Family (1946-48)		107
General Motors Promotion to North Bay, Ontario (1948-51)		123
Return to Oshawa, Ontario (1951-53)		157
Career Move to Preston, Ontario (1953-57)		169
A Father Gone Too Soon, 27 February 1957		189
Afterword:	Author's Reflections	203
Appendix A	The Memorial Cup Comes to Oshawa 1938-39	201
Appendix B	Cliff's WWII Army Records 1942-1946	225
Appendix C	Original Handwritten Letters	235
Appendix D	House Plan Drawings	277
Appendix E	Ancestry Summary Reports	289

Foreword

This book is a compilation of information about my father's life that I have discovered from family photos, letters, and personal memories. My efforts to place the photos in chronological order for this book required extensive searching of sources to verify information about the photos. Many of these sources such as birth, marriage, death, and census records as well as city directories, voters lists, passenger lists, war records, news clippings and maps are included within the text where I have also included websites, QR codes and my own personal reflections.

Through genealogy and even some DNA sleuthing I learned about my father Clifford, his parents' backgrounds, his early life in Wales and his emigration to Canada. I also discovered more about his years growing up in Oshawa, Ontario, Canada, his budding hockey career, his overseas service in the Royal Canadian Ordnance Corps (RCOC) during WWII, and his employment in the automotive industry. Most of all I enjoyed learning more about how he met my mother Dorothy and their early married years raising my sisters Susan, Deborah, and me.

It has been a joy to create this book in honour of my father. The process has afforded me the opportunity to learn more about the details of his life as well as delighted me in both reminiscence and discovery. I would like to thank those family and friends who provided encouragement and I give special thanks to my cousin Libby, and my sisters Sue and Deb for sharing treasured family photos. I also give special credit to son Matt who advised me with his technical know-how about writing and publishing, and to daughters Beth and Kate who showed great interest and appreciation. Finally, I especially want to thank my husband Joe who was always nearby during the many months of writing this book. He was there at Court of Palms, during our winter in Florida, to witness my excitement at new discoveries. Then, during the spring and summer months at our Uxbridge home, he gave me the space and time to write, as well as proofreading and coaching support during the editing process. Without Joe's encouragement, I could not have written **A Father Gone Too Soon**.

I hope you will enjoy reading this book and appreciate the detective work involved in creating a comprehensive history of my father's life. The people, places, dates, and details of activities were carefully confirmed and documented by the associated records and organized to tell the life story of **Clifford Ley Herbert Hinton**.

British Roots in England and Wales Up to 1922

Mother: Phyllis Hoad (1887-1974) — 5

Father: Herbert Hugh Melville Hinton (1891-1939) — 10

Parents' Marriage 28 April 1917 — 12

Family Move to Clydach, Wales 1919 — 13

Birth of Clifford Ley Herbert Hinton (1921-1957) — 15

Author's note: Thanks to my cousin Libby Clarke for sharing many of the early family photos and documents included in this book.

Clifford's Mother: Phyllis (Davies) Hoad 1887-1974

Phyllis Hoad, the eldest child of Martha Davies (1860-1950) and Walter John Hoad (1869-1896), was born 13 March 1887 at Pembroke Wales. She was registered with her mother's maiden surname.

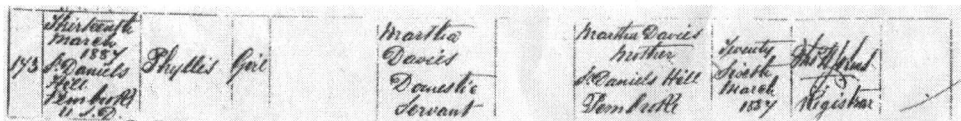

Her parents were married 5 months later, 3 September, at East Molesey Surrey England.

Phyllis soon had 2 brothers, Walter born in 1888, then Fred in 1889, and 2 sisters, Grace born in 1892, then Dorothy who was born in 1894 and died at 18 months. Phyllis's father Walter John Hoad also died in 1896. At age 36 her mother Martha was a widow with 4 children to support.

This photo was taken during their 1896 mourning period at their home in East Molesey Surrey England: Walter 8, Phyllis 9, Martha 36, Fred 7, and Grace 4.

Martha Davies 1860-1950

Martha Davies was the youngest child born at Pembroke Wales to parents John Davies (1815-1910) and Elizabeth Davies (1832-1891). She had 2 older brothers, John, and Frederick. By the 1881 census Martha was working as a domestic cook in Pembroke and by 1887 she gave birth to Phyllis the first of 5 children with her husband Walter John Hoad (in photo at right). She lived a long life to age 90.

Walter John Hoad 1869-1896

John Hoad was the 5th of 9 children born at Surrey England to parents Daniel Hoad (1840-1902) and Mary Ann Whittington (1842-1918). He began work in 1885 as a groom and somehow met Martha Davies age 25 with whom he conceived Phyllis Hoad in 1886 when he was age 17. They married in 1887 and after having 4 more children with Martha, he died in 1896, at age 26, of pulmonary tuberculosis.

1897: The year after her father died, Phyllis went to live in Pembroke Wales with the family of her Uncle John Davies Jr and her widowed grandfather John Davies Sr. The 1901 Census seen above, listed Phyllis at age 14 using her birth surname "Davies".

Meanwhile, Phyllis's siblings Walter 10, Fred 9 and Grace 6 were sent to rural Cowley Fields Residential School in Oxford County, England. They are listed there as pauper children in the 1901 census. That means they were taken in for care and education at a government funded institution. Phyllis's widowed mother Martha worked in Ealing, London where she appears in the 1901 Census as a cook at the Feathers Hotel. She would regularly take the 1-hr train north to her home in East Molesey where she appears in the electoral lists for years 1899-1902. It would then be a 2-hour train to Oxford to visit her 3 children at Cowley Fields and at least another 5-hour train to visit her daughter Phyllis and the Davies relatives at Pembroke Wales.

1902: While at the Cowley Fields Residential School, Grace became ill with tuberculosis. Martha moved to Oxford, England to care for her daughter. She soon arranged to send Grace for treatment at the Lymington House Sanatorium in Sandgate, Kent and to have Grace's portrait taken nearby at the Martin Jacolette Studio in Dover. Sadly, young Grace died in 1903, at age 10, of pulmonary tuberculosis. Phyllis must have soon joined her mother and brothers at Oxford, as evidenced by the portraits done at EC Hall Studio, St Clement, Oxford about 1903.

Phyllis Hoad's Mother and Siblings, about 1902-1904

Grace Hoad 1892-1903

Martha (Davies) Hoad 1860-1950

Phyllis Hoad 1887-1974

Walter Hoad 1888-1962

Fred Hoad 1889-1944

1903: Phyllis, Walter and Fred lived with their mother Martha at 7 Boulter St, St Clement, Oxford. This address is documented on Walter's records with Turner and Sons (1903-1910), and on Martha's 1905 marriage certificate when she married John Brinn on Christmas Day. Martha moved to her new husband's home at Pembroke's Orange Gardens, and they later moved to 2 Hamilton Terrace, Pembroke Wales. *(Brief histories for Fred, Walter, and Phyllis after 1905 are written below)*

Frederick Colling Hoad 1889-1944

After 1905: Fred age 16, left Oxford England after his mother's marriage to John Brinn and likely went with them to live at Pembroke. He next appears in the 1911 Census, working as a mineral water salesman and boarding with his Welsh cousins at 4 Rhosmaen St., Llandilo Wales. During WWI Fred served in the 4th Welsh regiment with Phyllis's future husband Melville Hinton and was a witness at their 1917 wedding. Fred became a constable with the Glamorgan Police Force as evidenced by electoral registers starting in 1919. In September 1925 Fred married Edith Evelyn Daniel at Glamorgan Wales. They had one son Griffith John Colin in 1926, and two daughters, Phyllis Madeleine in 1927, and Margaret in 1930. In 1934, at age 45, Fred became a widower with three young children. At age 50 in 1939 he retired as a Police Sergeant and died 5 February 1944 at Pembroke Wales.

Walter Alexander Hoad 1888-1962

After 1905: Walter age 17 continued to live in Oxford England until, at age 25, he emigrated to Canada. The 1911 Census lists Walter, a plumber, at 23 Alma Place off Cowley Road. Living nearby at 29 Boulter St in the 1901 and 1911 Census was his future bride Kate Ethel Beck (1888-1963). In early April 1913 Walter emigrated to Canada on the *SS Arabic* from Liverpool to Portland Maine and by train to Toronto, Ontario. He soon found work at the Toronto Furnace and Crematory Co and lodgings at 138 Huron Ave. The next spring, he brought his betrothed, Kate Beck, to join him. They were married 14 April 1914 at St James Cathedral, and they lived at 45 Kenilworth Ave where son Roy Alexander was born 1 May 1915. By 1917 they moved to their permanent residence at 24 Norway Ave where Walter was listed as a plumber in Might's Toronto Directory. The 1921 Canada Census confirms that Walter 32, Kate 32, and Roy 6 were living at 24 Norway Ave. in a semi-detached, 5 room, home they owned in Toronto. A second son Jack Walter was born 2 December 1922 when Clifford's family, newly emigrated from Wales, was visiting there.

Walter and Kate enjoyed living at 24 Norway Ave for many years. After their nephew Clifford Hinton's death in 1957 they were frequent visitors at the Hinton home in Etobicoke. Walter was very helpful with handyman jobs and Kate with Sunday dinners. Sadly, they died a year apart on 13 January 1962 and 11 February 1963 and were both buried at St John's Norway Cemetery on Woodbine Ave in Toronto. *See map* **Pg 29.**

> HOAD, Walter—Suddenly, at his residence, 24 Norway Ave., on Sat., Jan 13, 1962, Walter Hoad, beloved husband of Kate Beck, and dear father of Roy, loving grandfather of Linda, John and Elizabeth, brother of Phyllis Wootten. The late Mr. Hoad is resting at the funeral chapel of Austin J. Mack, 1986 Queen St. E. (at Waverley Rd.), where service will be held on Tues. at 2 p.m. In lieu of flowers, friends may send donations to Metropolitan Toronto Association for Retarded Children, 186 Beverley St. Interment St. John's cemetery, Norway

Phyllis Hoad 1887-1974

After 1905: Phyllis Hoad at age 18, had already begun her millinery apprenticeship. The next years are uncertain but by the 1911 census she had moved from Oxford to Bristol England.

Author's note: Her mother Martha gave this little figurine to Phyllis in 1907 when she completed her millinery apprenticeship. My grandmother gave her treasured millinery figurine to me 60 years later when I began teaching.

1911: In the 1911 Census, at 6 Clifton Vale, Bristol, England, Phyllis Hoad is listed as a visitor at the home of Rev Richard Morris. As a milliner she may have worked with his daughter Adela who was a millinery apprentice. Phyllis likely lived there with the Morris family or was boarding nearby.

1913: This portrait of Phyllis Hoad at age 26 was done by HM Veale & Co Artists in photography at 98 Victoria St. in Bristol England. While living in Bristol, Phyllis likely continued her visits to family in Wales and may have moved to Pembroke by about 1915. She met Melville Hinton through her brother Fred who served with Melville in the 4th Welsh Regiment, at Fort Scoveston, just 8 km from Pembroke, Wales.

9

Clifford's Father: Herbert Hugh Melville Hinton 1891-1939

1891: Herbert Hugh Melville (Stray) Hinton, the only child of Edith Maude Murray (1871-1920) and Benjamin Charles Herbert Stray (1868-1908), was born at Camberwell, London, England on 25 June 1891. His parents had been married about May 1890 (2nd quarter index) but after Edith became pregnant, they separated.

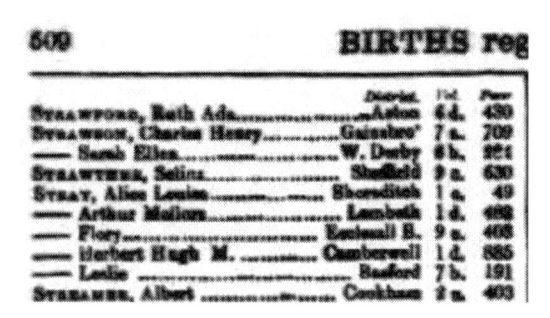

Melville Hinton's Parentage

While pregnant with Melville, Edith met and married Albert George Hinton (1872-1904). There are no records of a divorce for Edith from Benjamin Stray but there are 1st quarter index records for her marriage at age 18 with George Hinton age 19, at London in about February 1891. Their son's birth on June 25, 1891, was registered with the Stray surname, but Edith and George assumed their Hinton surname for him and the next year 1892, they had another son, Frederic Hinton. George Hinton worked as a cabman at London England until his death at age 31, in January 1904, at Oxford England. Edith's whereabouts, after her husband George died, is uncertain until she died, age 49, in early 1920.

While there has been some confusion about Melville Hinton's birth father, recent, DNA evidence has confirmed that Benjamin Charles Herbert Stray was indeed his biological father. Benjamin Stray's whereabouts is uncertain until he married Vanda Chrimes about 1905. Along with Benjamin's brother George Stray, they emigrated to Canada in 1906. Vanda gave birth to their son George Percival Stray while they were in Ontario before they settled that same year in Alberta. According to homesteader documents, Benjamin Stray died there at age 39 in 1908 at Lloydminster Alberta.

1901: In this Census at Regents Park, London, Melville is listed as son of George and Edith Hinton with younger brother Frederic, (ages 8, 9 were reversed in this census record). George age 30, was a cabman groom. Their family of 4 lived at 151 Stanhope St with his employer, cabman, Henry Brown.

1910: After his father George Hinton's 1904 death at Oxford, Melville's whereabouts is uncertain until this 1910 shipboard employment record seen below. Melville signed on with his correct birthplace at Peckham, London and the correct day and month but a wrong birth year, making him age 20 rather than his real age 19. His previous occupation was as a chauffeur, like his father, who was a cabman.

Herbert Hugh Melville Hinton worked aboard the Royal Navy ships, Vivid 1 and later Pomone until he was discharged in September 1911 to Shore OR likely at Dartmouth England.

1911: Melville was next listed as Herbert Hinton age 20 in this 1911 Census, employed with the Royal Navy as a Wardroom Steward at the Royal Navy College and Hospital at Dartmouth, England. It is unclear how long he was employed at Dartmouth before he appeared in WWI army service.

1915: This portrait of Herbert Hugh Melville Hinton about age 24, was taken when he served during WWI with the 4th Welsh regiment as an army private and later as Sergeant Instructor at Fort Scoveston where the army was protecting the dockyards of South Wales from attack.

Melville served there with Fred Hoad and was a welcomed visitor at the Brinn home in nearby Pembroke Wales where he met Fred's sister Phyllis. During their courtship Melville gave Phyllis this Portrait with "Best Love, Mall". Phyllis always referred to him as 'Mall'.

Marriage of Clifford's Parents

1917: On April 28, Clifford's parents, Phyllis Hoad 29 (really 30) of 2 Hamilton Terrace and Melville Hinton 26 residing at Fort Scoveston, were married at Wesleyan Chapel in Pembroke Wales. Witnesses were John Brinn Jr (eldest stepbrother of Phyllis) and Frederick Colling Hoad (he was Phyllis's younger brother and Melville's military friend).

1918: On May 19, a son, Douglas Melville Hinton (1918-2000) was born while Phyllis Hinton was still living at 2 Hamilton Terrace Pembroke with her mother Martha and stepfather John Brinn Sr. Phyllis's husband Melville Hinton was finishing military service at Fort Scoveston.

In the England and Wales 2nd quarter birth Index for April May and June 1918 Phyllis and Melville Hinton's first child is listed as Hinton, Douglas M with mother's maiden name of Hoad in District of Pembroke.

1918: Herbert Hugh Melville Hinton was listed as an absent voter at 2 Hamilton Terrace in St Mary Parish, Pembroke Wales, while he was still working for the Royal Navy at Scoveston. Melville's wife Phyllis and infant son Douglas Melville Hinton lived at 2 Hamilton Terrace with Phyllis's mother Martha and stepfather John Brinn Sr.

4692	Hall, Thomas	Elm Terrace	H.M. Dockyard, Bermuda	4692
4693	Hayes, John Henry	The Green	Pte., Lab. Corps	4693
4694	Hayward, Samuel	5, Orange Gardens	16724 L.-Cpl., 9th Welsh	4694
4695	Herring, Thomas	Travelling Caravan, Pem.	50424 Pte., 11th Welsh	4695
4696	Hinton, Herbert Hugh Melville	2, Hamilton Terrace	265806 Sgt., 4th Res. Welsh	4696
4697	Hitchcock, Percy Jno.	4, Upper Row	M.J.16598 A.B., H.M.S. Hyacinth	4697
4698	Hobson, William Henry	The Green	25703, 2 Cpl., R.E.	4698
4699	Howells, Stanley	16, Orange Gardens	T/2/11308 Dvr., A.S.C.	4699
4700	James, Geo. Arthur	5, Paradise Place	291687 Pte., 2/7th Welsh	4700
4701	James, Wm. Jno.	5, Paradise Place	7681 A.M.1, R.A.F.	4701
4702	Jenkins, Richd. Thos. Henry	Main Street	47529 Pte., 1st Monmouths	4702
4703	Jones-Lloyd, Owen Jno. Fredk.	Main Street	Lieut., R.A.F.	4703
4704	Jones, Richard	1, Golden Cottages	3626 A.B., H.M.S. Valiant	4704

1919, Move to Clydach Wales

When discharged from his WWI military service at Fort Scoveston, Melville found work as an engine fitter at the Mond Nickel Refinery at Clydach, 10 km north of Swansea Wales. Melville, Phyllis, and Douglas lived there at 88 Grove Rd., Clydach with her cousins Sarah Jane and Albert Davies. A second son Hugh Frederick Hinton (1919-1944) was born 14 December 1919 just in time for a Merry Christmas for the Hinton and Davies cousins at the 88 Grove Rd home before the Hintons moved to 40 Kelvin Rd.

https://www.genuki.org.uk/big/wal/GLA/Llangyfelach/Clydach

Clydach Wales

Clydach is on the Tawe River about 10 km north of Swansea. Melville Hinton worked there for three years at the Mond Nickel Refinery. Clydach was a factory town on the busy railway line.

The Hinton family homes, at 88 Grove Rd in 1919 and at 40 Kelvin Rd in 1920 to 1922 can be found in the top left section of the modern map on page 15.

Mond Nickel Works
https://coflein.gov.uk/en/site/301165/

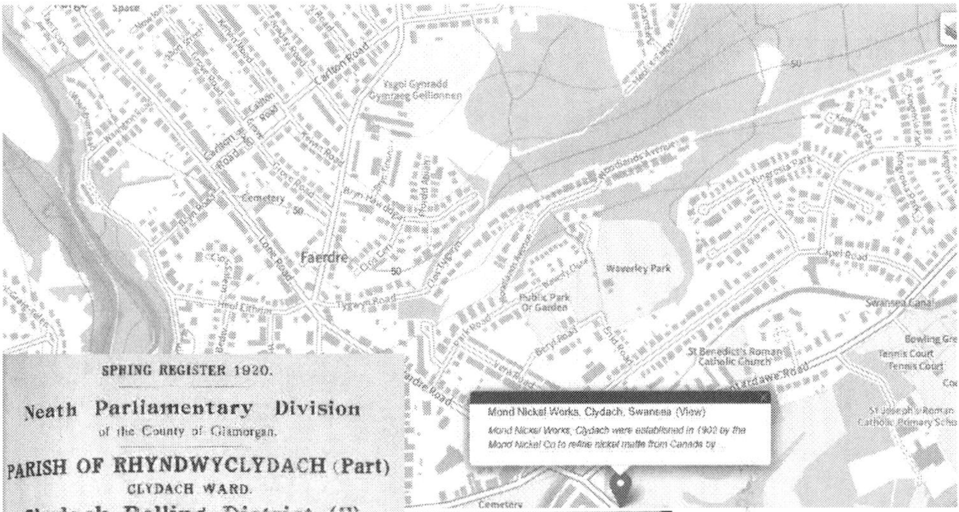

SPRING REGISTER 1920.

Neath Parliamentary Division
of the County of Glamorgan.

PARISH OF RHYNDWYCLYDACH (Part)
CLYDACH WARD.

POLLING DISTRICT E. CLYDACH WARD.

(1) No.	(2) Franchise. (a) Parlia- (b) Local mentary. Govt.	(3) Names in full. Surname first.	(4) Residence or Property abode of non-resident occupied of
1318	R O	Williamson, Edward	17 KELVIN ROAD
1357	H O H O	Murdock, Frederick Wm.	
1358	N M —	aMurdock, Joseph L.	39
1359	R O	Murdock, Peter Gordon	39
1360	R O	Hinton, Melville	40
1361	H O H O	Hinton, Phyllis	40
1362	H O H O		

1920: Phyllis and Melville Hinton would live for two years at 40 Kelvin Rd in Clydach Wales. They moved there in 1920 with their sons Douglas almost 2 and Hugh 4 months. They were soon expecting a third child.

Mond Nickel Works, Clydach, Swansea (View)
Mond Nickel Works, Clydach were established in 1902 by the Mond Nickel Co to refine nickel matte from Canada by

Clifford Ley Herbert Hinton 1921-1957

1921: On March 11, two days before Phyllis' 34th birthday, Clifford was born at 40 Kelvin Rd, Clydach, Glamorgan Wales, the third son of Phyllis and Herbert Hugh Melville Hinton.

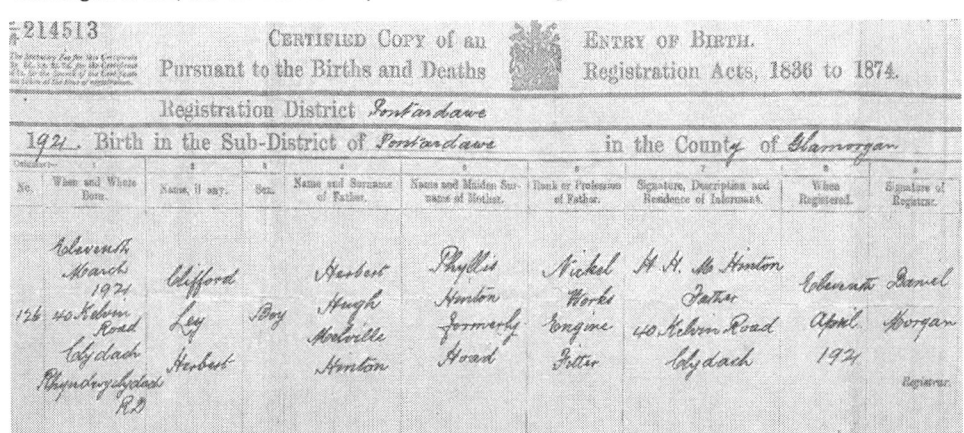

15

1921: This photo was taken at Clydach Wales June 25, for Melville's 30th birthday. They are likely on a Clydach hillside by the Tawe River.

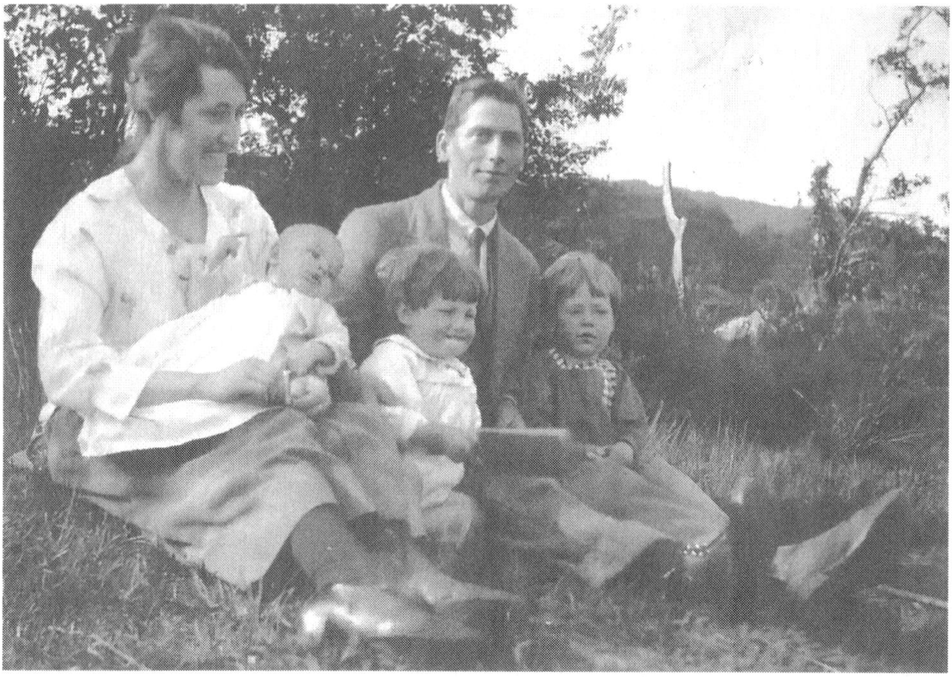

Phyllis 34, Clifford 3 months, Douglas age 3, Melville 30 and Hugh 1 ½ .

<u>**1921 Census**</u>

Author's note: I acquired this census record through my paid access to FindMyPast.co.uk. This company has an agreement with the National Archives to digitise and exclusively release the 1921 Census records until 2025 thus recouping their digitising costs.

This 1921 census record was to be a record of those present at 40 Kelvin Rd Clydach on Tawe Glamorganshire Wales on Sunday, 25th April 1921. It seems it was completed in early June when Clifford was 3 months old, before Melville's 30th birthday on 25th of June.

CENSUS, WALES & MONMOUTH, 1921.

SCHEDULE.

Prescribed by Regulations under the Census Act, 1920, as the form to be used in Wales and Monmouth for the purpose of returns in respect of (a) Private Households, (b) Hotels, Clubs, Boarding Houses, or Common or other Lodging Houses, and (c) Other persons in respect of whom no other form of schedule is prescribed.

This space to be filled up by the Enumerator.

Registration District.	Registration Sub-District.	Enumeration District.
593	1	35

Name of person responsible for making the return. Mr Herbert H M Hinton

Postal Address 40 Kelvin Road Clydach on Tawe Glam

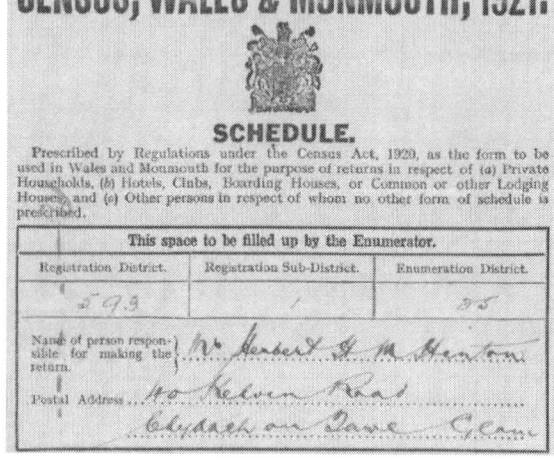

NAME and SURNAME	RELATIONSHIP to Head of Household	AGE	SEX	MARRIAGE or ORPHANHOOD	BIRTHPLACE
1. Herbert Hugh Melville Hinton	Head	29 10	M	Married	London / Peckham
2. Phyllis Hinton	Wife	32 2	F	Married	Pembrokeshire / Pembroke
3. Douglas Melville Hinton	Son	3 1	M	Both Alive	Pembrokeshire / Pembroke
4. Hugh Frederick Hinton	Son	1 6	M	Both Alive	Glamorganshire / Clydach
5. Clifford Ley Herbert Hinton	Son	3	M	Both Alive	Glamorganshire / Clydach

As recorder, Melville gave Phyllis age as 32 but it was really 34. Perhaps he did not know her real age or was being kind! He would rather have Phyllis be 3 years instead of 5 years older than him.

NATIONALITY	OCCUPATION and EMPLOYMENT		
	Personal Occupation	Employment	Place of Work
	Fitter's Mate, Lummer / Nickel Refinery	Mond Nickel Works / Nickel Refiners (out of work)	Clydach S.O. Glam / 9530 04
	Household Duties		

The 1921 Census notes Melville was employed by Mond Nickel Works at Clydach but was currently 'out of work'. His insecure employment was certainly a reason for considering emigration to Canada which they would soon begin planning.

Emigration to Toronto, Ontario, Canada 1922-1925

Plans for Emigration from Wales 1922	21
Toronto with Hoad Family	21
Passages to Canada 1922	22
Living in Toronto (1922-26)	28

Plans for Emigration to Canada

1922: Clifford's family moved back to the Brinn home at 2 Hamilton Terrace, Pembroke, while Melville and Phyllis made plans to move their family to Canada. They planned to join Phyllis's brother Walter Hoad, a plumber by trade, who had emigrated in 1913. Walter lived in Toronto, Ontario, Canada at 24 Norway Ave with his wife Kate and son Roy age 6. The two families had been communicating by letter and Walter was eager to have the Hinton family join them at their Toronto home. Melville planned to go first, to seek employment. Phyllis and their sons would follow in better summer travel conditions.

In February, (when Clifford was 11 months) Melville and Phyllis went to Somerset Place, Port of Swansea, Wales to make applications for their passages to Canada. The Passage date for Melville was to be April 1 on the *Canadian Pacific Steamship SS Melita*. The Passage date for Phyllis and their 3 boys was to be 4 months later, July 28, on the *CP Steamship SS Montrose*. They would be sailing from Swansea to Liverpool and then across the Atlantic Ocean to St John New Brunswick for Melville and to Montreal Quebec for Phyllis and sons Douglas age 4, Hugh age 2 and Clifford age 1. They would then take *Canadian Pacific Railroad* to Toronto.

Author's note: I found this website to be helpful for information about emigration. It also has ship and port photos.
www.norwayheritage.com/

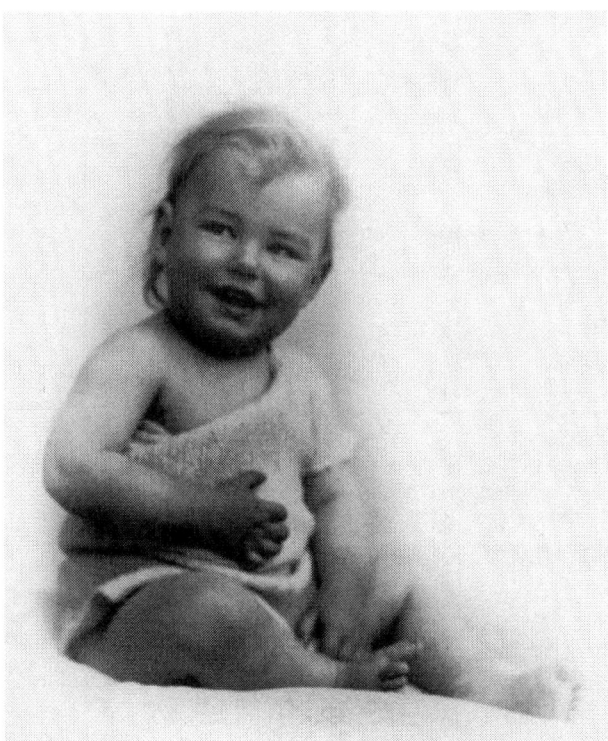

Portrait of Clifford

on his first birthday,

11 March 1922

Herbert Hugh Melville Hinton,

1 April 1922 Passage to Canada

FORM 30A — ORIGINAL

S.S. *Melita*   Class 3   Date of Sailing 1922 April 1

Inland routing _____ to _____

DECLARATION OF PASSENGER TO CANADA.   614

1. NAME: HINTON HERBERT HUGH MELVILLE   Age 30
2. Sex: Male   Are you married, single, widowed or divorced? Married
   If married, are you accompanied by husband or wife? If so, give name of husband or wife: —
3. Present occupation: Tiler   Intended occupation: Tiler
4. Birthplace: London   Race or people: British
5. Citizenship: British   Religion: Wesleyan
6. Object in going to Canada: To settle
7. Do you intend to remain permanently in Canada? Yes
8. Have you ever lived in Canada? —   If you have, give Canadian address: —
   Port of previous entry: —   Date: —
   Port of departure from Canada: —   Date: —
9. Why did you leave Canada? —
10. Money in possession belonging to passenger: £50
    (I am aware that I must have on my arrival in Canada the sum of $250.)
11. Can you read? Yes   What language? English
12. By whom was your passage paid? Myself
13. Ever refused entry to, or deported from Canada? No
14. Destined to: join brother-in-law W. A. New, 24 Norway Avenue, Toronto, Canada
15. By which Canadian railway are you travelling to destination? C.P.R.
16. Nearest relative in country from which you came: Wife
    Phyllis Hinton
    2 Hamilton Terrace, Pembroke, South Wales
17. Are you or any of your family mentally defective? No
    Tubercular? No   Physically defective? No
    Otherwise debarred under Canadian Immigration Law? No

Signature of passenger: H. H. M. Hinton

SWANSEA AGENT

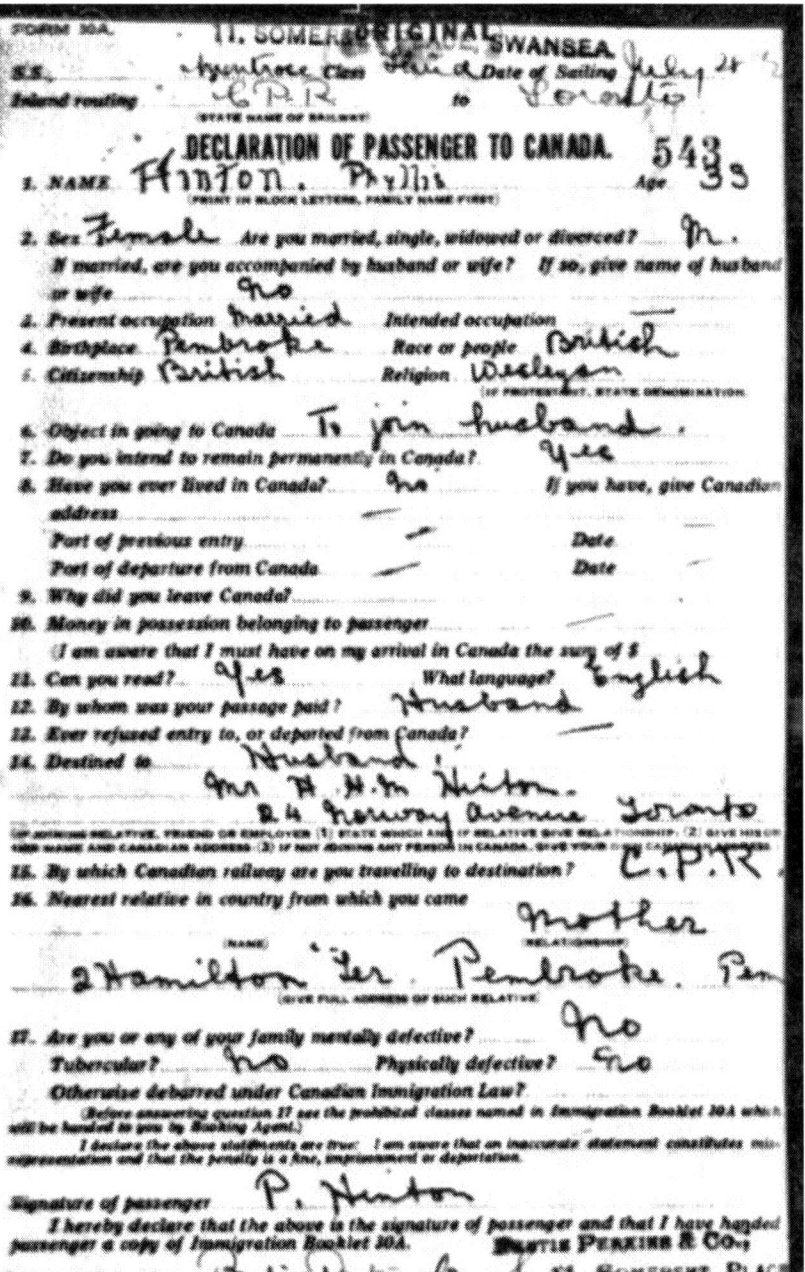

Phyllis Hinton, 28 July 1922 Passage to Canada

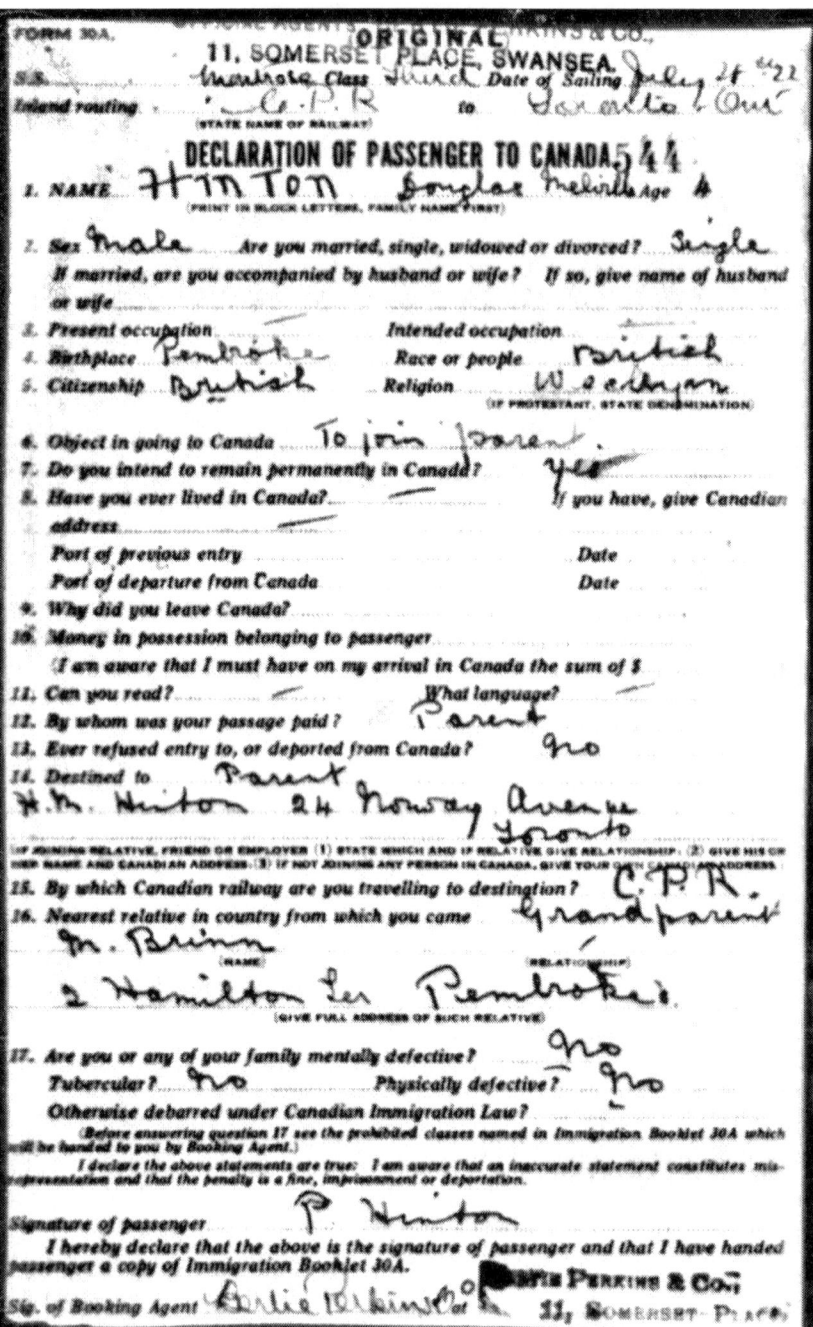

Douglas Melville Hinton, 28 July 1922 Passage to Canada

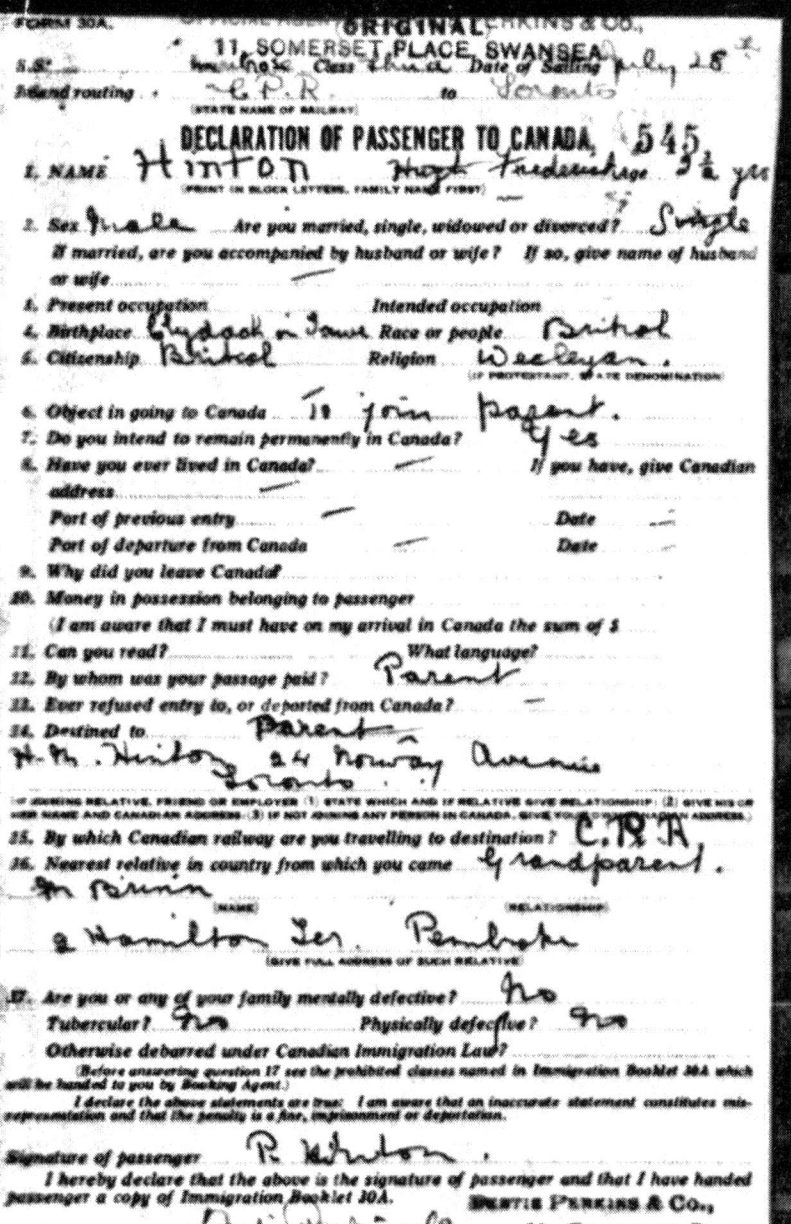

Hugh Frederick Hinton, 28 July 1922 Passage to Canada

Clifford Ley Herbert Hinton,

28 July 1922 Passage to Canada

FORM 30A.   (ORIGINAL)
S.S. _Montrose_   Class _Third_   Date of Sailing _July 29th 22_
Inland routing _C.P.R._ [STATE NAME OF RAILWAY]   to _Toronto_
546

DECLARATION OF PASSENGER TO CANADA

1. NAME _HINTON — Clifford Ley Herbert_   Age _11 mths_
   (PRINT IN BLOCK LETTERS, FAMILY NAME FIRST)

2. Sex _Male_ ... Are you married, single, widowed or divorced? _—_
   If married, are you accompanied by husband or wife? If so, give name of husband or wife _—_

3. Present occupation _—_   Intended occupation _—_
4. Birthplace _Clydach on Tawe_   Race or people _British_
5. Citizenship _British_   Religion _Wesleyan_
   (IF PROTESTANT STATE DENOMINATION)

6. Object in going to Canada _To join parent_
7. Do you intend to remain permanently in Canada? _Yes_
8. Have you ever lived in Canada? _—_   If you have, give Canadian address _—_
   Port of previous entry _—_   Date _—_
   Port of departure from Canada _—_   Date _—_
9. Why did you leave Canada? _—_
10. Money in possession belonging to passenger _—_
    (I am aware that I must have on my arrival in Canada the sum of $ _—_
11. Can you read? _—_   What language? _—_
12. By whom was your passage paid? _Parent_
13. Ever refused entry to, or deported from Canada? _—_
14. Destined to _Parent_
    24 Norway Avenue Toronto   Canada
    (IF JOINING RELATIVE, FRIEND OR EMPLOYER (1) STATE WHICH AND IF RELATIVE GIVE RELATIONSHIP. (2) GIVE HIS OR HER NAME AND CANADIAN ADDRESS (3) IF NOT JOINING ANY PERSON IN CANADA, GIVE YOUR OWN CANADIAN ADDRESS.)

16. Nearest relative in country from which you came _Grandparent_
    M. Brinn   _2 Hamilton Terrace_
    NAME   RELATIONSHIP
    Pembroke   South Wales.
    (GIVE FULL ADDRESS OF SUCH RELATIVE)

17. Are you or any of your family mentally defective? _No_
    Tubercular? _No_   Physically defective? _No_
    Otherwise debarred under Canadian Immigration Law? _No_
    (Before answering question 17 see the prohibited classes named in Immigration Booklet 30A which will be handed to you by Booking Agent.)
    I declare the above statements are true: I am aware that an inaccurate statement constitutes misrepresentation and that the penalty is a fine, imprisonment or deportation.

Signature of passenger _P. Hinton (Mother)_
    I hereby declare that the above is the signature of passenger and that I have handed passenger a copy of Immigration Booklet 30A.
    SOUTH PERKINS & Co.
    11 SOMERSET PLACE

26

Emigration to Canada

1922: On April 9, after his 8-day passage aboard the *SS Melita*, Clifford's father Melville arrived at St John NB and took a CPR train to Toronto. Melville lived with his brother-in-law Walter's family and soon found employment as a mechanic at WH Banfield and Sons Ltd, manufacturer of electrical devices at 370 Pape Ave Toronto, where he would be employed until 1926. See **Pg 28** for Hinton, Herbert M, in the 1925 Toronto directory.

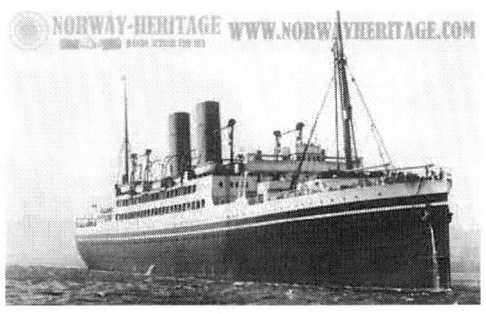

Canadian Pacific Steamship, SS Melita

WH Banfield and Sons Ltd., 370 Pape Ave.

Canadian Pacific Steamship, SS Montrose

3rd *class passage accommodation*

1922: On August 4, after 7 days aboard the *SS Montrose*, Phyllis and her three boys arrived at Quebec. They went by CPR train to Toronto, where Clifford's father and the Hoad family eagerly awaited their arrival. Clifford's Uncle Walter and Aunt Kate were expecting their second child, a sibling for Clifford's 7-year-old cousin Roy Hoad. Their son Jack Hoad was born on December 2, 1922, making it a very Merry Christmas for the young families at 24 Norway Ave.
See **Appendix D Pg 277** for the 24 Norway Ave house information.

Toronto, Ontario, Canada

1923: At some point in 1923, the Hinton family moved from 24 Norway Ave to 18 Ripon Road south of St Clair St E at Victoria Park Ave in East York. Their residence there is recorded on the back of Clifford's 1925 photo, and in this 1925 Toronto directory at right below.

Might's Toronto Directory 1923, Hoad p1039
https://archive.org/details/torontocitydirectory1923

Might's Toronto Directory 1925, Hinton p485

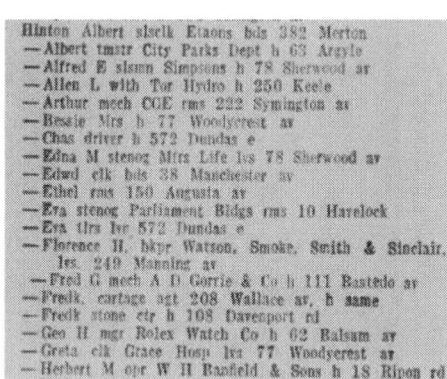

https://archive.org/details/torontocitydirectory1925

Many clues about employment and where the Hoad and Hinton families lived were found by searching the Might's Toronto Directory. The information was often delayed by a year.
https://archive.org/search?query=Toronto+directory

1923: Clifford's father went fishing at Frenchman's Bay, possibly with his brother-in-law Walter Hoad.

1925: Clifford was age 4 in the garden at 18 Ripon Road. The writing on the photo back shows it was taken on his brother Douglas's 7th birthday on May 19th. Their brother Hugh was age 5 ½.

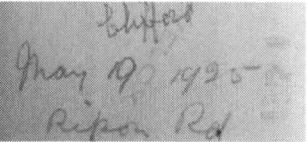

28

1921 Map of Toronto, Ward 8 (partial)

● Hoad home at 24 Norway Ave near Woodbine Rd

↑ Hinton home at 18 Ripon Rd near Victoria Park Ave

▊ St John's Norway Cemetery Kate and Walter Hoad are buried here

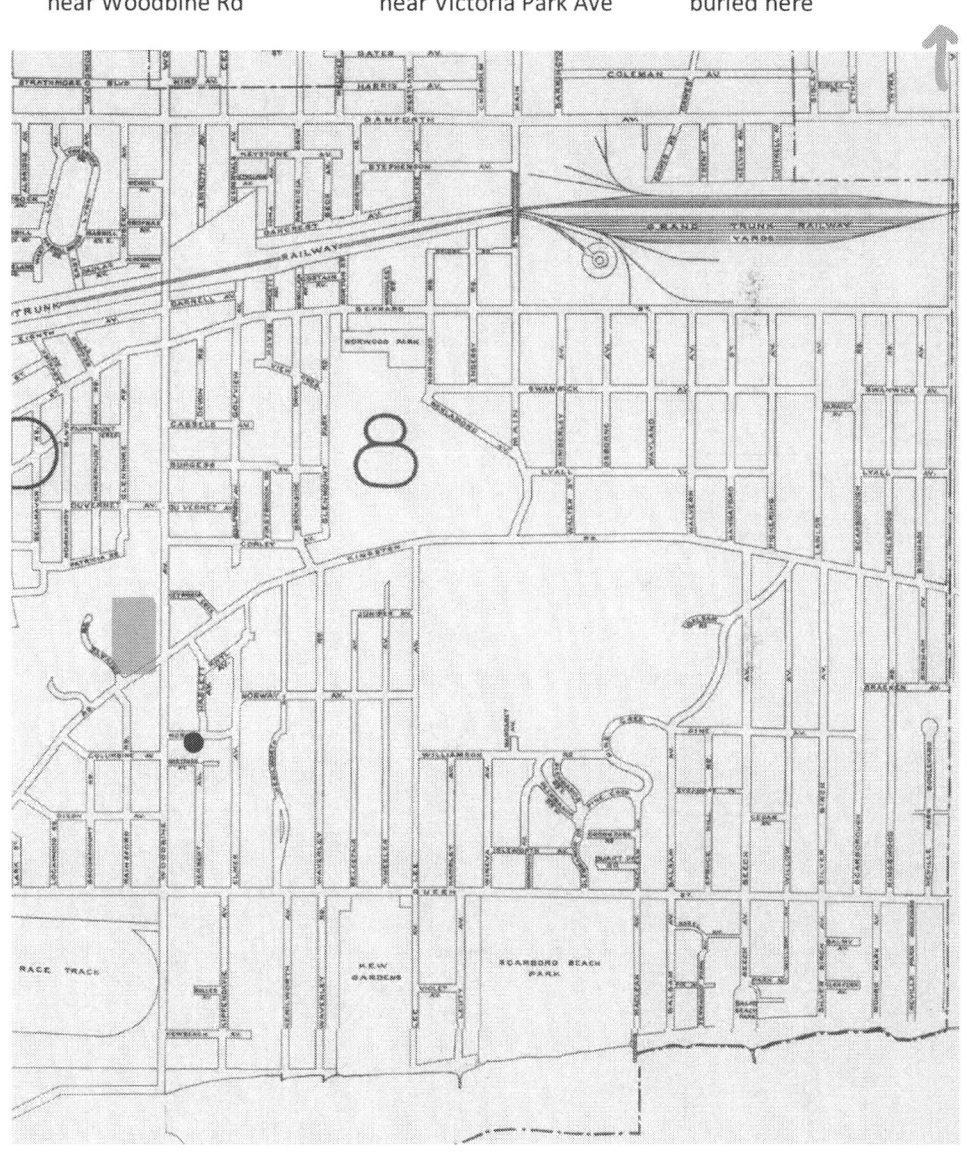

Growing up in Oshawa, Ontario, Canada 1926-1941

Hinton Family Move to Oshawa	33
General Motors Limited	35
24 Jones Ave, Oshawa (1928-36)	39
Teenage Years (1934-40)	47
General Motors Employment (1937-41)	54
Death of father, H H Melville Hinton, 23 August 1939	59
Passion for Hockey, Junior Bees (1940-41)	62

Move to Oshawa, Ontario, Canada

1926: When he was age 5, Clifford's family moved from Toronto to temporary rented rooms in the Hy Carey home at 236 Gliddon Ave in South Oshawa. This was near to the General Motors Plant on Ritson Road North where his father gained employment as an engine mechanic. They lived there for 2 years before they moved to a house at 24 Jones Ave.

Hinton residences were found in Vernon's Oshawa City Directory from 1928 to 1955. Hy Carey is listed in the 1929 directory at left.

GLIDDON AV, north side from Drew to Ritson rd s
O-204 E W Howard
O-208 John Wiggans
O-212 A W Hilts
O-216 Lionel Darks
O-218 Jas Kelly
O-220 Walter Rowden
O-226 Mrs H Luttrell
T-230 Burton Lighthall
O-234 Geo Redman
O-236 Hy Carey

https://archive.org/details/vernon1929oshawadirectory

General Motors is in the community stories link at right.

https://www.communitystories.ca/v2/oshawa-automotive-community_communaute-automobile/story/

1927: Through my research to identify the circumstances of this photo and the front porch photo on page 39, I learned more about the Small family, who from 1928 to 1930 lived on Jones Ave, next door to the Hinton family. This photo is of Clifford lower left, his father behind him and Hugh center. Beside Clifford's father, is Ebert Small with his arm on the shoulder of his younger brother Ross.

I believe that Cliff's eldest brother Douglas took this photo while they were at Lakeview Park in south Oshawa for a General Motors picnic. Ebert worked as a mechanic at GM with Melville and possibly encouraged the Hinton family's move in 1928 from their temporary rental at Gliddon Ave to a home beside the Small family on Jones Ave in northwest Oshawa. *See **Pg 35 and 39**.*

Author's note: Thanks to my sister Susan for sharing this and other photos for this book.

1927/28: These are Ritson Rd Public School photos of Douglas age 9 in Gr 4, Hugh age 7 or 8 in Gr 3, Clifford age 6 or 7 in Gr 1 taken when the Hinton family lived at 236 Glidden Ave. in Oshawa, Ontario.

Author's note: *Thanks to my sister Deborah for sharing these and other photos for this book.*

1928: Possibly at Easter, April 8, or on Mother's Day May 13, this photo was taken of Hugh, Douglas, Carey boy and girl, and Clifford in Mrs. Carey's Garden, Oshawa.

Vernon's Oshawa Directory (on page 33) lists Hy Carey at 236 Glidden Ave. Many neighbours on Glidden Ave also worked at the nearby GM factory.

Melville and others on 236 Gliddon Ave porch

34

> JONES AV. w from end
> of Simcoe n
> 3 new houses
> T-   Neil McEachern
> T-   L O Irwin
> O- 55 N E Knapp

1928: Vernon's Oshawa City Directory of Jones Ave lists 3 new houses. The Hinton home may have been one of these and not numbered until it was numbered 24 in the 1931 directory.

Hinton, Herbt H M (Phyllis) is listed as a mechanic at General Motors and living at Jones Ave.

https://archive.org/details/vernon1929oshawadirectory

> 232   VERNON'S DIRECTORY
>
> Hinds, Jas A (Clara), carp, h 98 Albert
> Hinds, Norman (Alice), wks Genl Motors, h 72 Simcoe n
> Hinds, Wm A (Clara), asst acct Hydro, 161 King e
> Hinkson, Burn W (Claretta), wks Fittings Ltd, h 39 Bruce
> Hinkson, Jas E (Julia), h 83 Centre
> Hinkson, Jas E jr, wks Genl Motors, 83 Centre
> Hinman, Clara M, 32 Park rd n
> Hinton, Herbt H M (Phyllis), mech Genl Motors, Jones av
> Hinton, John (Amy), carp Genl Motors, rms 136 Ritson rd s

Oshawa: Canada's Motor City

Oshawa General Motors assembly plants and administration offices were at Ritson Rd North and Bond St East in Oshawa. *See QR codes on next **Pg 36** for more information.*

35

General Motors Oshawa

https://www.communitystories.ca/v2/oshawa-automotive-community_communaute-automobile/story/

General Motors of Canada

In 1918 the McLaughlin family sold their McLaughlin-Buick and Chevrolet production to General Motors in the United States. Neither Sam nor George had sons who could head up the family business, and GM already owned 49 per cent of the McLaughlin Motorcar Company. While the Motorcar Company was doing well, it was dependent on Buick's performance. Sam McLaughlin remained as president of the newly formed General Motors of Canada, headquartered in downtown Oshawa.

https://www.tvo.org/article/how-oshawa-became-canadas-motor-city

A 1921 McLaughlin Special Sedan, better known as a "Whiskey Six".

In the early 1920s, the McLaughlin Special models became known for their speed and luxury. The performance of their six-cylinder engines made them popular with rum-runners for smuggling alcohol into the United States – they could outrun most police cars. They were dubbed "Whiskey Sixes," and some drivers claimed they could get up to almost 140 km/h (87 mph).

Through the 1920s the auto industry was evolving, and GM Canada had to evolve with it. The expensive Buick was losing customers to cheaper competitors like the Ford Model T, but the less-expensive Chevrolet line grew explosively. GM Canada added new product lines such as Oldsmobiles, Pontiacs, and Cadillacs.

General Motors Ad (1926)

2,000 General Motors Workers Now On Strike

Trimmers Joined by Other Piece Workers—Mass Meeting Held

CONCILIATION BOARD FOR OSHAWA STRIKE

General Motors Will Restore Old Scale and Men Go Back on Monday.

(Canadian Press Despatch.)
Oshawa, Ont., March 30.—The General Motors strike was ended this afternoon at a meeting in the armories when the men accepted the offer of...

MAJORITY OF OSHAWA STRIKERS SATISF[IED]

More Than Three Thous[and] Return to Work Pendi[ng] Negotiations

Meetings To Be Held [Next] Week to Further Unio[n] Organization

General Motors 1928 strike

www.communitystories.ca/v2/oshawa-automotive-community_communaute-automobile/story/strike-1928/

On March 26, 1928, 300 trimmers walked out on the job in protest. They were immediately fired. By the next morning another 1,200 employees had walked off the line, bringing the plant to a standstill.

The strike grew over the rest of the week, and by Friday the 30th all vehicle production in Oshawa had stopped. That day a group of 3,000 strikers gathering at the Oshawa Armoury voted to begin a union. Under pressure from the Ontario government, the striking workers, and the American Federation of Labor (AFL), the plant management gave in, giving the workers their original wages, rehiring all fired personnel, and allowing collective bargaining. As part of a large AFL network extending across North America, an Oshawa auto union had been born.

www.lakeviewparkoshawa_.wordpress.com

Despite its harsh policies, GM Canada took care of its own. Workers had injury insurance policies worth $1,000. They also had sports teams and a company choir, orchestra, literary society, and more. The annual company picnic, held through the 1920s, 1930s, and 1940s, regularly attracted 20,000 visitors to Lakeview Park every August. The land the park was built on had originally been donated to the City of Oshawa by Sam McLaughlin.

Visitors at the annual General Motors picnic in Lakeview Park, 14 August 1926

Living at 24 Jones Avenue, Oshawa

1928: In the spring or summer of 1928, the Hinton family moved to Jones Ave near to Simcoe Ave North and Ross Rd in Oshawa. This front porch photo includes new friend Ross Small 12, with Hinton brothers Douglas 10, Hugh 8, and Clifford 7. Ross Small's family and his dog lived next door (*at #59 later became #20*) from 1928 to 1930.

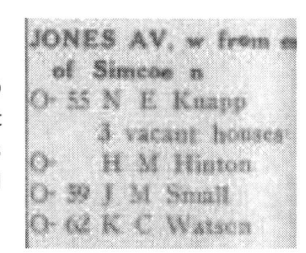

1929 Grandparents Martha and John Brinn Visit Toronto and Oshawa

1929: In May, Clifford's maternal grandparents, Martha and John Brinn Sr came by steamship from Pembroke Wales, to spend time with their son Walter's family at 24 Norway Ave in Toronto and with their daughter Phyllis's family at 24 Jones Ave in Oshawa. They would surely have delighted in spending the summer months in Canada, with their adult children and five handsome grandsons.

See Pg 41 for their travel records.

At right is a photo of Kate Hoad, Martha Brinn, and Phyllis Hinton at 24 Jones Ave.

1929: This happy reunion photo was taken in the Hinton family's garden at 24 Jones Ave. when grandparents Martha and John Brinn were visiting from Pembroke Wales. It may have been a party for Melville's 38th birthday June 25 and Kate's 41st birthday July 1.

Author's note: Thanks to my cousin Libby for sharing this and other photos for this book.

Melville 38, Kate 40, Walter 40, Phyllis 42, John 67, Martha 69,
Douglas 11, Clifford 8, Hugh 9, Jack 6 and Roy 14

1929: On May 31, Martha 69 and John Brinn 67 had departed from Liverpool on the Canadian Pacific Steamship, *Duchess of Bedford*, bound for Quebec and Montreal. From Montreal they took the CPR train to Oshawa where they reunited with family.

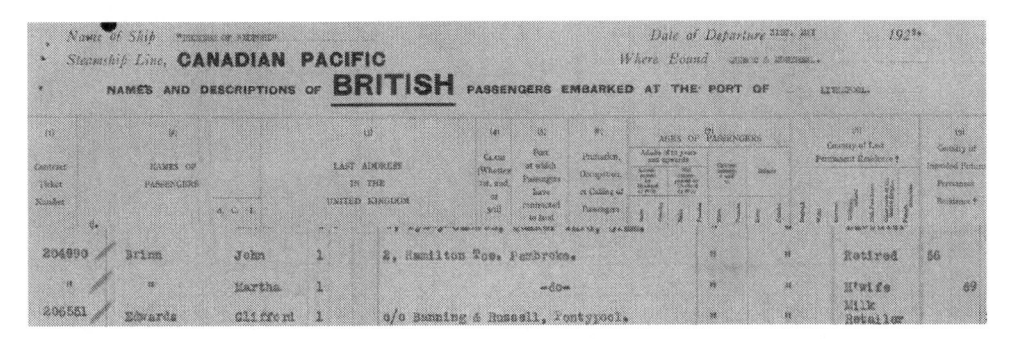

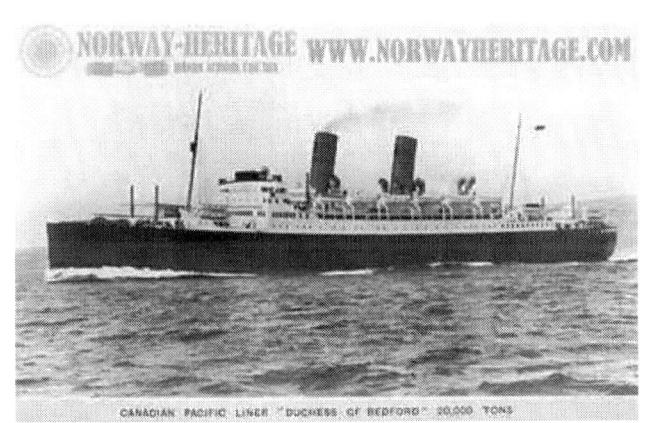

www.norwayheritage.com/

After a 3 month stay with family in Canada, Martha and John took the CPR train to Montreal and departed on the *Duchess of Bedford* bound for arrival at Liverpool on September 25. They would carry with them many happy memories of their time in Canada.

For 10 years, living in North Oshawa, Clifford and his brothers enjoyed an active outdoor life in this semi rural area near Oshawa Creek. They had new playmates, and a new puppy. They enjoyed activities such as hockey, tobogganing, swimming in Oshawa Creek and boy scout camping. They also enjoyed school life and they achieved academic success at the newly built North Simcoe PS (later renamed Dr S J Phillips) and at Oshawa CVI (later renamed O'Neill CVI).

1930: Melville, Phyllis, Hugh, Clifford on toboggan; Doug, Hugh, Clifford with sticks on Jones Ave. Hugh with their puppy and Clifford by their snow "dug out"

1931: In photos of swimming fun at Oshawa Creek, below left, are Melville, Clifford, Phyllis, young boy, and Hugh. To right is Clifford with the young boy, and below right is Roy Hoad and Doug Hinton.

1931: In the June 1st census, East Whitby is given as the location of the Hinton residence, but the Jones Avenue address is listed in the Vernon's city directory for Oshawa. This new northeast area of Oshawa may have been included in the East Whitby census for reasons of enumeration convenience. *Author's note: The 1931 Census (horizontal) record below has been clipped for clarity.*

The Hinton home was a 6-room single brick house valued at $4500. The family included Herbert M Hinton age 39, a line man at GM factory who earned $925 in 1930, who was currently laid off and unemployed for 26 weeks in 1931. Also included are Phyllis Hinton age 43 (really 44), a homemaker, Douglas 13, Hugh 11, and Clifford 10, all students. They were all from England in 1922, and religion is given as United Church. It's interesting that they had no radio. Not noted in the census but documented in his 1939 obituary on **Pg 59**, was Melville Hinton's active involvement with several community groups, sports, and choir.

This and some of the other Census, Birth, Marriage, Death, and Military documents as well as Voter's Lists, that are included in this book, were found through Ancestry.com.

1931: Phyllis and Melville encouraged their sons to achieve well at school and to be actively involved in community through sports, clubs, and volunteer work. Clifford stood 1st of 13 students in his grade 4 class at North Simcoe PS. (DR S J Phillips).

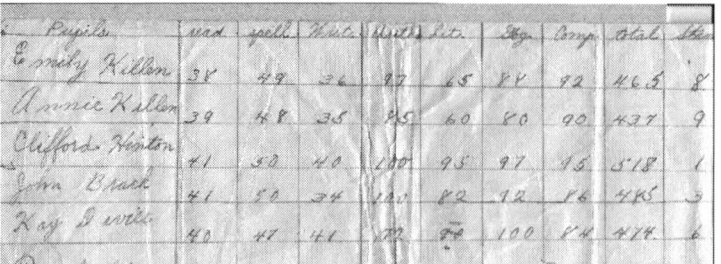

1932: The Hinton family spent time at Lakeview Park with recreation activities which were often sponsored by General Motors.

See Pg 38 for more about Lakeview Park.

Above left Phyllis is with Hugh and Clifford probably after playing baseball as evidenced by the bat and ball beside the unidentified friends in the photo above right. They may have travelled to the lake by the railway trolley that went from Ross Rd in north Oshawa down Simcoe St to Lakeview Park on the shore of Lake Ontario.
See **Pg 45** *for more about the Oshawa Street Railway.*

1933: The photo at right is of Clifford and his cousin Roy Hoad and likely taken in July at Lakeview Park.

44

Map of Oshawa, South of King St

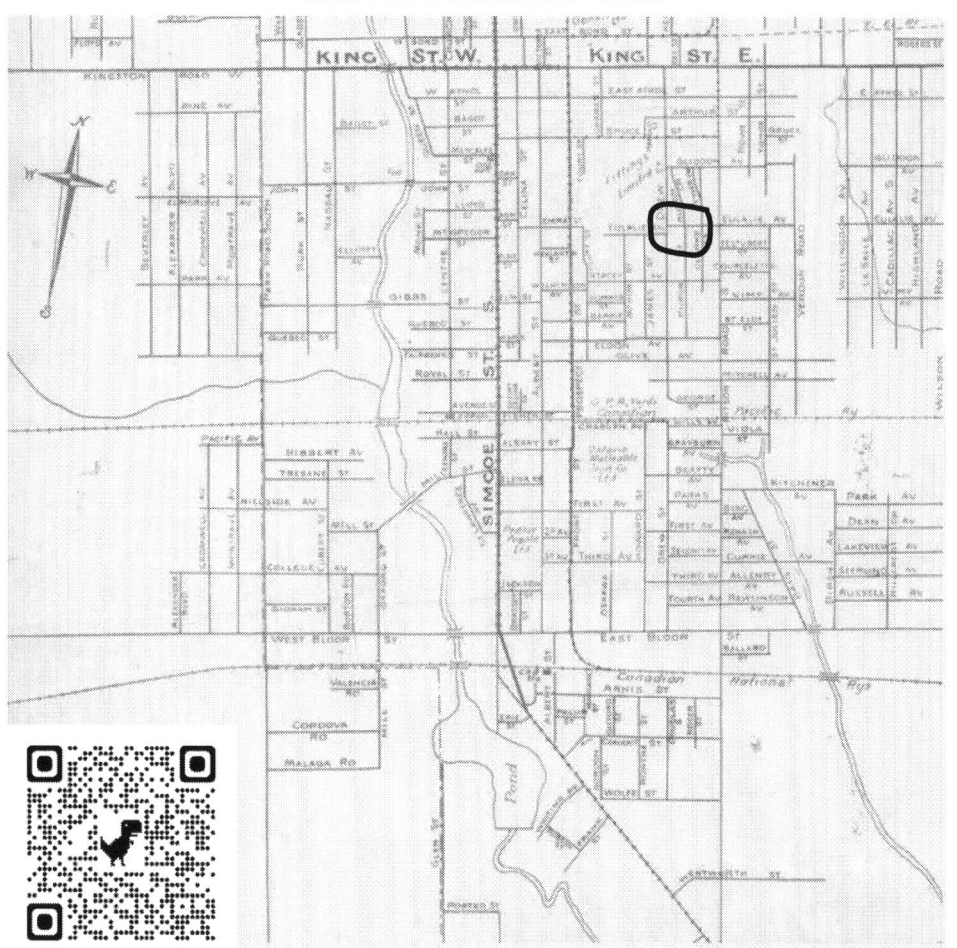

Image credit: Oshawa Museum Archival Collection

This map shows the streetcar railway line continuing down Simcoe St and angling southeast toward Lakeview Park at Lake Ontario. There was also the CPR and CNR line running East West with connections to the GM plants and other industries. The circle is at the location of the Hinton family's first Oshawa residence at 236 Glidden Ave. *(See better image at website here or the QR Code above.)*

https://lakeviewparkoshawa.wordpress.com/2020/05/11/oshawa-street-railway/

45

Map of Oshawa, North of King St

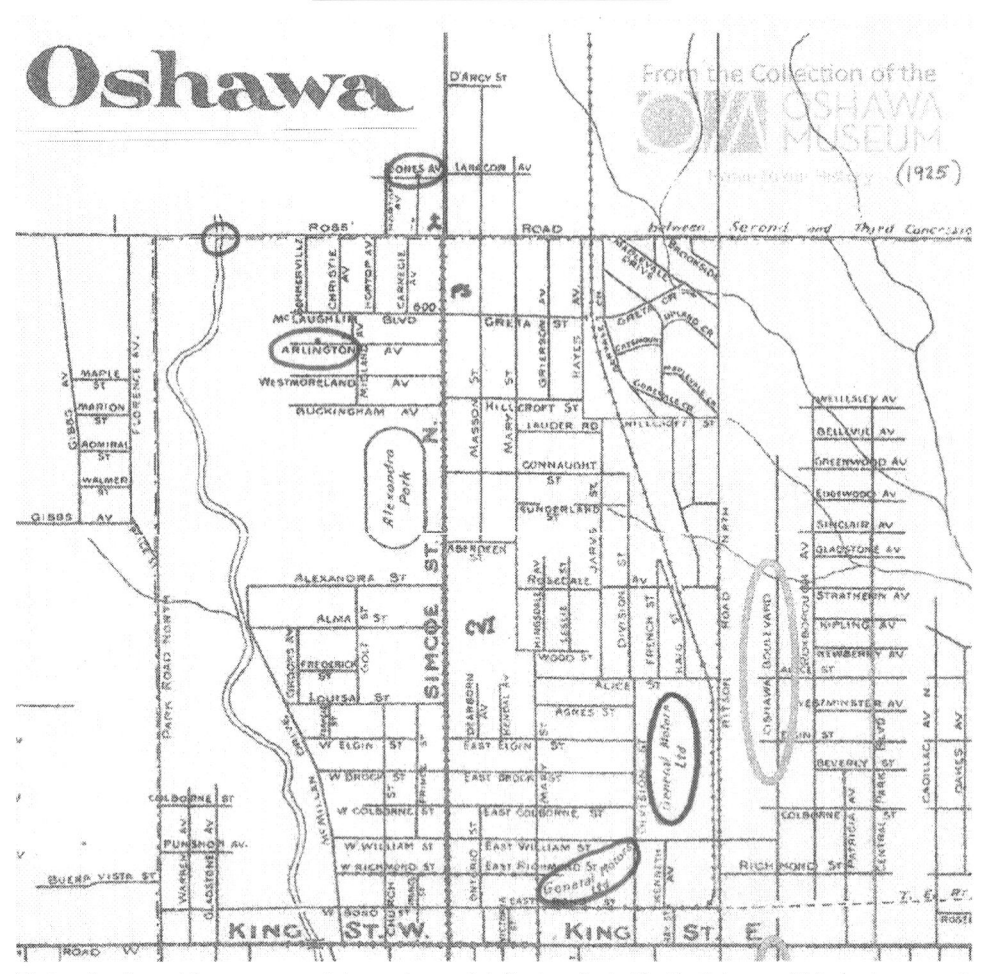

Hinton family residences were at Jones Av, and Arlington Av in North Oshawa; GM plants were at Bond St and Ritson Rd; North Simcoe PS and Northminster United Church were at Ross Rd and Simcoe St; Simcoe CVI was at Simcoe St and Rosedale Av; notice Oshawa Creek flows south under the Ross Rd bridge in North Oshawa. The river continued south to Lake Ontario. Also, going south to the Lake was an Oshawa railway line that carried passengers from Ross Rd down Simcoe St past Alexandria Park through the middle of Oshawa to Lakeview Park. Cliff's family may have used that service to go to Lakeview Park to attend sports and picnic events sponsored by General Motors.

https://oshawalibrary.ca/local-history-genealogy/

Cliff's Teenage Years

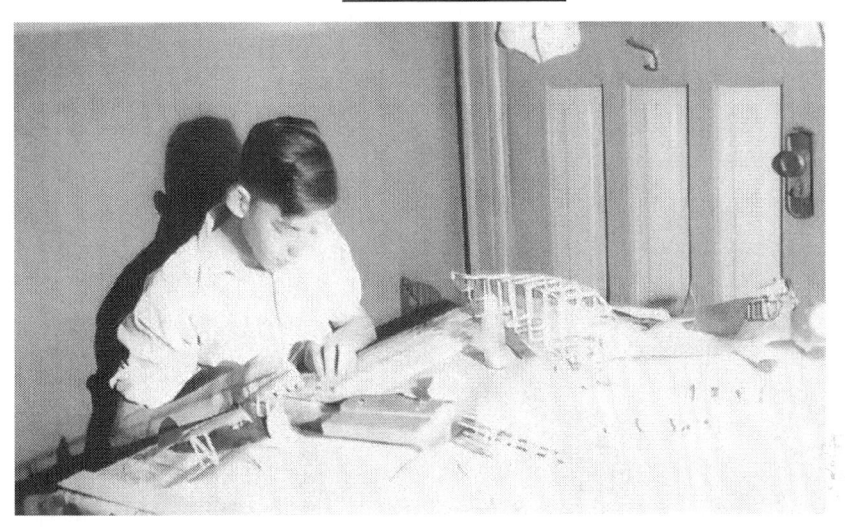

1934: Clifford at age 13, enjoyed one of his favourite hobbies. Here he is building a balsa wood aircraft model on the kitchen table at the Hinton's 24 Jones Ave home.

Like his father, Clifford was very interested in new technology. His interest in transportation, from airplanes to the latest in automobiles, was a natural family trait. His father Melville's background included work as a machinist at the Mond Nickel Refinery and as a mechanic at General Motors. Both his maternal and fraternal grandfathers' John Hoad and George Hinton had 'turn of the century' employment in transportation as busy London cabmen. It would be natural for Clifford to follow his ancestors as he developed his skills for the automotive industry.

In June 1934, the Oshawa Times Journal published these photos and a story about the 5th Oshawa Scout Troup enjoying scout training at an outdoor camp. It may have been at Brookside Park in north Oshawa. The 150-acre park was owned by Robert S McLaughlin until he donated it in 1943 to Scouts Canada. In 1946 it officially opened as Camp Samac.

See next page for larger images that can be read.

47

1934: Clifford's mom kept this clipping of his 1934 Scout Camp experience with the 5th Oshawa Troop. She marked him in both photos with an X and his friend, maybe Clifford's friend Alex Reid, with an O. Clifford is far right in the second row of the top photo which is identified as LEFT in the writeup. Clifford is far left in the bottom photo which is identified as RIGHT in the writeup.

Camp time for Scouts of the 5th Oshawa Troop is not just a spell of play while living under canvas, but is the period of the year when the boys manage to gain some real practical experience at the theory of scout training which they have received all during the year. Signalling flags can be waved properly in the open air, where there is no fear of striking against lights or ceiling; axemanship can be taught in camp much better than is ever possible in a backyard of a city,—so to camp go the Scouts and there The Telegram photographer found them busy learning from older scouts just how things are done. In the photographs above are shown: UPPER LEFT—a class in knotting, led by Patrol Leader Lloyd Annis; UPPER RIGHT—P. L. Bill Drake taking a class in signalling; LOWER LEFT—the 5th Oshawa Troop in camp "undress" togs; LOWER RIGHT—a little instruction in axemanship—at right, Douglas McDonald is showing Douglas Mechin the angle method of cutting, while Ralph Mechin is showing Clifford Hinton the use of a hand hatchet. —(Photographs by The Telegram's Oshawa Correspondent.)

48

1934 Phyllis Hinton's Trip 'Back Home' to England and Wales

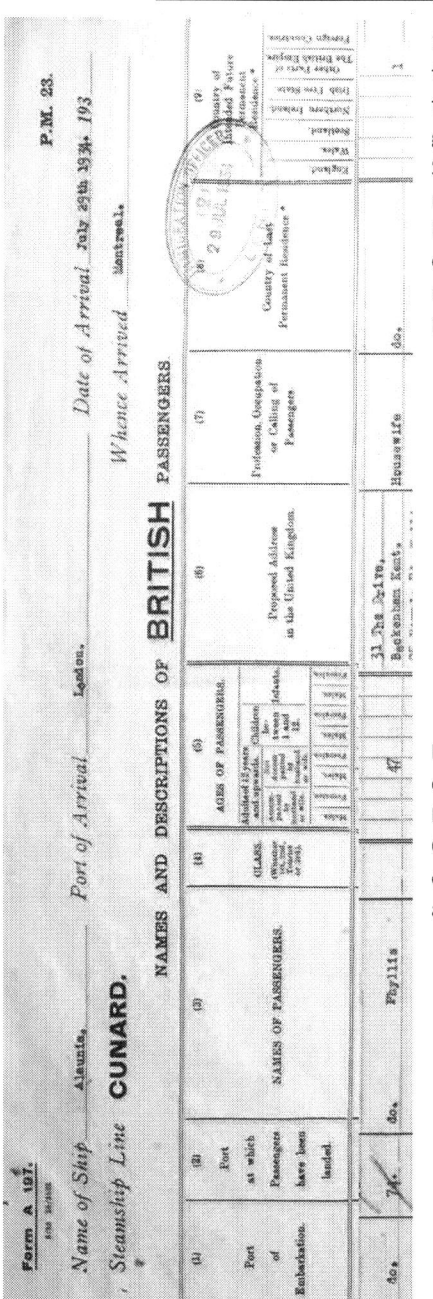

1934: In July, Clifford's mother Phyllis took the CPR train from Oshawa and sailed alone from Montreal aboard the *SS Alaunia*, arriving at London on July 29th. She was going to 31 The Drive in Beckenham, Kent. This is in South London and who she was visiting there is a mystery. It is very likely that while overseas she visited her youngest brother Fred Hoad and his young children Griffith 8, Madeline 6, and Margaret 4 while their mother, Phyllis's dear friend Edith, was dying in Llandough hospital in Wales.

Phyllis stayed a few weeks after Edith Hoad's August 21st death visiting her mother Martha and stepfather John Brinn Sr at Pembroke, before she returned in mid October aboard the *SS Athenia*, leaving from Liverpool on October 6, arriving at Quebec City on October 14th, and taking the CPR train to Oshawa.

1935: Clifford was an avid boy scout. This portrait was taken of him at age 14 in his scout uniform. Clifford's mother was proud to send it at Christmas 1935 to Clifford's Grandparents Martha and John Brinn Sr. Phyllis had visited them at 10 Hamilton Terrace in Pembroke Wales when she was in the UK the previous year.

Clifford finished grade 8 at North Simcoe P S, received his High School entrance certificate, and in September, began grade 9 at Oshawa CVI (O'Neill**).**

1935 Clifford at age 14, Graduated to Oshawa C.V.I.

Clifford and his brothers attended North Simcoe Public School, built in 1924 the same year that Oshawa became a city. (In 1962 it was renamed Dr S J Phillips PS.) After graduating elementary school, they attended Oshawa CVI which first opened in 1909 as Oshawa High School and after renovations, was renamed as Oshawa Collegiate and Vocational Institute. The Formal Opening was May 7-9, 1930, and was reported in a special edition of the Oshawa Daily Times.

https://archive.org/details/ocviopeningdailytimes_202002

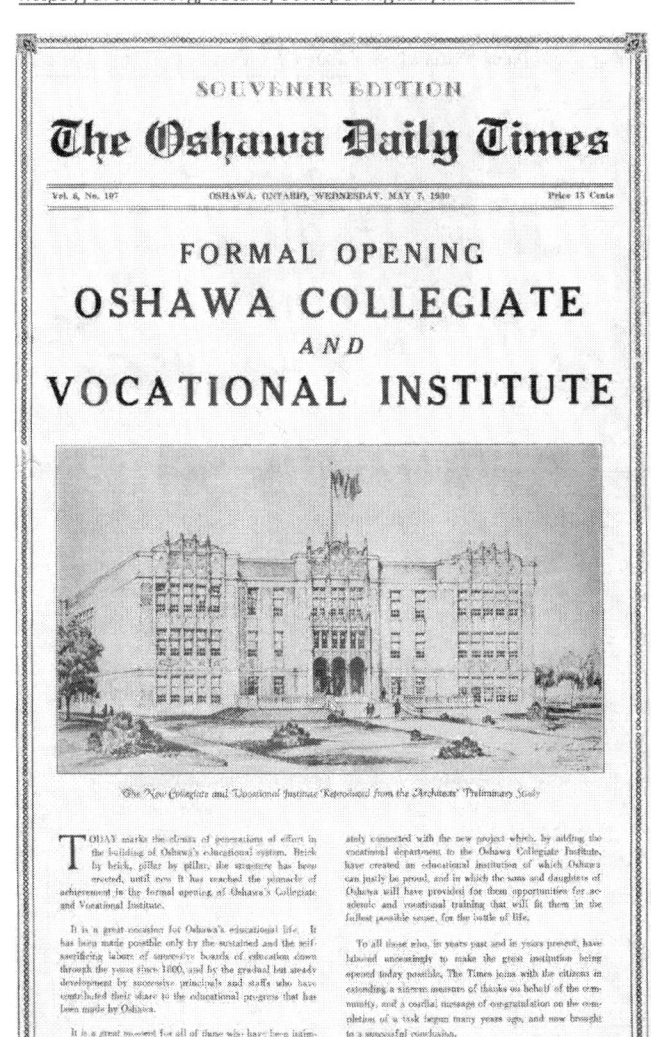

Douglas and Hugh had started attending OCVI in 1932 and 1933.

After WWII, in 1949, OCVI recognized former student veterans in a memorial, *'The Remembered'*. (QR link below) Clifford and Hugh are remembered in it. Douglas's secret service was not in this memorial. *See Pg 73*.

In 1959 OCVI was renamed O'Neill CVI.

1935/36: Clifford continued to achieve very well at Oshawa CVI. He stood 3rd in the first term with his class of 42 male students. Achievement lists were handwritten for each of the 42 students. There were no copy machines!

1936/37: The Hinton family moved to Arlington Ave, where they continued to live close to Oshawa Creek parklands. Clifford age 15, is in the first row, 3 from left, in this photo with his hockey team.

Kinsmen's Club Team Wins Oshawa Midget Title

A group of juvenile hockey players are champions in the midget of Oshawa Minor Hockey Association and were sponsored by Kinsmen Club. Club members are, from left to right, back row: n, executive; B. Suddard, J. Cameron, N. Raike, B. Hardie, J. McArthur, M. Fountain, J. Hobbs, D. Conlin, W. Brabin, "Ab" B coach, and W. Campbell, executive. Front row, left to right: R. Su J. Daniels, C. Hinton, R. Nash, F. Carey, G. Peters and I. Wilson. sent, Harold Luke, manager.

april 1937.

https://www.communitystories.ca/v2/oshawa-automotive-community_communaute-automobile/story/strike-1937/

Strikers meet in Memorial Park on a rainy day in 1937.

In 1937 Oshawa experienced a second major strike, one that would define labour in the city for the next 80 years. Between the 8th and 23rd of April more than 4,000 workers walked off the job, seeking an eight-hour workday, a seniority system, and most importantly recognition for the newly formed United Auto Workers (UAW). This group, which began in GM plants in Michigan, had been heavily suppressed by both plant management and the government of Ontario.

The 1937 strike led to changes at GM although it is unclear how this affected Clifford's family.

1937: Clifford's father, Melville Hinton, became very ill and was diagnosed with lung cancer. Perhaps his 2 years working at the Mond Nickel refinery in Clydach Wales had exposed him to the toxic chemicals that led to the cancerous lesions in his lungs.

With his father ill with lung cancer and often unable to work, Clifford left Oshawa CVI (O'Neill), to join his father and brother Douglas working at the Oshawa General Motors plant on Ritson Rd North. At age 16 Clifford started working as a clerk in the auto parts department.

Clifford played in a defence position with the Main Office team in the General Motors Inter-Departmental Hockey League. In the 1937-38 season the Main Office team were Champions winning the Highfield Trophy. See **Appendix A Pg 221** for more information.

1937-1938 Champions
GENERAL MOTORS INTER-DEPARTMENTAL HOCKEY LEAGUE
E. Frank Lint   L. Workman   J. Carter, Mgr.   R Joyce, Pres.   O. Lint, Sec.   F. Black, Coach   H. Kerr, Trainer
J. Jackson, L. Def.   C. Hinton, Sub.   E. Peterson, Sub.   J. Elliott, Sub.   G. Peterson, Centre   H. Foster, Sub.   Bill Conlin, Sub.   Reg. Burr, Sub.
Dick Toppings, R. Wing   Jim Toppings, L. Wing   Vic. Burr, Goal   Dick Conlin, Sub. (Capt.) Reg. Mills, R. Def.   Wally Wilson, Sub.
Winners of the J. B. Highfield Trophy

This photo of Clifford on ice at the Hambly Arena, was taken by his brother Hugh Hinton. This may be the Main Office team or the Canada Bread team as he played in both the GM league and City League during 1937-40 seasons.

The Hambly Arena had a unique roof held up by curved arches which did not block spectator views.

http:/oshawaexpress.ca/memories-of-the-oshawa-arena/

www.ohlarenaguide.com

1938: For his 47th birthday, June 25, Melville & Phyllis had photographs taken near Oshawa Creek at the Ross Road bridge, not far from their home at 105 Arlington Rd. This photo at right is my favourite. Phyllis was a wonderful caregiver for her dear husband 'Mall'.

1938/39: While working as a clerk in the auto parts department at the General Motors plant on Ritson Rd, Clifford secured a position playing defense for Canada Bread Juveniles in the Oshawa Minor Hockey League, also known as *"The City League"*. The Canada Bread Juveniles played their games at the nearby Hambly Arena at 140 King St W in Oshawa.

See **Appendix A Pg 219** for more information.

Oshawa's Future Hockey Stars
By W. H. "Bill" Campbell

The Oshawa Minor Hockey League known as "The City League" was organized in 1934 following a proposal by Bill Hancock then coach of Oshawa hockey teams. Through the co-operation of Les McLaughlin, of McLaughlin Coal, Lou Beaton of Beaton's Dairy, Wm. Jack of Canada Bread and Oshawa's three service clubs Kiwanis, Rotary and Kinsmen, the venture was successfully launched.

The Oshawa arena co-operated by allowing the teams that were completely outfitted, use of the arena on Thursday evenings. The first executive comprised S. E. McTavish, president, Lloyd Workman, vice-president and the writer as secretary-treasurer. The present president is Walter Branch and most of the men originally associated with the league still hold office. The league is comprised of six teams, McLaughlin Coal, Beaton's Dairy, Canada Bread, Rotary, Kiwanis and Kinsmen split into juvenile and midget sections. The winning midget team receive the Jack Worrall Memorial Cup while the C. E. McTavish trophy goes to the winning juvenile team.

The juvenile winner also enters the O.J.H.A. playoffs and as a tribute to the calibre of hockey played Beaton's Dairy reached the finals in 1937, McLaughlin Coal won the all Provincial title in 1938 while this year Canada Bread were defeated in the semi-finals by Waterloo McPhails who won the Ontario title. Members of the Canada Bread championship team this season included: Goal—Jakie Nash. Defense—Cliff Hinton, Gord Wilson, Frank Keleman, Butch Suddard, Jack Wetherup. Forwards—Sam Stark, Louie Lott, Norm McBrien, Buck Davies, Lyle McIntyre, Doug Furey. Coach—Joe Patterson. Manager—Bill Jack.

The season is annually brought to a close with a banquet at which all teams are present, when the cups are presented and individual crests given to each player of the winning teams. A real breeding ground, the league has developed many of Oshawa's hockey stars besides instilling into the youths the value of clean sportsmanship and good living.

Clifford kept a 1938-39 Commemorative book, **Memorial Cup winners: the Oshawa Generals** which can be seen in **Appendix A on Pg 201-224**. Cliff's team is mentioned in the sample clip above, which came from page 16 of the 20-page booklet.

Hockey was important to Clifford. He excelled as a defensive player and made many friends in the various teams and leagues in which he played hockey.

1939 Canada Bread Juveniles, at Hambly Arena, Oshawa, March 22

Due to late arrival of the Midland team, only two periods were played in this semi-final game with only one goal scored by the Oshawa Juvenile "Canada Bread" team.

"The rival defences turned in fair efforts although the homesters were more adept at clearing loose pucks and skating-off the in-coming playmakers."

Prov. Semi-Finals

Midland Team Is Late
Only Two Periods Played —
Whitby Fixture Follows

Visiting Goalie Allows Only One Goal, Foiling Many Attempts by Locals

FINALLY SCORE

Weatherup Scores With Only Three Minutes to End of Second Period

Oshawa Canada Bread Juveniles won their first game in the provincial semi-finals when they defeated Midland by the narrow margin of one goal, the only one scored in an abbreviated 2-period arena was leased for another O.H. The game which was "billed" for eight p.m., was late in starting due to the late arrival of the Midland team's equipment, and as the arena was leased for another O.H. A. playoff game at 9:30 it was found necessary to cut the Juvenile tilt down to two periods. However, judging from the play of the contestants the deleted period was probably a blessing in disguise for Midland. The Canada Bread lads made a slow and shaky start but as the game progressed, they improved remarkably and had it not been for the sensational goalkeeping of Brownell, in the Midland nets, the score would have been much higher.

The local "City League" champions were almost complete masters of the territorial play, particularly in the second period, but the visiting goalie stopped everything that came his way except the orphan tally that spoiled his shutout. On it he had very little chance, coming as the result of a combination effort that brought McBrien and Weatherup right to the edge of his goal-crease. Wilson, tall Canada Bread defenceman, carried the puck into the Midland defensive area where he passed to McBrien. In the ensuing scramble McBrien managed to get the disc over to Weatherup who gave Brownell no chance.

The scoreless first period was slow and listless at times with the Midland team, coached by Bert Corbeau, checking the local boys' every move. Offsides were frequent and the constant whistle-tooting spoiled the play somewhat. Although the Canada Bread boys had the better of the play, the visitors did break through the Oshawa defence frequently to test Goalie Nash. In the second and last stanza the locals put on a little more pressure. They carried the majority of the play. Centreman Stark and Wingers Lott and McBrien especially giving Brownell a lot of anxious moments. They had a man advantage once when Todd drew a rest for a trip but over-anxiousness and poor marksmanship spoiled their chances. The Midland lads were consistent back-checkers and a great many times when Oshawa forwards seemed to have an almost sure goal on their sticks after beating the Midland defence, an opposing forward would scoop in from "nowhere" to help out their great little goalie.

Although Canada Bread's second line of McIntyre, Davies and Weatherup held up their end well when on the ice, it was the first trio of Stark, Lott, and McBrien particularly, that seemed to stand out the more. The latter player spent the greater part of the last period on the ice and was a frequent puck-carrier and constant threat to the Midland goalie. The rival defences turned in fair efforts although the homesters were more adept at clearing loose pucks and skating-off the in-coming playmakers. No fault could be found with the work of Nash in the local nets, but his rival, Brownell, shaded him to some extent, having had a great deal more to do. Out in the front lines, the Midland team showed their most promising material in Nesbitt, a good centreman, and Todd and Jeffery, wingmen.

The teams:
MIDLAND—Goal, Brownell; defence, Gerrow and Ryan; centre, Nesbitt; wings, Todd and Simpson; alternates, Gilbert, Joffery, Quinn, Simpell, Woods and Roberts.
CANADA BREAD—Goal, Nash; defence, Wilson and Hinton; centre, Stark; wings, Lott and McBrien; alts., McIntyre, Davies, Weatherup and Suddard.
Referees—"Bill" Morrison, Oshawa; "Bob" Dodds, Midland.

SUMMARY
First Period
No score. Penalties—none.
Second Period
1.—Oshawa, Weatherup (McBrien, Wilson) 17:00
Penalties—Todd, Davies.
No third period played.

1939 Canada Bread Juveniles, at Midland, March 27

Oshawa Canada Bread Juveniles won their second game 4 to 3, to oust Midland and advance to the Round Robin Series in the O.J.H.A. playoffs. It was a tense game with aggressive goal tending. Defenseman Cliff had penalties in the 1st and 3rd periods.

Canada Bread Juveniles Oust Midland in Hectic Game and Now Advance to Round-Robin Series

Oshawa Kids Build Up Lead in First Two Periods and Manage to Hang on in Third Despite Midland's Desperate Ganging

DAVIES GETS TWO

Midland Tied Game Score With Only 30 Seconds Left to Play But McBrien Broke Away to Clinch Round for Oshawa Just 5 Seconds Before Finish

MIDLAND, Mar. 28. — Over one thousand noisy hockey fans crowded the local Arena last night, and should their heads off in desperation as their only remaining hockey team, the Juvenile Lions, went down to elimination at the hands of Oshawa "Canada Bread" Juveniles, in the second game of their goals to count series.

Down one goal as the result of an Oshawa win last week, it was evident from the first "everything goes, only get that goal back" attitude was being taken, and the final 4 to 3 victory that Oshawa scored came after one of the most bitterly fought juvenile contests seen here for a long time.

Oshawa Scores First

The visitors opened the scoring after twelve minutes of the first period when hustling "Buck" Davies batted the puck into the cage past Brownell during one of many scrambles in front of the Midland goalkeeper, to give the Baker Boys a two goal margin on the round, and it proved to be "the straw that broke the camel's back" as far as Midland was concerned.

It was the signal for a terrific offensive that was heightened by three straight Oshawa penalties, and a savage series of power plays were put on by the homesters. Nash in the Oshawa cage turning in a sensational game to hold them off, but it was not until both teams were at full strength that Simpson gave the Midland fans their first opportunity to cheer since the series began, when he took Nesbitt's pass to swing around the Oshawa defence and send a low angle shot into the far corner of the nets.

Rough Tactics Used

Tied on the game, and one goal down on the round, the Midland team practically went berserk as they hooked, chopped and slashed their way to the Oshawa goalmouth. Even when Nash had stopped the puck and was holding it to ease the tension, the Midland forward Gilbert, persisted in chopping at his face and shoulders in an effort to make him drop the puck. The game was held up for a short time while Nash got over the effects of a tap on the head during one of these attacks.

The breaking point came half way through the second period, when Wood was sent off for holding, for the first Midland penalty of the game. Davies scored his second goal, combining with McIntyre and Weatherup during an Oshawa power play, and Furey duplicated it a minute later, on a precisely similar play on a pass from Weatherup.

The Midland defense of Gerow and Ryan, two juveniles with extremely large ideas when it came to bodychecking, had a field day spreading the light Oshawa forwards in no uncertain fashion, Gerow in particular making himself very unpopular with the visitors.

Come Very Close

Gerow scored Midland's second goal late in the final period, giving Midland's finalist ambitions another belated boost, and when Nesbitt scored the tying counter a bare two minutes later, bedlam really broke loose in the Midland ice palace, Coach Bert Corbeau putting on four forwards in a frontic effort to tie the round in the remaining five minutes of play. But once again, penalties spelled disaster for the Midlanders. Gilbert was sent off for boarding, and McBrien took Stark's pass to break away for Oshawa's fourth and last goal of the game.

The visitors started a near riot in the last few minutes of the game when Goalkeeper Nash went down swinging, after one of the Midland forwards struck at him with a stick. It was but one of many such attacks that had been going on during the entire game, and Nash's hair-trigger temper finally broke. Referee Squeak Morrison was a very unpopular man in Midland when he failed to send Nash to the cooler.

Penalties Costly

Gilbert, of Midland's second line, received a five minute penalty in the last three minutes of the game, when he told Referee Morrison a few things, and this was the final blow to the Midland hopes. This lad Gilbert, with plenty of size but rather short on condition and grey matter, was a very poor example of Midland juveniles.

McBrien, Davies and Stark starred for Oshawa, with Nash holding a considerable edge over his netminding rival Brownell, but the entire team turned in heads-up performances, and showed up well in clearing the puck out of danger when pressed hard. For Midland Brownell, Nesbitt, Todd and Simpson were dangerous throughout, with Quinn and Wood showing up well, but the lads marred an otherwise good display by an overdose of enthusiasm in the wrong places.

The Teams:

MIDLAND—Goal, Brownell; defense, Gerow and Ryan; centre, Nesbitt; wings, Todd and Simpson; subs, Quinn, Gilbert, Wood, Beteau, Jeffrey and Duncan.

OSHAWA—Goal, Nash; defense, Wetherup and Hinton; centre, Stark; wings, McBrien and Lott; subs, McIntyre, Davies, Furey, Willson, Keleman, Suddard.

Referees—"Bill" Morrison, Oshawa, and "Bob" Dodds, Midland.

THE SUMMARY

First Period
1 Oshawa, Davies.
Penalties—Hinton and Stark.

Second Period
2 Midland, Simpson (Nesbitt).
3 Oshawa, Davies (Wetherup-McIntyre).
4 Oshawa, Furey (Wetherup).
Penalties—McIntyre, Wood and Willson.

Third Period
5 Midland, Gerow.
6 Midland, Nesbitt.
7 Oshawa, McBrien (Stark).
Penalties—Willson, Gerow, Hinton and Gilbert (5 minutes).

See **on Previous Pg 56** *for* Bill Campbell's article about the City League (page 16 of The Memorial Cup booklet), "Canada Bread were defeated in the semi-finals by Waterloo McPhails who won the Ontario Title."

The Oshawa Generals won the Memorial Cup, the Canadian Junior Hockey Championship 1938-39. Oshawa's Hambly arena *'was the home of legendary Generals teams of the 1930s and 1940s, who dominated junior hockey like no team before or since.'* Clifford's hockey photo on page 65 was taken at Hambly Arena in front of a composite photo of his favourite team, The Oshawa Generals.

58

1939: June 25, Hugh 19 and Douglas 21 were with their father to celebrate Melville's 48th birthday. These photos were likely taken by young Clifford at age 18. Phyllis and their friend Helen Wootton who had lived at 28 Jones Ave next to the Hintons, (*Pg 122*), are with Hugh by the porch at 105 Arlington Ave. It seems to be a happy time just before Melville's health declined.

Clifford's father Melville Hinton died August 23 at age 48. His funeral was held at Northminster United Church, officiated by Reverend Frank Wootton. Melville Hinton was buried at Mount Lawn Cemetery in Whitby and a lengthy obituary was published in The Oshawa Times Journal newspaper.

LENGTHY ILLNESS PROVES FATAL TO WELFARE MEMBER

H. Melville Hinton Dies — Served Throughout War Without Wound

Seriously ill for more than eight months, H. Melville Hinton, member of the Oshawa Welfare Board, and veteran of the Great War with the record of having served throughout the entire period of hostilities from 1914 to 1918, died late yesterday at his home, 105 Arlington avenue.

He was an active worker in a wide range of interests during his 12 years residence in Oshawa. He was born in London, England, June 25, 1891, and was 48 years old at the time of his death. He came to Canada 17 years ago and after living in Toronto for five years came to Oshawa. He was employed on the General Motors truck assembly line until he became ill. He was a member of the United Automobile Workers of American, local 222 and of the General Motors War Veterans Club.

He took a keen interest in sports, especially hockey, baseball and fishing but was also interested in music. In this capacity he was a member of the former Welsh Male Choir of Oshawa, and he was also secretary of St. David's Society of Oshawa.

He served overseas with the Welsh Regiment as a sergeant from 1914 to 1918, seeing active service throughout the entire period of the Great War, coming through the conflict without being wounded. At the conclusion of the war he was promoted to the rank of sergeant-major. He was appointed to the Oshawa Welfare Board in 1938 and was reappointed this year.

In fraternal interests he was a member of Lebanon Masonic Lodge of Oshawa and of Local Essex No. 4 Lodge of Sons of England. In the latter organization he was a past district deputy having had the unique distinction of serving two years as district deputy of that lodge. He twice was representative to the Sons of England convention which is held every two years in Canada. He was an honorary life member of the Marine degree of Sons of England.

In religion he was a member of Northminster United church.

The surviving members of the family are his wife, formerly Phyl-
(Continued on Page 10, Col. 2)

LENGTHY ILLNESS PROVES FATAL TO WELFARE MEMBER

(Continued from Page 1)

lis Hoad, and three sons, Douglas, Hugh and Clifford, all at home. Hugh is a supervisor for the Oshawa Playground Association. One brother, Frederick Hinton of Manchester, England, also survives.

The body is resting at the Armstrong Funeral Home, King street east, until Friday afternoon when the funeral will be held from Northminster United church, at 2:00 p.m., with the pastor Rev. F. M. Wootton in charge of the service. Interment will be made in Mountlawn cemetery. Members of England Lodge, Essex No. 4 will be in attendance at the funeral.

1939 Herbert Hugh Melville Hinton Ontario death certificate.

There is a lot of information, given by his son Douglas, and recorded on this registration of death. Herbert Hugh Melville was a Canadian citizen born at London England on June 25, 1891. His parents were George Hinton and Edith Murray. He died at home on August 23, 1939, after August 12th gastrostomy surgery. He had been ill with lung carcinoma for several years and with recent bronchial pneumonia. He was living at 105 Arlington Ave, married to Phyllis Hoad, and he had lived in the city of Oshawa in the township of East Whitby for 12 years and in Ontario, Canada for 17 years. He had last worked on the General Motors truck assembly line in December 1938. Melville was buried at Mount Lawn Cemetery on August 25, 1939.

1939: On August 25, Melville Hinton was buried at Mount Lawn Cemetery located at Garrard Road and Dundas Street East in Whitby, Ontario.

After Melville's death, Phyllis and her sons continued to live at 105 Arlington Ave. Phyllis had her family, friends, and her United Church community for support. Clifford, Hugh, and Doug ambitiously pursued employment while they continued to enjoy their active life in Oshawa.

Clifford (Cliff as he was known by friends and family) at age 18, was having fun in his brother Hugh's hat while they were being photographed in the garden at 105 Arlington Ave. Hugh was home from Queen's University to attend Toronto Normal School for teacher training.

61

Passion for Hockey

1940: Cliff, at age 19, pictured below in his favourite hockey jacket, played defence for the Oshawa Bees, a Junior B Hockey team. Their home ice was Oshawa's Hambly Arena. The Bees played from 1938-53, in various leagues during the early formation of the OHA. Their best year was in 1940-41 when the Bees lost the provincial final to the Brantford Lions. *See **Pg 66-68** for Cliff's game reports.*

1941 Clifford at age 20, Oshawa Bees O.H.A Junior "B" team

This team photo was taken by the entrance to Hambly Arena at 140 King St W in Oshawa.

OSHAWA "BEES"
O.H.A. JUNIOR "B" FINALISTS 1940-41

Back Row—Roy Painter, Art Ladd, Cliff Hinton, Don Bouckley, Frank Black, Jim Galbraith, Andy McMullen, Ken Davies, Walter Kilsuck, Ross Wilson.

Front Row—O. H. A. Luke, Jack McMullen, Norm McBrien, Phil Burkhart, Lyle McIntyre, Doug Furey, George Easton.

Absent—Den Sawyer, Frank Foley

1941: For Cliff's 20th birthday on March 11th, his friends, *"Junior Bee Fans"*, wrote a poem celebrating his hockey fame and potential.

HAPPY BIRTHDAY   HAPPY BIRTHDAY   HAPPY BIRTHDAY

Here's to our chum and friend Cliffie
Who has turned out to be a great Junior B
He sure knows how to mow them down
Even though his name is not "Stanowski"

Then of course there was Eddie Shore
Who always came bouncing back for more
He's over here now, as a Big League scout
And we're almost sure that he'll pick you out

We also know of a guy named Orlando
But needless to say, he's a man though (21)
Just one more year for that kid Hinton
And in Senior ranks he'll really "hip them"

Happy Birthday to Defenceman Hinton
Who, if they come straight at him, can really hit them
He's fairly tall and a little lean
But say, those eyes, they really gleam.

These verses we know, are not in rhyme
But we just thought this the proper time
To say "HAPPY BIRTHDAY".

         Junior Bee Fans

HAPPY BIRTHDAY   HAPPY BIRTHDAY   HAPPY BIRTHDAY

1941 Clifford at age 20 plays for Oshawa Bees O.H.A Junior "B" team.

This photo was taken inside Hambly Arena, 140 King St W, Oshawa. *See QR for Hambly Arena*

1941 Oshawa Bees, O.H.A. Junior B finals, April 8

This QR code is for a playoff games report for the 1940-41 Sutherland Cup Championship.

Below is one of Cliff's many clippings from The Oshawa Daily Times.

"Oshawa Junior Bees made Good Friday live up to its name as they walloped St. Catherines….by the score of 12 to 5 on Friday night."

"Oshawa now meet Brantford for the Ontario Championship." The Bees and Lions would be competing to win the best 3 of 5 games for the Sutherland Cup.

THE OSHAWA DAILY TIMES, MONDAY, APRIL 14, 1941

Oshawa Jrs. "Bees" Reach O.H.A. Finals Again

Motor City Kids Will Again Play in Junior "B" Finals; Win 12-5 Right in St. Kitts

Galbraith Paces Oshawa "Bees" in Clean-Cut Victory Over St. Catharines Saints, Right on Their Own Ice

MEET BRANTFORD IN O.H.A. FINALS

Win Clinches Second Place for Frank Black's Team and Right to Meet Brantford's Strong Team for Provincial Honors

(By D. B. C.)

Led by the great work of burly Jim Galbraith, who alone scored five goals, Oshawa Junior "Bees" made Good Friday live up to its name as they walloped St. Catharines "Mason Saints" right in St. Kitts by the score of 12 to 5 on Friday night. The "Bees" stung hard and often as a too confident St. Kitts team played right into their hands by trying to skate with the faster and better coached Oshawa team. The game had a little of everything, including a real Donnybrook with every player on the ice including the two goaltenders swinging punches at one another. Phil Burkhart, classy Oshawa net minder, starred alongside Galbraith with a sensational display of goaltending. The husky "Bee" goalie kept the Saints at bay in every period when their power plays threatened to even up the score.

Opened Fast

Play opened at a fast clip with the Saints on the attack. Lyle McIntyre started the fireworks after 1 minute and 55 seconds when he poked the puck away from Scotty Wallace and slipped it over to reliable Normie McBrien and Normie made no mistake with a sizzling shot to the corner. Less than three minutes later Galbraith started his parade by stickhandling through the entire St. Catharines team to beat Burrell with a hot drive. Doug Furey made it three for Oshawa as he took Bouckley's pass clipped in on the St. Kitts ...

... corner on a beautiful shot ... showed ... and ... Burrell never had a chance. Crocker finally scored ... homesters on a power play after Scotty Wallace set it up. Galbraith got that one back before the period ended when he took McIntyre's pass and made no mistake. Burrell in the Saints' net, should have come out to clear as the puck got ahead of Galbraith but the goalie elected to try and stop the shot and lost. Bouckley then missed a perfect setup when he overskated the puck just before the period ended. The period ended with the "Bees" with value for a 4 to 1 lead.

Oshawa All Way

It was all Oshawa again in the second period as the Saints pressed hard and forgot to cover up. Jim Galbraith scored his third one after 7 minutes from Buck Davies. St. Catharines then put up on a sustained power play and Burkhart rose to great heights to keep the puck out. McComb finally scored at 11.35 on a pass from Vines. St. Kitts continued the ganging attack only to have McIntyre and McBrien combine on a breakaway with Normie McBrien again scoring. Not satisfied with that lesson, the "Saints" continued to press and Normie McBrien again outfoxed them and stole the puck. Lyle McIntyre sank the goal after going right in. McIntyre and McBrien played brilliantly in this period.

Hectic "Donnybrook"

The final period carried all the attractions of a three-ring circus as the St. Kitts players grew desperate and Frank Black's well-coached squad toyed with them as tempers frayed and the Saints started roughing it. Eight goals were counted before the period ended, five penalties, among them 3 majors and one misconduct, a free for all and St. Kitts tried out a new goalie and in the space of the twenty minutes. St. Kitts scored first but then Oshawa rapped in four straight as Galbraith, Davies, McIntyre and finally Art Ladd tallied for the Bees. Nelson got one back for the Saints and then Jim Galbraith scored his fifth goal. Vine ended the scoring at the 19 minute mark. The tempers which had bubbled all night boiled over when Andy McMullen and Melville started swapping punches and that started a real free for all. Melville talked back to referee Beef Mackay and had a misconduct tacked on to his major. St. Kitts swapped goal tenders in an effort to halt the Oshawa attack but young Percy Fovelle, who replaced Bobby Burrell fared no better.

Meet Brantford

Oshawa now meet Brantford for the Ontario championship and the Bees are hopeful of garnering their first championship. All players came out of the game in fair condition with Burkhart and Davies bruised a little and Cliff Hinton and Art Ladd nursing sore ankles. Don Sawyer who although not scoring, played a whale of a game with his checking and speed, also was banged around a little.

The teams:

ST. CATHARINES — Goal, Burrell and Favelle; defense, Crocker and Welch; centre, Wallace; wings, Nelson and McComb subs, Melville, Webstock, Vine, A. Crocker, Parker.

OSHAWA BEES — Goal, Burkhart; defense, Hinton and Galbraith; centre, McIntyre; wings, McBrien and Furey; subs, Davies, A. McMullen, Sawyer, Ladd, J. McMullen, Bouckley, Kilnuck, sub goal.

Referee—Gordon "Beef" Mackay of Hamilton.

First Period
1—Oshawa, McBrien (McIntyre) 1.55
2—Oshawa, Galbraith 4.41
3—Oshawa, Furey (Bouckley) 9.13
4—St. Kitts, Crocker (Wallace) 11.56
5—Oshawa, Galbraith (McIntyre) 19.15
Penalties—McComb, A. McMullen, Welch, Hinton.

Second Period
6—Oshawa, Galbraith (Davies) 7.10
7—St. Kitts, McComb (Vine) 11.35
8—Oshawa, McBrien (McIntyre) 16.37
9—Oshawa, McIntyre (McBrien) 17.15
Penalties—Welch, A. McMullen.

Third Period
10—St. Kitts, Wallace (Nelson, McComb) 3.22
11—Oshawa, Galbraith 10.05
12—Oshawa, Davies 10.40
13—Oshawa, McIntyre (McBrien, Furey) 12.30
14—Oshawa, Ladd (McBrien) 12.50
15—St. Kitts, Nelson (Crocker, Parker) 13.25
16—Oshawa, Galbraith (McBrien) 14.36
17—St. Kitts, Vine (Parker).
Penalties — J. McMullen, McComb, Davies, A. McMullen (major), Melville (major and misconduct).

1941 Oshawa Bees, O.H.A. Junior B finals, April 14

The Bees were defeated by the Brantford Lions 10 to 4, giving the win to the Lions in this first of 5 championship final games. *See QR Code below.*

Brantford's Strong 'B' Team Wins First Game of Finals

Oshawa Kids Lose Tilt on St. Catharines' Ice When Lions Roar Into Lead With First Period Splurge

St. Catharines, April 15. — Displaying a fast-breaking and close-checking brand of puck chasing, Brantford Lions captured the first game of the O.H.A. Junior "B" finals here last night when they defeated Oshawa Bees, 10-4.

Lions packed too much early foot for Frank Black's charges, who left their rally until too late. Only in the final did Bees outscore Brants at 2-1, as both teams tossed in a deal of heavy bodying, a wealth of holding and various trips. The spice of the night was inserted late in the second when Butcher and Furey tangled and Referee McKay had to plunge into the fray to hold off the rivals, who were keen to get involved. Both starters drew majors.

BRANTFORD LIONS — Goal, Wilson; defense, Reise, Butcher; centre, Pigeon; wings, Kennedy, Campbell; subs., Strongman, Linn, Horeck, Bailas, Plumley, Aslin, McNicholl.

OSHAWA BEES—Goal, Burkhart; defense, Galbraith, Hinton; centre, McIntyre; wings, Furey, McBrien; subs., Davies, Sawyer, A. and J. McMullen, Ladd, Bouckley, Klimeck.

The Summary

First Period
1—Brants, Kennedy .... :45
2—Brants, Strongman (Linn, Horeck) 17:25
3—Brants, Reise 19:59

Second Period
4—Brants, Kennedy (Reise) 2:10
5—Oshawa, Furey (Galbraith) 3:10
6—Brants, Horeck (Strongman) 6:15
7—Brants, Reise 7:43
8—Oshawa, McIntyre 10:15
9—Brants, Reise (Horeck) .. 15:06
10—Brants, Kennedy (Pigeon) 16:02
11—Brants, Campbell (Kennedy) 19:20
Penalties—Butcher (major), Furey (major).

Third Period
12—Oshawa, Sawyer (Furey) 12:30
13—Oshawa, Furey 13:05
14—Brants, Pigeon (Kennedy) 19:59
Penalties—Hinton 2, Aslin.

https://icehockey.fandom.com/wiki/1940-41_Sutherland_Cup_Championship

1941 Oshawa Bees, O.H.A. Junior B finals, April 16

"Brantford Lions moved one step closer to the O.H.A. Junior "B" championship here last night when they defeated Oshawa's 'Motor City Bees' by a score of 8 to 6 for their second straight win of the 5-game final…. the third game will be played in Brantford on Friday night, when a win for the Lions will decide the championship." It seems the 'Bees' lost that Friday April 18 game 8 to 3 and the Sutherland Cup Championship. Cliff did not have that newsclip in his collection.

Oshawa Kids Scare Lions Right In Their Own Den

Motor City Bees Had Early Lead and Outplayed Homesters in 3rd Frame Too, But Second Stanza Proved Disastrous Play Again Friday Night in Brantford

(Special to The Times)

Brantford, April 17 — Brantford Lions moved one step closer to the O.H.A. Junior "B" championship here last night when they defeated Oshawa "Bees" by a score of 8 to 6, for their second-straight win of the 5-game final series.

In a neffort to clean up the long drawn-out hockey season, the third game will be played in Brantford on Friday night, when a win for the Lions will decide the championship.

Oshawa Took Lead

The Motor City kids burst out in front with a 3-goal scoring splurge in the opening period but the determined homesters came on in the second period with a sudden rush to wipe out this deficit and go on to build up a substantial lead, which they successfully defended although outplayed again in the third period.

The Lions drew down the major share of the penalties, six against Oshawa's mere two. These penalties proved costly to the homesters, with Reise being in the penalty box twice in the first and twice in the third periods. It was these penalties that helped Oshawa to outscore the Lions in both periods.

Second Period Rally

Lions were too good for the Oshawa team in the second period. The Motor City Bees showed plenty of fight and zip but they couldn't cope with the Lions' superior weight on the smaller ice surface. Burkhart played a whale of a game for the visiting Oshawans, with McBrien, Furey and McIntyre shining on the attack. Galbraith and Hinton also toiled well on the rearguard.

Oshawa Bees buzzed around at a great rate and stung the Lions with three neat goals in the first stanza, McBrien, J. McMullen and McBrien again, doing the scoring.

Brantford's key men, Kennery, Butcher and Pigeon pulled them out of the slump with their grand work in the second period. In the last period, McIntyre and Aandy Strongman got one for the Lions.

Wilson, in the Brantford nets, turned in a great game too to match Burkhart's fine play. He "stalled" via the drink-of-water system repeatedly when the Oshawa team got the Lions up in the air near the finish of the game but urged on by a large and very rabid audience the Brantford boys managed to survive.

Oshawa played the right type of game to win against the husky Lions and but for a brief but costly lapse in their tactics, during the second period, the Motor City boys would have tied up the series.

The Summary

BRANTFORD LIONS—Goal, T. Wilson; defense, L. Reise, J. Butcher; centre, Pigeon; wings, W. Campbell, Kennedy; subs., Ballas, Strongman, Horrock, Aslin, Linn, Plumley; sub-goalie, McNicol.

OSHAWA—Goal, Burkhart; defense, Hinton, Galbraith; centre, McIntyre; wings, McBrien, Furey; subs., J. McMullen, A. McMullen, Davies, Sawyer, Ladd, Painter; sub-goalie, Kilmuck.

First Period.
1—Oshawa, McBrien 7:23
2—Oshawa, J. McMullen ... 11:25
3—Oshawa, McBrien (Painter) 16:25
4—Brantford, Pigeon (Kennedy) 17:40
Penalties—Reise 2.

Second Period.
5—Brantford, Kennedy (Reise, Campbell) .... :48
6—Brantford, Butcher (Pigeon, Kennedy) 3:52
7—Brantford, Kennedy (Pigeon) 14:36
8—Oshawa, Furey (McBrien) 15:14
9—Brantford, Pigeon 16:04
10—Brantford, Linn (Horeck, Strongman) 18:40
11—Brantford, Kennedy (Pigeon) 19:46
Penalties—Horeck, J. McMullen.

Third Period.
12—Oshawa, McIntyre (Davies) 7:08
13—Brantford, Strongman ... 17:23
14—Oshawa, A. McMullen (Furey) 18:37
Penalties—Butcher 2, Reise, Galbraith.

1941: In the back row are Cliff, Jack Hoad, Hugh, and Walter Hoad. In the front row are Phyllis and Kate Hoad, with friends Kay, John and their son who were visiting at 105 Arlington Avenue, a year since Melville's death. Doug likely took the photo above.

Cliff, at age 20, with his brothers Doug 23 and Hugh 21. There was surely talk about current employment, with Cliff at General Motors, Doug at Bell Telephone Company and Hugh teaching. As well there was likely talk of the escalating war in Europe and imminent enlistment possibilities.

Employment at General Motors, Oshawa

1941: For 4 years prior to his WWII enlistment, Cliff worked as a clerk in the Oshawa General Motors Parts Department. This General Motors Office Team photo was likely taken in autumn of 1941, before Cliff enlisted for army service. He is in back row 3rd from right where he can be seen sporting a newly grown mustache.

World War II Years
1941-1945

Brother: Douglas Melville Hinton (1918-2000)	73
Brother: Hugh Frederick Hinton (1919-1944)	75
Cousin: Roy Alexander Hoad (1915-1997)	76
Cousin: Jack Walter Hoad (1922-1944)	76
Clifford Ley Herbert Hinton (1921-1957)	77
RCOC Overseas Service, England, Sicily, Italy	78
Brother Hugh Killed at Normandy, 12 August 1944	80
Cousin Jack Killed at Gimli Manitoba 17 October 1944	85
Cliff's Return to Canada, 15 July 1945	86

Douglas Melville Hinton 1918-2000

Cliff's brother Doug left GM in 1941 to work at Bell Telephone. From there he was recruited by the British Security Co-Ordination (BSC) to work on communication intelligence activities. He was instrumental in setting up and operating the communication systems at the secret Camp X training facility at Whitby, Ontario. Military records are not available, but several US border crossing records note his work with BSC at 5th Ave New York. During the war years Doug did important work in surveillance and communication. *See* **Camp X** *on next Pg 74.*

In 1945, When Cliff returned from his overseas wartime service, he visited Doug in New York City where he was working on covert operations with the BSC. *See* **Pg 86** *and Phyllis's note below.*

When WWII activities ended Doug returned to work (and continued his secret intel?) at the Bell Telephone offices in Oshawa where he met Doris Evelyn Hele. Doug and Doris married 27 September 1949, at Oshawa. They lived there at 17 Quebec St. and by 1952 at 764 Grierson Ave. In 1955 Doug and Doris moved to Ville St Laurent, Montreal, Quebec. They had three children: Dale born 3 September 1950, Robert born 8 October 1954 and Beverly born 11 August 1958. During the cold war years, Doug worked on the planning and the 1957 installation of the DEW (Distant Early Warning) radar stations in Northern Canada. By 1970 Doug moved his family to 16 Plaza Square in Belleville. His work as a "communication specialist" with Bell Telephone took him to countries around the world where his expertise was well appreciated. Douglas Melville Hinton died age 82 at Belleville 24 February 2000. Doris died age 89 at Belleville 22 May 2017.

Camp X at Whitby Ontario

From 1942 to 1946 Camp X, was a secret spy training school STS103 in south Whitby. It also served as a secret communication and surveillance facility during WWII. There are many resources at the **Camp-x.com** official site to help us learn about Camp X. The site's creator, Lynn Philip Hodgson, has extensively researched Camp X history since he first discovered its location in 1977. Lynn's well researched books can be found at https://www.camp-x.com/.

Lynn Hodgson and his wife Marlene met Doug Hinton at a 1979 Camp X reunion. They acquired this photo of Doug in the communication room, from Doug's friend Bill Hardcastle. They told me that Doug's headphones are on display in a Camp X exhibit at Casa Loma, Toronto. Available through Camp-x.com is a link to the book **How to Be a Spy**. At this QR code, CampX info is on Pg 11-17 in the book preview.

There is also information at the Wikipedia QR code links available on **Pg 86**.

Below is a quote from Lynn's Hodgson's 2013 book **Inside CampX** about the 'Field of Rhombic Antennae' in the photo at left.

In 1942, were you to take a walk through the Camp and buildings, you would start at Thornton Road. Here you would find a wooden sign nailed to an old and weathered post about four feet high. The sign simply announced, PROHIBITED AREA - DEPARTMENT OF NATIONAL DEFENCE. From this point, you would walk westward along the original farm road into Glenrath. The road was a typical country gravel road about ten feet wide. You would have to pass a small unassuming guardhouse with a swing gate beyond which no one proceeded without proper orders. This was the only gate to the camp.

Approximately three hundred feet from Thornton Road and to the left would be the old original apple orchard. Directly south of that, as you looked toward Lake Ontario, you would be able to see the giant Rhombic Antennae, which could originate or pluck coded Morse traffic from the ionosphere.

Hugh Frederick Hinton 1919-1944

Cliff's brother Hugh finished 4 years at Oshawa CVI, working summers as a playground leader, swim instructor and at an Oshawa Funeral Home. After his father's death, Hugh left his studies at Queens University to complete a year at Toronto Normal School for teacher qualification. He taught briefly before duty called and he enrolled for army reserve training at Newmarket and Camp Borden. On October 28, 1941, Hugh enlisted at Camp Borden for active army service and was attached to the RHLI (Royal Hamilton Light Infantry). By November he was promoted to corporal and given a 14-day furlough to visit family in Oshawa. In July, after Officer Training at Brockville, Hugh was back at Camp Borden as 2nd lieutenant, and he was promoted to full lieutenant on November 14, 1942.

While they were both at Camp Borden, he and Cliff were able to spend time together (photo). They also enjoyed a few days leave over New Years which they spent at home in Oshawa with their mother Phyllis and brother Doug.

As a lieutenant with the Royal Hamilton Light Infantry, Hugh was sent for overseas active duty in March 1943. Sadly, on 12 August 1944, he suffered a fatal second casualty in Normandy field action. He is buried at Bretteville-sur-Laize, Canadian War Cemetery in France. See **Pg 80-85** for information.

LT. HUGH F. HINTON son of Mrs. H. M. Hinton and the late Mr. Hinton, who is overseas, and today celebrating his 24th birthday. Born in Wales, he has been a resident of Oshawa since 1928. He attended North Oshawa Public School and the O.C.V.I. and was employed by M. F. Armstrong and Son. He received his first class teacher's certificate on completing his course at the Toronto Normal School just before his enlistment in April, 1941. A leader of the Sunday Morning Class for teen-age boys at Northminster United Church, he also acted as a city playground supervisor for several years. He received his basic training at Newmarket and Camp Borden and in November 1941 was promoted to corporal. In April 1942 he went to the officers' training centre at Brockville and graduated as a second lieutenant in July. Two months later he became a full lieutenant. He went overseas in March of this year. His mother resides at the Edwards Apartments and his brother, Cliff, is also overseas.

Clifford's Cousin: Roy Alexander Hoad 1915-1999

Kate and Walter Hoad's first child, Roy Alexander Hoad was born May 1, 1915. While growing up at 24 Norway Ave, Roy went to Norway Public School and later Malvern Collegiate in the Beaches area of East Toronto. It appears, from Toronto directory records, that Roy worked for about 8 years from 1934 to 1941, as a clerk and salesman for Macdonald Mfg., producer of graphic tin products, at 401 Richmond St W in Toronto.

Roy and Norah Elizabeth Finley were married 27 June 1942 at St Aidan's Church on Queen St E and lived with Norah's family at 10 Balsam Ave in the Toronto Beaches area. Roy worked briefly at DeHavilland Aircraft before his Royal Canadian Air Force enlistment.

The photo at right of Roy Hoad with his parents Kate and Walter and with his Aunt Phyllis may have been taken at 10 Balsam Ave after Roy and Norah's 1942 wedding.

Roy and Norah's daughter, Linda Margaret, was born 27 January 1944. When his wartime service ended Roy returned to work at DeHavilland Aircraft and moved his family to 111 Redpath Ave. Their son, John Alexander was born 2 October 1947. In 1951 Roy moved his family to 249 Melrose Ave. and their daughter, Elizabeth Catherine was born 19 January 1952. By 1957 they moved to 54 Melrose Ave where Roy's family resided for many years. When DeHavilland closed operation in the mid 1960s Roy was employed at Douglas Aircraft until he retired at age 65 in 1980. Roy Hoad died 17 December 1997 His wife Norah died two years later and was buried with him at St. John's Norway Cemetery at Woodbine Ave. *See map **Pg 29**.*

Clifford's Cousin: Jack Walter Hoad 1922-1944

Kate and Walter Hoad's second child, Jack Walter Hoad was born 2 December 1922 while the Hinton family were staying with the Hoad family at 24 Norway Ave. Like his brother, Jack enjoyed growing up in the Beaches community, attending Norway Public School, Malvern Collegiate and Central Technical School studying aircraft. 1940-42 Jack worked in aircraft assembly at DeHavilland and had his pilot licence before he enlisted in the Royal Canadian Air Force and became a flying instructor.

Jack Hoad and Pauline Ruth Black were married 23 June 1943 at Toronto and were living together in Gimli Manitoba when he died 27 October 1944, in a crash during flying operations. *See **Pg 85**.*

Clifford Ley Herbert Hinton 1921-1957

1942: On March 20, at age 21, Cliff enlisted at Canadian Military offices in Toronto. He was given No B9203, rank of Private and assigned to No 2 detachment of Royal Canadian Army Ordnance Corps (RCOC) for introductory training at Toronto. His records noted brown eyes, height 5' 10", weight 154.5 lbs, good hearing acuity, education Gr 12 at age 16, 4 years auto parts clerk at GM, and hobbies of sports and model building. In April, Cliff was posted to the No 3A Kingston, Ontario, Army Tank Ordnance Field, where he met Joe Forsythe (the nephew of Dorothy Auld, his future bride).
See **Appendix B Pg 225** for Cliff's enlistment and service documents.

1942: On June 16, Cliff was posted, for a year, to CFB Camp Borden, 23 km west of Barrie Ontario. While there for Army Ordnance training Cliff saw his brother Hugh who was also there, training for Lieutenant rank qualification. See **Pg 75** for Cliff and Hugh's Camp Borden photo.

In late December, Cliff and Hugh had New Year's leave from Camp Borden to be at home in Oshawa. It was certainly an emotional time for Phyllis to have her sons with her before they were sent to active duty overseas. Phyllis and Doug then moved from 105 Arlington Ave to #9 Edwards Apartments at 17 Quebec St in Oshawa while Doug was working nearby at Camp X in Whitby, Ontario. Photos below are Phyllis with Hugh at Arlington Ave, Cliff center and at right is Doug with Phyllis at 17 Quebec St.

1943: On June 16, Pte Cliff Hinton was sent overseas to England. While there he likely had leave to visit his relatives in Wales. See **Pg 123, 124, and 134**.

By September Cliff was in Sicily with the CMF, Central Mediterranean Forces.

1944: In February, Cliff received his mother's letter telling him about the February 5th death of her brother Frederick Hoad at Pembroke Wales.

On April 15, Cliff was posted to eastern Italy near Pesaro, Marche, on the Adriatic Sea, for army ordnance services with the AAI (Allied Armies Italy). *See Italy photos at right.*

1944: In April, Cliff's mother still lived at Quebec St. in Oshawa and Doug was often away on secret BSC communication projects in New York and elsewhere. Friends Jack Durie, Leone Palmer, Charlie Johnston, and his wife Marion visited Phyllis before the young men would soon be called to military service in Europe. Jack is reading news reports while Phyllis knits.

The Oshawa times Gazette reported news about the Normandy Campaign on 6 June 1944, the day it started with the D-Day invasion.
https://archive.org/details/timesgazette19440606 *see below right*.
https://archive.org/details/timesgazette19440608 *see below centre*.

This link above left has information and firsthand D-Day accounts:
https://www.thecanadianencyclopedia.ca/en/article/normandy-invasion

Hugh's Royal Hamilton Light Infantry unit was with the 2nd Canadian Division which had been held in reserve in England during the Normandy Invasion. They were sent late in June to join efforts to weaken the German occupation but before that Hugh sent a letter to his brother Cliff. Hugh's transcribed June 23 letter and Cliff's August 22 reply letter are on the next two pages.
See handwritten letters in **Appendix C on Pgs. 237 and 240.**

Hugh's 23 June 1944 Letter to Brother Cliff

Addressed to: B 9203 Pte Hinton C
                      1st Cdn Corps & Army Tps
                      Sub Park, R.C.O.C, C.M.F. (passed by Censor 3830)

23 June 1944

Dear Cliff,

You will be surprised to know that I have not seen any action yet. I am afraid everyone back home is thinking of me in the invasion and hell I am still in England.

About the only thing of interest that has happened is the robot planes loaded with explosives that the Germans have been sending over. They come in very fast then their motors are cut, and they drop to earth apparently exploding on impact. Although I have not seen any yet, they have been dropping all around us the last few days. They are not very devastating, and the people regard them as a novelty. Their blast effect is great but unless they get a direct hit, the damage is slight.

I received a letter from Jack Durie last week. He tells me Charlie Johnson is in the Army now and that he also may be reboarded and obliged to join up. They certainly are draining the best out of Canada. It is going to be a struggle after the war.

The war seems to be going well in all parts, and if this continues, Montgomery's prophecy will become a reality. He said the war would be over by Christmas. I hope he is right for I am dying to go home.

There is nothing else that I can say Cliff so I shall say goodbye and good luck.

Hugh

During 'Operation Spring', on July 25-27, Hugh suffered mortar wounds to his back during field combat. By August 3 Hugh had healed enough to be returned to his unit at Falaise. They were engaged in a series of fierce battles during the August 8-9 'Operation Totalize' when Hugh suffered fatal wounds. He died on August 12, 1944, and was later buried at Bretteville-Sur-Laize Canadian War Cemetery.

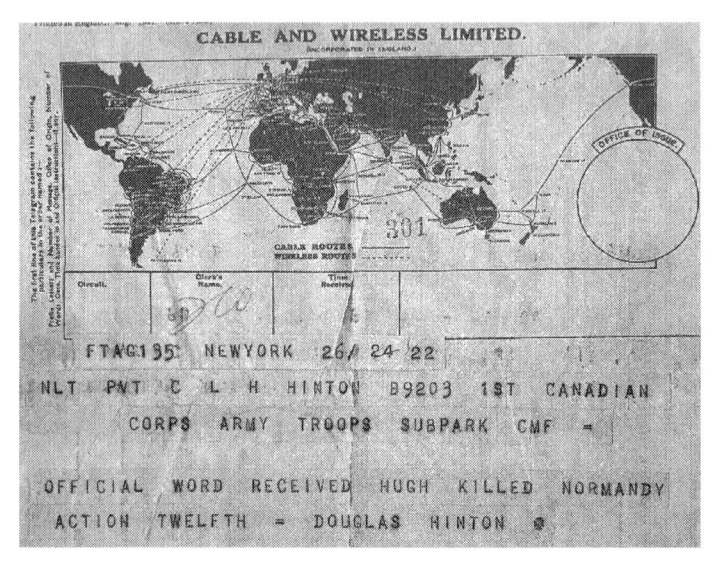

80

Cliff's 22 August 1944 Letter to Brother Hugh

Addressed to: Lieut H F Hinton
                     RHLI, Canadian Army Overseas

August 22nd (1944)

Dear Hugh:

Please forgive me for not writing sooner. I received your last letter, you wrote June 23rd, quite some time ago. And as usual, I delayed in dropping you a few lines.

I received two airmails from Mother to-day, containing the disheartening news of your injuries. Hugh, I want to tell you how proud I am of you and am hoping so much that your injuries are slight and that you will be on your feet again soon. I have read a few reports of your regiment in the paper and my thoughts were with you. I would give anything to have been with you.

Mother seemed quite cheerful in her letters, but she must be worrying, about you very much. I was very glad to hear that Doug was able to get home from New York for a few days. Kay and John were very kind to her also. Mother mentioned about the story in the Toronto paper of your exploits during your patrols. You deserve a lot Hugh, for your courage. I know, pretty well, what you have gone through. It really burns me up to think of the small effort I am turning in. I applied for a transfer to the Combined American and Canadian Special Service Corps, a few weeks ago, without any luck. I like my unit very much, also my work, but at times such as this I am very discontented. I know its too late to ever think of joining you now, but I want you to know that my thoughts are always with you and I'm hoping that it will all end soon, and we can get together again. I'll have so much to tell you.

You must wonder, Hugh, why I haven't got ahead in the Army. Its not because of my behaviour. I haven't been up for orders since I left Canada. I've had a few chances for promotion, but so far, I've felt that the work I have turned in for my unit is more deserving than what they have ever offered. I know you'll say I have been very foolish but that is the way I feel. When I missed out on my commission in leaving Canada a few weeks too soon, I was very disappointed. But now all I'm looking forward to is a speedy finish to this mess we are in.

Well Hugh, it's getting late, so I must cut this short. Take care of yourself and I hope this letter finds you back on your feet again and happy. I won't fail to write you again in a few days.

All the best,
Your kid brother, Cliff

Cliff's August 22 letter did not reach Hugh but was returned to sender. Two days after he sent this letter to his brother, Cliff learned of Hugh's August 12th death. He received the shocking new in a brief August 24 cable sent from New York City by his brother Doug. *Seen on previous **Pg 80**.*

1944 Hugh Frederick Hinton registration of death at France in WWII

PROVINCE OF ONTARIO
VITAL STATISTICS ACT
REGISTRATION OF DEATH

Registration Number: **705962**

1. **PLACE OF DEATH** — City, Town or Village of **IN THE FIELD (FRANCE)**
2. **LENGTH OF STAY**
3. **PRINT FULL NAME OF DECEASED**: **HINTON**, **Hugh Frederick**
4. **PERMANENT RESIDENCE OF DECEASED**: City — **Oshawa**, Street — **105 Arlington Avenue**, Province of **Ontario**
5. **SEX**: M
6. **CITIZENSHIP**:
7. **RACIAL ORIGIN**:
8. **Single**, Married, Widowed or Divorced
9. **BIRTHPLACE**: **Wales**
10. **Date of Birth**: **December 14, 1919**
11. **AGE**: 24
12. (a) Trade, profession: **School teacher**
19. I certify the foregoing to be true and correct to the best of my knowledge and belief.
   Given under my hand at **Ottawa**, this **8** day of **October** 19**45**
   Address: **Director of Records, Dept. of National Defence**
20. Burial, Cremation or Removal: **France**

MEDICAL CERTIFICATE OF DEATH

23. **DATE OF DEATH**: **August 12, 1944**

CAUSE OF DEATH
(a) **Killed in action**
(b) **OVERSEAS CASUALTY**
    CANADIAN ARMY

1944 Cliff's brother Hugh Frederick Hinton, Killed in Action near Falaise, France.

In Memory of

Lieutenant

Hugh Frederick Hinton

1st Bn., Royal Hamilton Light Infantry, R.C.I.C. Age 25

Son of Herbert Hugh Melville Hinton and Phyllis Hinton, of Pembroke, Wales.

Remembered with Honour
Bretteville-Sur-Laize Canadian War Cemetery

Commemorated in perpetuity by
the Commonwealth War Graves Commission

https://www.veterans.gc.ca/eng/remembrance/memorials/overseas/second-world-war/france/bretteville

1944 H F Hinton at Bretteville-Sur-Laize Canadian War Cemetery

These early crosses were later replaced with stone monuments.

84

1944: More sad news for the Hinton/Hoad family was received after October 17, when Cliff's 21-year-old cousin Jack Walter Hoad died in a RCAF flying operation at Gimli Manitoba.

F.O. JACK WALTER HOAD, R.C.A.F., son of Mr. and Mrs. Walter Alexander Hoad, Norway Ave., was killed in flying operations near Gimli, Manitoba, on Friday. In June, 1943, F.O. Hoad married Miss Pauline Ruth Black, daughter of Mr. and Mrs. L. H. Black, Wineva Ave., and she has been in the west with her husband since December. F.O. Hoad enlisted in August, 1942, and received his wings and commission at Camp Borden, Oct. 15, 1943. He has been instructing for the past year at Weyburn, Sask., and Gimli. The funeral will take place in Toronto.

FO. JACK W. HOAD

FO. Jack Walter Hoad, 21, RCAF, was killed Oct. 27, on active service during flying operations near Gimli, Man., where he had been an instructor since February, according to word received by his wife, Pauline Ruth Black Hoad, of 18 Wineva Ave.

Enlisting in Aug., 1942, he received his wings at Camp Borden in Oct., 1943, and before going to Gimli was an instructor at Weyburn, Sask. Born in Toronto, he attended Norway Public School, Malvern Collegiate and Central Technical. Before enlistment he was employed by the de Havilland Aircraft of Canada Ltd., and had been a student in flying at the Toronto Flying Club.

Surviving besides his wife are his parents, Mr. and Mrs. William A. Hoad, 24 Norway Ave., and a brother, LAC. Roy Hoad, overseas.

HOAD, JACK WALTER F/O(P) J36990. From Toronto, Ontario. Killed Oct.27/44 age 21. #18 Service Flying Training School, Gimli, Manitoba. F/O.s Hoad and J.R. Lawlor were engaged in instrument flying and practising spins under the hood and were killed when Harvard aircraft # 3770 failed to recover from a spin and crashed near Gimli. Flying Officer Pilot Hoad is buried in the St. John's Norway Cemetery at Toronto, Ontario.

1945: In February, Cliff was deployed to Northwest Europe for Army Ordnance services in France and The Netherlands. He was a qualified store man working to supply the field troops.

With the war ending in Europe, Cliff returned to England on June 22, 1945, and from there was shipped home to Canada on July 15. He was granted special leave July 25 to August 23. During that leave he visited his brother Doug who was working on a 'communications intelligence project' at the British Securities Offices in New York City. See **Pg 73** for photo of Cliff and Doug in NYC. The photo at right was taken by Doug while walking with Cliff and friends near Rockefeller Center. Cliff's mother Phyllis wrote the note on the back of the photo and may have known Eileen Knox, from Oshawa.

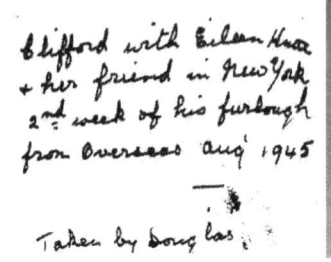

Clifford with Eileen Knox + her friend in New York 2nd week of his furlough from Overseas aug 1945

Taken by Douglas

Below are QR codes that link Wikipedia pages for British Securities Coordination offices and covert operations at Rockefeller Center in NYC. There are references to CampX and Wm Stephenson.

| BSC | Rockefeller | CampX | William Stephenson |

Cliff Returns to Oshawa, Family, Friends, and Hockey

Cliff's Return to Oshawa 1945	89
Legionnaires Hockey Team (1945-46)	90
Discharge 10 January 1946	94
General Motors Employment	94
Meeting Dorothy Marguerite Auld (1919-2004)	96
Cliff and Dodie at Kingston	105

Return to Oshawa, Family, Friends and Hockey

1945: In August, Cliff reconnected with family and friends; spending time with them in Oshawa, Toronto, and Utica, Ontario. At left He is in Oshawa with Scotty Reid and 3 other friends.

In September, Cliff was granted an extended unpaid military leave from September 30, 1945, to March 29, 1946.

Phyllis and Cliff visited with friends who lived in Utica. While sightseeing they stopped at the Foster Memorial near Uxbridge, Ontario. It's also possible that Cliff was there playing hockey with the Legionnaires at the Uxbridge Arena. He would later play a January 1946, game at Uxbridge. *See* **Pg 95** *for game report.*

At right, Cliff and Phyllis are with Doug and an unknown dog at their Quebec Street apartment.

1945: Cliff was back in his favourite hockey jacket in this photo, likely taken in front of Scotty Reid's Arlington Ave home. Eager to get back to playing hockey, he and Scotty joined the Oshawa Legionnaires. In 1946 Scotty left the Legionnaires joining his brother James Reid to play with the Oshawa Red Raiders team. The Reid family had been Arington Ave neighbours of the Hintons. Their father was the custodian at the nearby North Simcoe Public School.

Cliff and his friend Alex (aka Scotty) Reid played hockey with the Oshawa Legionnaires. Alex is top left player and Cliff is 2nd from left on the bench

1945 Oshawa Legionnaires

'Canadian Legionnaires, Oshawa's all veteran entry in the Big Four OHA Intermediate A grouping who are making a splendid showing this season.'

The team photo (see page 86) was used in this Oshawa Times-Gazette issue likely in December of 1945. It's included here as it has the names of players, coaches, and others.

During the winter months, the Oshawa Legionnaires played in the Intermediate A, OHA playoff games against the Peterborough Petes, the Oshawa Red Raiders, the Belleville Redmen, and the Kingston Locos. Cliff played defense in every game that season.

Home ice was Hambly Arena at 140 King ST W in Oshawa.

www.ohlarenaguide.com

1946 Oshawa Legionnaires at Omemee, January 5

'The Oshawa Legionnaires opened their Intermediate "A" O.H.A. schedule against the Peterborough Petes'. They played at Omemee on slushy ice. The Motor City squad put up a sterling battle in their first appearance of the season but lost to the Petes in a 4-3 decision. Cliff played defense with a penalty in the third period.

PROGRAMME

#	OSHAWA "LEGIONNAIRES"	#	PETERBOROUGH "PETES"
1.	"Rube" Waddell (RCAF)	1.	R. Harding
2.	"Cliff" Hinton (ARMY)	2.	F. Parson
3.	"Jr" McMullen (RCAF)	3.	L. Burton
4.	"Spud" Murphy (RCAF)	4.	A. Jamieson
5.	"Andy" McMullen (RCAF)	5.	B. Kingdon
6.	"Red" Regan (RCAF)	6.	A. Hool
7.	"Red" Krantz (RCAF)	7.	H. Thompkins
8.	"Regina" Tisdall (ARMY)	8.	R. Creighton
9.	"Doug" Furey (ARMY)	9.	J. Blewet
10.	"Stan" Fraser (RCAF)	10.	
11.	"Whitey" White (RCAF)	11.	E. Vitarelli
12.	"Bob" Hicks (RCAF)	12.	T. Parson
14.	"Gar" Peters (ARMY)	13.	K. Bradley
15.	"Lylo" McIntyre (ARMY)	14.	R. Ellis
	"Cliff" Maundrell (NAVY)	15.	R. Wakelin
16.	"Perce" Berriage (ARMY)	16.	C. Brooks

Manager:
  "Buck" Hobbs (RCAF)

Coach:
  "Ken" Sanders (ARMY)

THE TIMES-GAZETTE
Saturday, January 5, 1946

PETES EDGE LEGION TEAM AT OMEMEE

The Oshawa Legionnaires opened their Intermediate "A" O.H.A. schedule against Peterborough, out at Omemee, last night and while the Motor City squad put up a sterling battle in their first appearance of the season, they dropped a close 4-3 decision, in a game played on slush.

Jack Regan opened the scoring for Oshawa on a pass from White, but Parsons tied it up on a pass from Honey Tompkins a few minutes later.

In the second stanza, Bun Kingdon from Ned Vitarelli and Blewett unassisted, made it 3-1 with Oshawa serving three of four penalties in that frame.

Doug. Furey scored on a pass from Regina Tisdale and Andy McMullen popped one near the end of the period on a pass from Regan to tie the score but with only 12 seconds left to play, Red Creighton scored on a pass from Blewett to break the deadlock and give the Petes the decision.

Oshawa: Goal, Waddell; defense, Hinton and J. McMullen; centre, Krantz; wings, Tisdall and Furey; alternates, Murphy, Fraser, White, A. McMullen, Regan and McIntyre.

Petes—Goal, Harding; defense, Burton and F. Parsons; centre, Kingdon; wings, Tompkins and E. Creighton; alternates, Ellis, Blewett, Bradley, T. Parsons and Vitarelli.

First Period
Oshawa—Regan (White) 8:20
Petes—T. Parsons (Tompkins) 12:35
Penalties—Vitarelli, Burton and Murphy.

Second Period
Petes—Kingdon (Vitarelli) ... 5:06
Petes—Blewett 18:00
Penalties—White, Murphy, Furey and Vitarelli.

Third Period
Oshawa—Furey (Tisdale) 7:50
Oshawa—A. McMullen (Regan) 15:45
Petes—Creighton (Blewett) 19:48
Penalties—F. Parsons, Tisdale and Hinton.

Referee: Williams, Peterboro.

1946 Oshawa Legionnaires Arena, Hambly Arena, Oshawa, January 6

'The Oshawa Legionnaires made their bow before a good crowd of about 2,000 fans' at the Hambly Arena at 140 King St W in Oshawa.

Kingston Locos Score Win Over Oshawa Legionnaires In Local Inter. "A" Opener

Limestone City Squad Show Benefit of Previous Games — Andy McMullen Scores Oshawa's 4 Goals — Rival Goalies Shine — Big Crowd on Hand for Opener, Sees Fast Clean Game

Oshawa Legionnaires made their bow before a good crowd of about 2,000 fans, at the Oshawa Arena last night and although they dropped their Intermediate "A" schedule opener to Kingston Locos by 6 to 4, they gave promise of some interesting hockey competition before this particular O.H.A. group title is settled.

Smoother passing and team-play plus superior staying power and speed were the deciding factors, all present with the Limestone City team because they had more games under their belts—the Van Horne series and one previous league fixture—than had the Motor City Legionnaires, who were playing their first actual competition of the season.

Smooth and Fast

The Locos proved smooth and fast. Up front they had speed galore and their snappy passing attack was of high order and brought results.

Aitken, a speedy left-winger with a smart change of pace and a top gear that was really fast, proved very effective beside Paris, but it was Kingston's starting line of McGregor at centre, flanked by Scruton and Kennie McNaught that really produced most of the Kingston scoring punch.

Right-winger Scruton potted three goals and McGregor got a couple besides chalking up two assists. Kennie McNaught got a couple of "helpers". Aitken and Paris combined for their other tally.

Four for Andy McMullan

Andy McMullan was the big gun for the locals. Outside of Andy, the rest of the boys couldn't beat the sensational net-minding served up by by Glen Udall, the bespectacled goalie. He was terrific in spots and robbed Oshawa snipers on sizzling shots and smothered close-in scrambles with rare effect.

Andy had two scoring spasms, one in the first three minutes and the other in the last three minutes of the game. Each spasm produced two goals. Oshawa was leading 2-0 before the 9-minute mark, on successive goals by McMullan, both on assists by Regan. Then after the visitors had made it 6-2, McMullen scored one at the 17.15 mark on help from White and Regan and just 21 seconds later, he notched his and Oshawa's fourth goal of the night, with White and Hicks getting the assists this time.

Oshawa enjoyed a slight edge in the first period but when the pace began to tell in the second frame, Kingston took a 3-2 lead. They ran in three more goals in succession in the 3rd period, before McMullan moved in again.

Both Goalies Shine

Both goalies earned star rating. Barrage, in the Oshawa nets, saved many times when left all alone. But for Barrage, the Kingston total would have been much higher, but then it was Udall who kept Kingston in front too for the play was wide-open and ranged from goalmouth to goal-mouth.

Oshawa fans took a keen interest in Kennie McNaught and Bill Mortimer, both former Oshawa Generals and they served up good hockey, especially defenceman Bill, with his fast rushes and cool playmaking. For Oshawa, Hinton showed well on defence while Doug. Purey, Regan, White and Regina Tisdall all turned in very useful games.

Referee Earl Hurst meted out only four minor penalties. The boys stuck strictly to hockey, and there wasn't anything that bordered on dirty checking. It was rugged but very clean.

KINGSTON LOCOS — Goal, Udall; defense, Lay and Mortimer; centre, McGregor; wings, Scruton and McNaught; alternates, Paris, Aitken, Bearame and Watts.

OSHAWA LEGIONNAIRES — Goal, Barrage; defense, Hinton and J. McMullan; centre, White; wings, A. McMullan and Regan; alternates, Kinaird, Purey, Tisdall, Murphy, Fraser and Hicks.

Referee, "Pep" Hurst, of Oshawa.

The Summary

First Period
1—Oshawa, A. McMullan (Regan) 1.33
2—Oshawa, A. McMullan (Regan) 8.50
No penalties.

Second Period
3—Kingston, Scruton (McGregor) 9.13
4—Kingston, McGregor (McNaught) 8.40
5—Kingston, Scruton (Mortimer) 13.45
Penalties—McGregor and White.

Third Period
6—Kingston, Aitken (Paris) ... 1.20
7—Kingston, McGregor (McNaught) 7.16
8—Kingston, Scruton (McNaught) 12.43
9—Oshawa, A. McMullan (White, Regan) 17.15
10—Oshawa, A. McMullan (White, Hicks) 17.37
Penalties—Watts and J. McMullan.

Travelling Salesman

1946: On January 7, Cliff was recalled from leave for a meeting at Toronto to discuss his future. He declared his plan to return to employment at General Motors Ltd. and was formally discharged from military service on January 10, 1946. *See **Appendix B Pg 231-234***

Cliff returned to his job at Oshawa GM and was soon promoted to auto part sales. He drove a 1946 Chevrolet sport coupe. *See Pg 184 and the QR code below left.*

Cliff reconnected with Oshawa friends Scotty Reid, Jack Durie and Charlie Johnston with Cliff in the photo at right.

ttps://classiccarcatalogue.com/CHEVROLET_1946.html

Cliff and Scotty worked together at General Motors. In the photo below they are having fun as Clark Gable impersonators 'Going My Way?'!

94

1946 Oshawa Legionnaires at Uxbridge, January 18
The Legionnaires defeated the Oshawa AAA Red Raiders 12-1 at Uxbridge. Cliff played against Oshawa friends, Alex, and James Reid among others on the Red Raider team. The photo below is of Cliff and his childhood friend Alex 'Scotty' Reid.

Cliff Meets Dorothy Auld at Kingston

1946 Oshawa Legionnaires at Jock Harty Arena, Kingston, January 26

The Oshawa Times -Gazette wrote *'defensemen Hinton was a Star'* in this game at Kingston against the Locos who won a 10-5 triumph over the Legionnaires. This seems to be Cliff's first game at Kingston; and likely when he met Dorothy Auld, possibly at the Jock Harty arena. Cliff would have known and connected with his wartime RCOC friend Joe Forsythe who was Dorothy's nephew just 3 years younger than his mother Helen's sister Dodie.

Dodie told stories about meeting Cliff and his visits to the Auld farm when he was in Kingston for hockey games. Her family welcomed him to come for dinner and being polite he had difficulty refusing although a big meal was not wise to have before a game! Dad soon became a favourite visitor at the Auld house. See **Appendix D Pg 280-281** *for Auld house information.*

QR Code for Jock Harty Arena

LEGIONNAIRES DROP ANOTHER

Oshawa Legionnaires dropped a 10-5 decision in Kingston on Saturday but not before they had given the Kingston "Limestone City Locos" a real scare for two periods and given Kingston puck patrons a swell hockey game as entertainment.

Breaking from the barrier with a rare burst of speed that featured sparkling combination play and dutiful back-checking, the Oshawa Legion team ran up a 3-1 lead in the opening stanza. The Locos came back to outscore Oshawa 3-1 in the second stanza to tie up the count at 4-4. In the final frame, Kingston showed more "legs" and condition than the Motor City puck-chasers and roared through to register their 10-5 triumph.

Doug. Furey took a pass from "Gar" Peters to open the scoring early in the game and Andy McMillan made it 2-0 on passes from Cliff Hinton and White. Aitkens scored on a 3-way passing play with Partis and Scrutton helping out and a minute later Andy McMullan scored again with Hinton's help.

Goals by Aitkens and Lay tied it up at 3-3 and then Bill Mortimer scored with Carr-Harris and Catlin assisting. Gar Peters came right back on a rush by Hinton to make it 4-4.

During this second period, when the homesters enjoyed an edge in territorial play as well as scoring success and throughout the entire third period, when the Legionnaires wilted badly and the hometown "Locos" pressed eagerly to the attack, "Rube" Waddell turned in a sensational display of goal-minding to keep the Oshawa boys in the running.

Kingston Homebrews Star

In the third-period drive that brought victory to the Locos, a group of Kingston homebrew puck stars, graduates of Kingston's great little Junior "B" teams of a few years back, took things into their own hands to bring about the parade of goals. Carr-Harris, McGregor, Aitkens, Joey Catlin, Ken Partis, all were very much to the fore, as the score-sheet indicates. Catlin scored three goals in succession to turn victory into a rout, late in the period.

"Red" Regan on a pass from A. McMullan, got Oshawa's only goal of the period, at the 18-minute mark.

There wasn't a single penalty issued in the entire game, as officials "Mike" Rodden and "Yip" Radley of Kingston took a lenient view of play in general and just made certain that the boys kept their checking within legal bounds.

In addition to goalie Waddell, defenseman Hinton was another star, along with Furey, McMullan, Regan and Peters. The entire Kingston team starred and all but Kennie McNaught got into the scoring column.

OSHAWA LEGIONNAIRES — Goal, Wadell; defense, Hinton and J. McMullen; centre, Krantz; wings, Furey and Peters; alternates, White, A. McMullan Regan, Murphy, Praser, McIntyre and Barriage, (sub-goal).

KINGSTON LOCOS—Goal, Udall; defense, Watts and Lay; centre, Partis; wings, Catlin and Carr-Harris; alternates, McGregor, Aitken, Scrutton, Murphy, McNaught and Mortimer.

Officials—"Mike" Rodden and "Yip" Radley, both of Kingston.

First Period
1—Oshawa, Furey (Peters) 2.35
2—Oshawa, A. McMullan (Hinton, White) 6.35
3—Kingston, Aitken (Partis, Scrutton) 13.48
4—Oshawa, A. McMullan (Hinton) 16.45
No penalties.

Second Period
5—Kingston, Aitken (McGregor, Watts) 6.06
6—Kingston, Lay (Aitken) 10.22
7—Kingston, Mortimer, (Carr, Harris, Catlin) 13.05
8—Oshawa, Peters (Hinton) 14.17
No penalties.

Third Period
9—Kingston, Carr-Harris (Catlin) 4.45
10—Kingston, McGregor (Aitken, Murphy) 6.02
11—Kingston, Catlin (Partis, Carr-Harris) 9.35
12—Kingston, (McGregor) 14.17
13—Kingston Catlin (Partis, Carr-Harris) 17.20
14—Oshawa, Regan (A. McMullan) 18.00
15—Kingston, Watts (McGregor) 18.24
No penalties.

96

1946 Oshawa Legionnaires at Hambly Arena, Oshawa, February 4

LEGIONNAIRES WHIP RED RAIDERS

Local Puck Squads Stage Wild Hockey Scramble to Give Fans Real Thriller

Not Much Good Hockey But Plenty of Rugged Checking and Bumping Gives Crowd Laughs and Excitement — Jack Tisdall Grabs Scoring Limelight With 4 and 3 — Cooke and Crandall Tally for Losers

The game that all the Oshawa Inter. "A" hockey fans had been waiting for, was played at the Oshawa Arena last night and the boys waded through it to the tune of "This Is Worth Fighting For" with the Legionnaires coming out on top with a handy 10-2 victory.

While the Legion team was winning two points here, Kingston Lonos were winning over in Whitby and so the Oshawa Legionnaires are now practically assured of a playoff berth, as they have 3rd place by a 1-game margin over Whitby and Belleville is back in 5th place and not likely to upset things either.

Wild and Rugged

The two teams started off fast with Peters opening the scoring for the winners, and Krantz and Tisdall adding to the total before the halfway mark in the period. Cooke on Alex Reid's pass, made it 3-1 before the period ended.

The boys really got the chips up on their shoulders in plain sight in the second stanza and the action was fast, hectic and rugged.

A follow-through play by Furey and Tisdall made it 4-1 after a dozen minutes of speedy action in which play ranged from end to end and all hands elected to toss weight and "hickory" around with rare abandon. In the last minute of play, with the ranks depleted due to 5-minute terms meted to Alex Reid and "Red" Krantz for scrapping, Legion punched in two quick goals.

There had been plenty of spirited elbowing and high-sticking and slashing up until then but the lid was off in the third period, "Crabby" Crandall came down right wing to take a nice pass from "Jake" Jackson and fire the puck past Perc. Barrage from a sharp angle. This made it 6-2 but it was the closest "Red Raiders" could get.

Three-In-Row For Tisdall

As the rugged checking increased, scrambles became more frequent and they were usually in front of Bob Forester's citadel. The spirited goalie, like most of the others, was taking time out to wave his stick a little or leave a stray foot extended where it would do the most "good" but he was kept pretty busy all-told.

Andy McMullan slid the puck into the empty cage after Forester had slid out in a vain attempt to smother. Then in the last half of the period, "Regina" Tisdall moved casually up beside the Red Raider cage and proceeded to get himself three goals. While the other boys were throwing out flying tackles and body-blocks, Tisdall just coasted in and around waiting for the loose pucks to come his way and when they did, he promptly flipped them into the cage. He collected three goals in succession to bring his night's total to 4 goals and 3 assists, which of course made him the big gun of the night.

Other than Tisdall, there wasn't much chance to pick any outstanding stars because it was that kind of a game where they were all into the thick of it, all the time. Few of the forwards worried about position. They just waded into the puck-carrier where they could find him and swooped after the disc when it was loose, regardless of the territory.

Defensemen Jackson of Raiders and Hinton of Legion were particularly strong with the Reid brothers, Trimm, Crandall and Sutton all working hard. For that matter—they all worked hard. So did all the Legionnaires, especially White, Furey, Peters and Krantz.

The Summary

First Period
1—Legion, Peters (Tisdall, Furey) 1.17
2—Legion, Krantz, (White) . 4.35
3—Legion, Tisdall (Peters) . 9.40
4—Raiders, Cooke (A. Reid) 17.40
Penalties—Crandall and A. Reid.

Second Period
5—Legion, Furey (Tisdall) . 13.03
6—Legion, J. McMullan (Peters, Hinton) 19.31
7—Legion, Peters (Tisdall) .. 19.54
Penalties—Trimm, Krantz (major), A. Reid (major).

Third Period
8—Raiders, Crandall (Jackson) 2.02
9—Legion, A. McMullan (White, Krantz) 2.55
10—Legion, Tisdall (Furey, Peters) 11.49
11—Legion, Tisdall (Murphy) 16.50
12—Legion, Tisdall (Hinton) . 19.27
Penalties—Regan, Trimm, Furey (major), J. Reid (major), Crandall and Murphy.

The summary:
OSHAWA "RED RAIDERS" — Goal, Forester; defense, McArthur and Jackson; centre, Crandall; wings, A. Reid and Trimm; alternates, J. Reid, Cooke, Childerhose, Dionne, Logeman, Sutton and Nash, (sub-goal).

OSHAWA "LEGIONNAIRES" — Goal, Barrage; defense, Hinton and J. McMullan; centre, Tisdall; wings, Furey and Peters; alternates, A. McMullan, Regan, White, Hicks, Krantz, Murphy and Waddell, (sub-goal).

Referee, "Peg" Hurst; linesman, "Doug." Love, both of Oshawa.

1946 Oshawa Legionnaires at Belleville, February 8

An 8-7 win against the Belleville Redmen puts the Oshawa Legionnaires firmly in fourth place of the Intermediate O.H.A. race.

Oshawa Legionnaires Move Up Into Third Place With 8-7 Win Play Belleville Again, Here Mon.

"Buck" Davies Proves Help to Legionnaires — Walt. Gerow Is Standout For Redmen — Oshawa's Win Puts Them In 3rd Place — Deciding Game of Schedule Here on Monday Night

THE TIMES-GAZETTE, Saturday, February 9, 1946

Belleville, Feb. 9.—Oshawa Legionnaires took a firm hold of fourth place in the Intermediate O.H.A. race here last night defeating the Belleville Redmen by 8-7 in one of the hardest fought games of the season.

Belleville must now defeat the Legion in their last game of the season to gain a mathematical chance in the playoffs. This all-important game will be played in the Oshawa Arena on Monday night.

Oshawa scored in the first eight seconds and were never headed, although the Redmen fighting desperately tied the score at the end of the second period, 6-6.

The visitors flashed a sustained offensive in the third period, scoring two goals early in the session and were hard put to hold their lead. The Reds struck back midway through the third, but the Legionnaires clung desperately to their lead.

Walt Gerow, Leo Goyer and Tim Williams starred for the Reds, figuring in all the scoring. Gerow got eight points. Cook, the Red goaler, was sensational, with Waddell, Oshawa net-minder, saving his team consistently. White, Davies and A. McMullen were the best for the visitors.

OSHAWA LEGION—Goal, Waddell; defense, Hinton, J. McMullen; centre, Tisdall; wings, Furey, Peters; alternates, White, A. McMullen, Davies, Krantz, Murphy, Hooks, Barrigar.

BELLEVILLE — Goal, Cook; defense, V. Goyer, St. Louis; centre, L. Goyer; wings, Gerow, Williams; alternates, McPherson, B. Meagher, A. Meagher, L. Moffit.

Officials—Referee, "Mike" Rodden, Kingston; linesman, "Toots" Hollaway, Belleville.

First Period
1—Oshawa Legion, Tisdall (Peters) .08
2—Belleville, L. Goyer (Gerow, St. Louis) 3.24
3—Oshawa Legion, Furey (Tisdall) 6.32
4—Belleville, L. Goyer (Gerow) 11.20
5—Belleville, Gerow (L. Goyer, Williams) 12.34
6—Oshawa, Davies (White) 12.44
7—Oshawa, Davies (Krantz) 15.51
Penalty—None.

Second Period
8—Oshawa, Davies (White) 6.15
9—Belleville, Gerow 7.30
10—Oshawa, White (A. McMullen) 8.42
11—Belleville, Williams (Gerow, L. Goyer) 10.04
12—Belleville, V. Goyer (Gerow, Williams) 19.30
Penalty—V. Goyer.

Third Period
13—Oshawa, White (Murphy) 6.55
14—Oshawa, Peters (J. McMullen) 8.20
15—Belleville, L. Goyer (Gerow) 8.45
Penalty—None.

Inter. "A" Loop Standing

The O.H.A. Intermediate "A" Lakeshore Group standing is as follows and it is official. Only remaining games will be played on Monday night, with the group playoffs starting almost immediately.

Teams	W	L	F	A	Pts
Kingston	9	1	90	36	18
Peterboro	7	2	68	34	14
Oshawa Legion	4	5	51	49	8
Whitby	4	6	40	61	8
Belleville	3	6	59	65	8
Oshawa A.A.	1	8	17	80	2

Remaining Games
Feb. 11—Belleville Redmen at Oshawa Legionnaires; Peterborough at Oshawa "Red Raiders."

PLAYOFFS—First and third teams, second and fourth teams in semi-finals, 3-out-of-5 games, starting Feb. 13, 15, 18, 20 and 22nd.

1946 Oshawa Legionnaires at Hambly Arena, Oshawa, February 11

A 10-8 win against the Belleville Redmen clinches third place for Oshawa Legionnaires. *'For Oshawa, former local Juniors were to the fore, Cliff Maundrell got a couple of goals, so did Andy McMulland and Regina Tisdall. Buck Davies, Krantz, White, Hinton and Furey all figured in the scoring column, and they all played a big part in the win.'*

QR Code for Hambly Arena

LEGIONNAIRES OUST BELLEVILLE

Oshawa Legion Squad Wins Over Belleville Redmen In Wide Open Scoring Session

Win Clinches 3rd Spot for Oshawa Team, Means Elimination for Belleville and Keeps Whitby In Playoffs, 4th Place—Visiting Redmen Make Great Bid to Avoid Scrap Pile With Leo. Goyer Scoring 5 Goals — Total of 8 Goals Within 7 Minutes During 3rd Period

Trotting out a strong line-up for their crucial contest last night at the Oshawa Arena, the local "Legionnaires" clinched 3rd place in the O.H.A. Intermediate "A" Lakeshore Group standing when they defeated Belleville Redmen 10-6.

It was the final game of the schedule and proved a very important tussle, which is why the fans were treated to so much lively action and wide-open hockey that featured offensive thrusts and goals galore.

Belleville Eliminated

Defeat meant the end of the O.H.A. season for the Redmen as they ended up with only three wins for 6 points, back in 5th place, two points behind Whitby Donald Motors, who held on to 4th place, the last playoff berth, by successfully hoping for an Oshawa win. The win clinched third place for the Legionnaires and now they will meet Kingston Locos in a 3-out-of-5 game group semi-final playoff series.

In the other semi-final playoff, Peterboro will tangle with Whitby. "Petes" had 2nd place clinched before they concluded their schedule last night over in Uxbridge but they ran up a 14-4 triumph over the Oshawa "Red Raiders" just by way of sharpening up their goal-scoring technique for the approaching series with the County Town team.

Facing elimination, the Belleville team went all out in quest of goals but that technique proved their undoing for while they were stressing offensive play and with fairly successful results, they were at the same time leaving themselves wide open to the counter-thrusts of the local Legionnaires. Oshawa broke in front in the first stanza and although the visitors twice tied up the count and were always within reach, they couldn't quite make the grade.

Free-Wheeling Attacks

About the only two players who did much defensively were the goalies. It wasn't that the rearguard men didn't try hard but play raced back-and-forth so fast and so often that they had little chance to get set in position. They were always on the move and the forwards went at it in free-wheeling fashion, wide-open from face-off to siren.

Cliff Maundrell opened the scoring with a nice shot early in the game and Leo. Goyer came back on Labonne's assist to make it 1-1. From there on, it was L. Goyer and Labonne who carried the mail for the desperate Redmen. Playing at top speed, this pair carried the attack time-and-again into Oshawa territory said but for the fact that they were short in stamina to withstand the pace, it would have been even closer.

Keith Krantz scored with Furey's help to break the first deadlock and then Andy McMullan made it 3-1 on White's help only to have Labonne come back 15 seconds later and score on a pass from L. Goyer.

Few Penalties Meted Out

Referee "Peg" Hurst let the two teams battle it out in their important elimination test. The teams themselves played hard and rugged but there was little dirty and tempers flared only once, when Hinton and Goyer tangled a little midway through the final frame.

Oshawa increased their lead to 6-4 in the second period but it was L. Goyer who scored first in the period, to make it 3-3 and this time Walt. Gerow and "Speedy" St. Louis got the assists. Andy McMullen got his second one on help from Davies and White and then Maundrell got his second one, again unassisted, to make it 5-3. Cliff Hinton scored with a pass from "Buck" Davies and L. Goyer got his one back on a combined effort with Gerow.

Thick and Fast

Goals came thick and fast in the third period, in fact each team scored a total of 3 goals and they were all scored within a space of 7 minutes. The splurge started just after Hinton and Leo Goyer were thumbed to the sin-bin for roughing.

Regina Tisdalle made it 7-4 and t'en less than a minute later, Vern Goyer scored with Labonne's help. Just 33 seconds later Tisdall scored on a pass from Krantz and by this time the defensemen might as well have left the ice. The forwards were paying no attention to them. 23 seconds after Tisdall's second goal, L. Goyer got another on a play by Williams. That made it 8-6 and then White made the mistake of passing the puck in front of his own net. Barrett, parked there, snaffled it up and let go a shot. Barriage, nearly, making it 8-7.

White Redeems Self

Right there is where this Belleville Redmen lost their big chance. The Legionnaires were almost as m L. up for his boner, grabbed the puck from the face-off, sprinted through the Belleville team and scored just 22 seconds after his "give-away" tally at the other end. That put Oshawa back 2 goals up again. "Bunk" Davies got one when he was out in front to slap in A. McMullan's pass -out from the corner. That made it 10-7 and Leo Goyer and Gene Labonne once again repeated their pet play for the final goal of the night, at the 16.15 mark, just 5 minutes and 55 seconds after Tisdall had got the first of the period's 8 goals.

That proved Belleville's last kick. they went down battling gamely but they were lucky the score wasn't worse. They sent everybody up and three times in the last three minutes Oshawa had clean breakaways, Maundrell, Murphy, and Krantz all getting away with only the goalie to beat—but Cook did just that, each time.

Leo Goyer and Gene Labonne were easily the standouts for the visitors. Goyer scored five goals and had one assist while Labonne scored once and earned three assists. Vern Goyer scored once and Wait. Gerow had two assists.

For Oshawa, former local Juniors were to the fore. Cliff. Maundrell got a couple of goals, so did Andy McMullan and Regina Tisdall. Buck Davies, Krantz, White, Hinton and Furey all figured in the scoring column and they all played a big part in the win, with Barriage doing well in the netsconsidering the barrage of rubber he faced at times.

BELLEVILLE REDMEN: Goal, Cook; defense, V. Goyer and St. Louis; centre, L. Goyer; wings, Labonne and Gerow. Alts., Barrett, Williams, A. Meagher, B. Meagher, Moffatt and McPherson.

OSHAWA LEGIONNAIRES: Goal, Barriage; defense, Hinton and J. McMullan; centre, Tisdall; wings, Furey and Regan. Alts., A. McMullan, White, Maundrell, Murphy, Krantz and Davies.

Referee: "Peg" Hurst; Linesman, Doug Love, both of Oshawa.

First Period
1, Oshawa, Maundrell 4.17
2, Belleville, L. Goyer
   (Labonne) 9.15
3, Oshawa, Krantz (Furey) 14.11
4, Oshawa, A. McMullan
   (White) 18.40
5, Belleville, Labonne
   (L. Goyer) 18.55
No Penalties.

Second Period
6, Oshawa, L. Goyer
   (Gerow, St. Louis) 3.32
7, Oshawa, A. McMullan
   (Davies, White) 9.25
8, Oshawa, Maundrell 11.22
9, Oshawa, Hinton (Davies) 14.00
10, Belleville, L. Goyer
   (Gerow) 19.00
Penalty: Hinton

Third Period
11, Oshawa, Tisdall 9.27
12, Belleville, V. Goyer
   (Labonne) 10.07
13, Oshawa, Tisdall (Krantz) 10.40
14, Belleville, L. Goyer
   (Williams) 11.03
15, Belleville, Barrett 12.10
16, Oshawa, White 12.32
17, Oshawa, Davies (A.
   McMullan) 13.55
18, Belleville, L. Goyer
   (Labonne) 16.15
Penalties: Hinton and L. Goyer.

1946 Oshawa Legionnaires at Hambly Arena, Oshawa, February 15

Oshawa Legionnaires Upset Kingston Locos In 1st Game Of Semi-Final Group Series

THE TIMES-GAZETTE, Saturday, February 16, 1946

Homesters Outplay and Outcheck Classy Limestone City Squad—White and Tisdall Lead Their Lines In Fine Offensive Display — "Rube" Waddell Stars In Nets—Kingston Players Show Resentment in 3rd Period

Coming up with their best display of the season, a very timely "blue chip" performance, Oshawa Legionnaires turned back Kingston "Locos" 8-4 at the Oshawa Arena last night in the first game of their group playoffs, a 3-out-of-5 semi-final series. The two teams go at it again tonight down in the Limestone City.

The Motor City squad was full value for their win, outplaying the visiting Kingston team all down the line and matching their down-grade speed with a brand of sparkling offensive and diligent checking that produced desired results.

Locals Scored First

The Legionnaires opened the scoring, after holding off the Locos for three successive Oshawa penalties in the first ten minutes. The McMullan brothers and Fraser were all thumbed to the sin-bin in succession but the homesters still held on and had enough left to take command of the game. Actually they won it right there.

Regina Tisdall opened the scoring with Hinton's help when they broke away from a pressure play while Fraser was serving his term. About seven minutes later, Andy McMullan capitalized on a nifty three-way passing play with Fraser and White helping out. This one came during a ganging act while Kennie McNaught was doing time. Near the end of the period, Kingston's smart trio of Partis, Catlin and Carr-Harris combined for a pretty goal, the former doing the scoring.

Wide-Open Action

Play was of the wide-open, end-to-end variety in the second stanza and it was in this frame that the visiting Locos made their supreme bid for victory. Aitken on Scrutton's pass, scoring right after the face-off and a half-minute later, Cliff Maundrell got it back with help from Peters and Tisdall. It was a pretty goal. The clock had reached the 3-minute mark when Catlin scored on a pass from Partis to make it 3-all and just 58 seconds later, Aitken scoring on a pass from McNaught. Hinton was in the penalty pews when this happened.

Kingston's 1-goal lead, only time all night they were ahead, lasted only a minute and a half. White drifted up the centre to take Andy McMullan's pass-out and he fired the puck home before Udall could get set.

About two minutes later Junior McMullan fired one into the strings from well out, during a ganging play, with Maundrell feeding him the puck for the shot.

For the last 12 minutes of the middle canto, both teams went at it hammer-and-tongs. Rival goalies, Udall and Waddell were called on for sparkling saves. Oshawa had an edge in territorial play and they missed two great scoring chances when Andy McMullan and Gar Peters both went in flanked by teammates with only one defenseman to beat and in, both cases, the puck-carrier shot from well out, rather than pass to a mate, who was in better position.

Locos Display Temper

Cliff Maundrell whistled one of his good shots home on a three-way play with his line-mates, Peters and Tisdall, right after the 3rd-period face-off. About two minutes later, Bill Mortimer lifted Maundrell's stick from behind, right at the Kingston goal-mouth. Maundrell was accidentally cut on the face and Mortimer drew a 5-minute major. Obviously unintentional, it looked as if a minor sentence would have been adequate.

As it was, the Kingston boys started to wield their sticks and elbows in lusty fashion, especially Nicholson, Scrutton and McNaught. Nicholson soon followed Mortimer to the penalty bench and while both were off, Buck Davies brought the puck from the corner along the back-boards and passed out to the goal-mouth where Tisdall was waiting and he promptly slapped it into the net.

Nicholson continued his vicious checking after this, ripped Hinton in the mouth and handed out some elbows to White and Peters, but there were no more penalties given out.

Partis, Catlin, Aitken and Bill Mortimer all kept trying real hard to get Kingston back into the running but Oshawa's fine back-checking and nice defense work kept them at bay and when they did get in, Waddell handled their shots in superb fashion. Near the end, Peters potted one with Furey and Tisdall helping out, to conclude the scoring.

Cliff Maundrell and Regina Tisdall with two apiece, headed the Oshawa goal-getters but almost everybody on the team got into the scoring column, indicating the will-to-win which the entire Legion team displayed. White stood out for Oshawa in the closing stages with his checking and Hinton, J. McMullan and Murphy were especially good on defense, all turning in their best games of the season, while goalie Waddell was sensational throughout. Lay and Mortimer also did yeoman blue-line work for their team. Aitken scored two goals while Partis got one. McGregor, Catlin and Carr-Harris were all good up front for Locos.

The Teams

KINGSTON "LOCOS":—Goal, Udall; defense, Lay and Mortimer; centre, Partis; wings, Carr-Harris and Catlin. Alts.: Scrutton, Aitken, McGregor, Nicholson, McNaught and Murphy.

OSHAWA "LEGIONNAIRES":—Goal, Waddell; defense, Hinton and J. McMullan; centre, Tisdall; wings, Maundrell and afters. Alts.: Davies, White, A. McMullan, Murphy, Fraser and Furey.

Referee: "Jim" Primeau; Linesman: "Eddie" Mepham, both of Toronto.

First Period

1—Oshawa, Tisdall (Hinton) .. 9:04
2—Oshawa, A. McMullan (Fraser, White) 15:02
3—Kingston, Partis (Catlin, Carr-Harris) 19:05
Penalties: J. McMullan, A. McMullan, Fraser, Murphy and McNaught.

Second Period

4—Kingston, Aitken (Scrutton) :30
5—Oshawa, Maundrell (Peters, Tisdall) 1:25
6—Kingston, Catlin (Partis) 3:22
7—Kingston, Aitken (McNaught) 4:20
8—Oshawa, White (A. McMullan) 6:90
9—Oshawa, A. McMullan (Maundrell) 7:52
Penalty: Hinton.

Third Period

10—Oshawa, Maundrell (Tisdall, Peters) .... .24
11—Oshawa, Tisdall (Davies) 5:20
12—Oshawa, Peters (Furey, Tisdall) 13:31
Penalties: Mortimer (major), and Nicholson.

LEGIONNAIRES LOSE AT KINGSTON

FEB-19/46

Kingston "Locos" Run Wild In Third Period; Inter. "A" Semi-Final Series Tied Up

1946 Oshawa Legionnaires at Jock Harty Arena, Kingston,

February 16

Score All Tied In Second Period But Oshawa Legion Fades Badly In 3rd Frame — J. McMullen and Maundrell Put Out by Injuries—Three Goals in Last 40 Seconds Gives Locos One-Sided Total—Play Again Tonight at Kingston and Here Friday

Kingston, Feb. 19.— (Special)— Kingston Locos rapped in three goals in the last 40 seconds of the game here Saturday night to trounce Oshawa Legionnaires 10-4 in the second game of their 3-out-of-5 semi-final group play-offs.

The two teams will clash again on Tuesday (tonight) at Kingston with the fourth game of the series booked for the Oshawa Arena on Friday night.

All Even In Second

In tying up the round, "Locos" flashed more speed in scoring punch than the visitors from Oshawa, but it wasn't until the third period that they made their margin sure.

The homesters ran in three goals in the first period with a flock of penalties being a big help, especially two major penalties to Andy McMullen. The first came in a tangle with Watts of Kingston, the Loco player getting only a minor. McMullen hadn't quite finished his 5-minute term when Carr-Harris opened the scoring. McMullan's second major penalty came with the score 2-0 and an automatic misconduct penalty with it, to keep out of action for more than half of the second period as well.

Catlin made it 3-0 with McMullan off the second time and Maundrell from Tisdall made it 3-1 before the period ended, shortly after Bill Mortimer had been given a minor penalty.

In the second stanza, Legion showed their best hockey to tie up the score at 4-4. Maundrell got his second on a three-way play and then after Carr-Harris had made it 4-2 Tisdall scored on Maundrell's pass and a few minutes later, Maundrell made it 4-4 unassisted.

Play roughened up then and Catlin's goal on Mortimer's pass made it as the second stanza ended.

All Kingston In Third

It was all Kingston's game in the third period. Play was rough and rugged and Oshawa suffered badly with injuries. Cliff Maundrell suffered a twisted leg and had to leave the game and Junior McMullen was cut over the eye with a high stick and he had to leave the action too.

Their play-strength thus reduced, the Legionnaires couldn't keep up the dazzling pace the Locos maintained, urged on by a large crowd of howling fans.

After goals by Carr-Harris and McNaught had made it 7-4, the Oshawa team collapsed completely. Barrage held out until the last minute and then Locos rapped in three goals in just 30 seconds, Aitkin, Scrutton and MacGregor doing the scoring.

Ref. Kenny Holmeshaw took a lenient view of the rugged tactics employed by the homesters in the hard-checking game and the weary Legionnaires just couldn't stay in the running. The Limestone City fans enjoyed the game thoroughly, of course.

The Teams

OSHAWA LEGION—goal, Barriage; defence, Hinton and J. McMullan; centre, Tisdall; wings, Maundrell and Peters; alts. Murphy, A. McMullan, Kravia, Pavey, Fraser and White.

KINGSTON LOCOS—goal, Udall; defence, Mortimer and McNaught; centre, Partis; wings, Catlin and Carr-Harris; alts. Watts, Aitken, McGregor, Scrutton, Murphy and Nicholson.

Referee, Kenny Holmeshaw, of Toronto; Linesman, "Speedy" St. Louis, of Belleville.

First Period
1. Locos, Carr-Harris (McNaught) 3.03
2. Locos, Carr-Harris (Partis, Catlin) 11.20
3. Locos, Catlin (Partis, Carr-Harris) 15.65
4. Legion, Maundrell (Tisdall) 17.20
Penalties: Watts, (2 minors) A. McMullan (3 majors and a misc.), Nicholson and Mortimer.

Second Period
5. Legion, Maundrell (Tisdall, Peters) 2.55
6. Locos, Carr-Harris 6.32
7. Legion, Tisdall (Maundrell) 7.00
8. Legion, Maundrell 13.15
9. Locos, Catlin (Mortimer) 13.35
Penalties: Nicholson and Hinton.

Third Period
10. Locos, Carr-Harris (Mortimer) 2.55
11. Locos, McNaught (Catlin, Carr-Harris) .. 5.27
12. Locos, Aitkin (MacGregor) 19.20
13. Locos, Scrutton (Watts) .. 19.42
14. Locos, MacGregor (Nicholson) 19.50
Penalties, Watts and Fuery.

QR Code for Jock Harty Arena

1946 Oshawa Legionnaires at Jock Harty Arena, Kingston, February 19

QR Code for Jock Harty Arena

LEGIONNAIRES EKE OUT GREAT WIN IN KINGSTON

Oshawa Inters. Come from Behind With 2 Goals Late In 3rd Period Edge "Locos" 3-2 to Lead Series

"Gor" Peters Ties Score at 14-Minute Mark and "Andy" McMullan Scores Winner On a Pass From "Buck" Davies With Only 2 Minutes Left While Catlin Serves Costly Penalty — Oshawa Defensemen Play Big Part in Valuable Win and Waddell Stars in Goal — Kingston "Locos" Must Win Here Friday — Or Else!

The Summary

First Period
1—Legion, A. McMullan (White, Peters) 6.10
Penalties—Watts and Hinton 2.

Second Period
2—Locos, Paris (Catlin, Carr-Harris) .... .25
No penalties.

Third Period
3—Locos, Paris (Mariner) .... .87
4—Legion, Peters (White) 14.20
5—Legion, A. McMullan (Davies) 17.35
Penalties—Nicholson, Hinton and Catlin.

Oshawa Legionnaires performed a valiant chore on Tuesday night when they nosed out the Kingston "Locos" 3-2 in the third game of their 2-out-of-3 semi-final group playoff series, right in the Limestone City, to take a lead in the series, two games to one.

Kingston Locos headed the Inter. "A" group race throughout the entire schedule with only one defeat but they'll have their backs to the elimination wall when they play here at the Oshawa Arena on Friday (tomorrow) night in the 4th game of the series, for the Locos are faced with the ash-can bogey. They must win—or else! Another win for the Oshawa Legion team will complete the big semi-final series in a real upset and send the Motor City "vets" into the group finals against the "Petes".

Close and Hard-Fought

Tuesday night's game in Kingston was a real thriller-diller from start to finish, with the much-improved Legionnaires winning the game by dint of their diligent back-checking and sustained pressure.

The Legionnaires never quit skating. Kingston's classy forwards, many of whom have starred in what they are pleased to refer to as "fast-er leagues", were held rigidly under control by Oshawa's defensive checking and the Oshawa team showed just enough alertness and scoring punch to cash in on their chances to squeeze out the 3-2 win. And they did it without Cliff Maundrell, who was forced to sit this one out due to a leg injury, but who is expected to be back in top shape for tomorrow night's game here in Oshawa.

Goals were scarce, speed was the by-word and checking was hard and rugged in the thrilling contest. The Limestone City lads certainly saw a rousing game but the defeat was only a bitter pill for the Kingston fans but the Locos too, did a lot of grumbling.

Oshawa's victory was directly traceable to their fine defensive play. Not only did all the forwards check hard and earnestly but Goalie "Rube" Waddell was sensational in the Oshawa nets. In front of him, Cliff Hinton, did yeoman service on defense. He was Oshawa's blue-line bulwark and was given grand support by "Junior" McMullan and "Spud" Murphy, who turned in what was by far his best game of the season to date.

Goals Were Scarce

The Locos checked just as hard and effectively as did the Legion boys and as a result, goals were scarce and came only as a result of the breaks.

"Andy" McMullan topped off a three-way play with his line-mates, White and Peters, to get the only goal of the first period, fairly early. It came while defenseman Watts of Locos was serving a penalty. Cliff Hinton drew down two minors in this frame in quick succession but Waddell and his battling mates kept the desperate Locos out.

There were no penalties in the second period and Kingston tied up the score at 1-1 when Paris scored from his two mates, almost from the face-off, at the 47-second mark. For the remainder of the period, the teams battled away in ding-dong fashion without either gaining any edge.

Exciting Finish

Locos sent the Kingston fans into a frenzy of delight right from the face-off, in just 52 seconds, when Paris scored on a rush by Bill Mortimer and his pass.

The even-steven play continued and finally "Gor" Peters evened up the count at the 14:30 mark, on a nice play by White. Prior to this Locos had held the Legionnaires out while Nicholson serving a penalty and Legion in turn held the home-sters off while Hinton did some time.

The "big break" came at the 17:30 mark when Joey Catlin drew down a penalty for tripping. Oshawa swarmed to the attack and their ganging act paid off when Andy McMullan took a pass from "Buck" Davies, who made a pretty play for the set-up and McMullan fired the puck past Udall to make it 3-2.

Kingston fought back grimly but they had all they could do to keep Legion from adding another and when Catlin returned there was only 30 seconds left to play and the ball sounded before Locos could get back on even terms.

Every player starred in the hard-fought contest, especially the goalies and defensemen, but there was not a weak spot on either team.

THE TEAMS:
OSHAWA LEGIONNAIRES — Goal, Waddell; defense, Hinton and Murphy; centre, White; wings, A. McMullan and Peters; alternates, Tisdall, Davies, J. McMullan, Krantz, Regan and Fuoco.
KINGSTON LOCOS—Goal, Udall; defense, Mortimer and Watts; centre, Paris; wings, Catlin and Carr-Harris; alternates, McKnight, Aiken, MacGregor, Scruton, Murphy and Nicholson.

Referee—Kenny Holodinsky, of Toronto; linesmen, "Spunky" St. Louis, of Belleville.

1946 Oshawa Legionnaires at Hambly Arena, Oshawa, February 21

KINGSTON LOCOS TIE UP SERIES ON OSHAWA ICE

Limestone City Pucksters Smother Local Legionnaires With Speed, Scoring Punch

6-Goal Rally in Speed-Crammed 2nd Period Gives Visitors Clean-Cut Margin—Legion Held 2-1 Lead for Only Few Minutes — Locos Too Fast and Too Smart for Locals — Carr - Harris Proves Hero

Kingston Locos came into Oshawa last night with elimination staring them in the face but with fire in their eyes, they put forth an Oshawa Legionnaires for loose pucks and unreeled a second-period display of dazzling speed and goal-scoring finesse that put them back on even terms, as they fashioned a 10-3 victory, to tie up their O.H.A. Intermediate "A" group semi-final series at two wins apiece.

The 5th and deciding game of this crucial series will be played in Kingston on Monday night.

Deserved Their Win

The "Locos" richly deserved their victory. They were much the better team in the important tussle here last night and the fact that they stepped right into Oshawa with the old "sch-osh" yawning and then came up with their best hockey game of the season is proof enough of their competitive spirit, not to mention their amazing speed and scoring punch.

It wasn't that there was much wrong with the Legionnaires. No doubt their defense was prone to back in behind the blue-line, which enabled the speedy Kingston puck-carriers to promptly put all their mates on-side the moment they got into Oshawa territory and perhaps goalie Waddell wasn't as brilliant as he has been in some games, but there is no denying that every member of the Oshawa team tried hard. Regtus Tindall skated himself almost into exhaustion while White, Hinton, the McMullen brothers, Peters, Davies and the rest gave everything they had. Chief Meininghi's leg wasn't right and he had to give up in the last half, after trying hard to share the load.

The whole story was that it wasn't good enough last night. Certainly they were not over-confident but they were up against a team of determined puck-chasers who individually and collectively fancied what they themselves admitted, after the game, was their best performance of the season. They were too fast and too smart for the locals and in that second-period splurge, the brand of speed they displayed was simply terrific. They literally dusted the barnstorm dizzy and their accuracy (and good-fortune) around the Oshawa net was the final touch.

They got their shots away with the least possible delay, usually just changing the direction of the puck as it came to them and three of their goals were scored from close quarter scrambles in just this way.

All Happened in 2nd

It was the kind of thriller-diller display the fans had expected, in the first period, and the largest Intermediate crowd of the season was on hand to see the game.

Johnny Carr-Harris, Kingston's hero in their "million-dollar win", opened the scoring with help from Joey Caffin and Lay. That one came after the middle mark and with only a little over a minute left, "Andy" Davies tied it up.

Right from the face-off as the second period opened, the Legion took the lead—for the only time in the game. It just took six seconds for "Gus" Peters to flash down his side and take a pass from Waddell and then he beat Glynn Udall with a scorching shot.

Then the roof fell in! At the 9:32 mark Carr-Harris took a pass from Parkin and scored to tie. It was Legion lineup on for about 4 odd minutes and then Johnny Carr-Harris scored a pretty solo goal to make it 3-2. Two minutes later Murphy batted in Aitken's pass-out and the parade had really swung into high gear.

It was "Bill" Mortimer, a former Oshawa General, who struck the deciding blow. Incidentally, Mortimer spear-headed his team's attack and was a bulwark on defense all night. He shared honors with Carr-Harris as the two Locos most responsible for the victory.

Caffin cleared the puck to Mortimer from an Oshawa power-play and Mortimer broke fast. Murphy almost got to him but he batted the puck at Waddell and it bounced off the goalie into the top of the net to make it 5-2. Nicholson slapped one in from well out in a scramble a few minutes later and in the last half-minute, Mortimer punched in a third after Waddell had moved away from the post to conclude the 6-goal rally of the period, making it 7-2.

Penalties Scarce

There wasn't a single penalty in this hard-packed second stanza. As a matter of fact, up until tempers flared in the last half, both teams stuck right to their hockey and tried to dog on for the ice. There wasn't a "dirty" check made in the game.

In the third period, Parkin and McNaught scored in quick succession to run up the total to 9-2 and then at the half-way mark, White fired home Tindall's pass on a nice breakaway rush, for Oshawa's last goal.

Parkin got this one back with a pretty piece of stick-handling, in front of the Oshawa net, firing the puck past Waddell just as he was bumped off his feet.

Ronny McNaught high-sticked Andy McMullen and then they tangled in a brief spot that brought a minor and major to McNaught and a major to the Oshawa winger. Aitken got a misconduct penalty from the referee when he argued Peneacca Mapura's calling on a blue-line critter in vivid language.

Right down the line, the Kingston team starred, Carr-Harris and Mortimer were standouts but Caffin, Parkin, McGregor, Murphy, Lay, Watt, Nicholson and goalie Udall were all in top form. They not only skated like whirlwinds but their plays were heady and their accurate passing made their win seem almost easy.

Every player, except goalie Udall, of the Kingston team, collected at least one scoring point—proof that they all contributed to the win.

The teams:

KINGSTON LOCOS—goal, Udall; defense, Mortimer and McNaught; centre, Parkin; wings, Caffin and Carr-Harris; alts.,- Aitken, McGregor, Murphy, Lay, Watt and Nicholson.

OSHAWA LEGIONNAIRES—goal, Waddell; defense, Hinton and Rumsey; centre, White; wings, A. McMullen and Peters; alts.; Tindall, Shamdrell, Davies, J. McMullen, Furey and Regan.

Referee, "Sis" Princeau; Linesman, Eddie Mapines, both of Toronto.

First Period
1. Kingston, Carr-Harris (Caffin, Lay) 12.18
2. Oshawa, Davies 18.16

Penalties; Hinton and Watt.

Second Period
3. Oshawa, Peters (White) .. .06
4. Kingston, Carr-Harris (Parkin) 9.32
5. Kingston, Carr-Harris 9.15
6. Kingston, Murphy (Aitken) 11.12
7. Kingston, Mortimer (Caffin) 11.12
8. Kingston, Nicholson (Murphy) 17.44
9. Kingston, Mortimer (Parkin) 19.30

Third Period
10. Kingston, Aitken (McGregor, Watt) 2.12
11. Kingston, Mellinghi (Carr-Harris, Parkin) 3.57
12. Oshawa, White (Tindall) .. 10.23
13. Kingston, Parkin (Carr-Harris) 12.20

Penalties; Watt, A. McMullen (major), McNaught (minor and major), and Aitken (misconduct).

QR Codes for Hambly Arena

1946 Oshawa Legionnaires at Jock Harty Arena, Kingston, February 26

KINGSTON LOCOS OUST OSHAWA LEGION IN DECIDING 5th GAME

Limestone City Pucksters Will Now Take On "Petes" In Finals
Group Winner May Win O.H.A. Title

Motor City Legionnaires Bow Out After Gallant Bid for Victory In Thrilling Battle — Joey Catlin Scores 4 Goals In Kingston's 5-3 — "Buck" Davies Scored In Last Minute But Catlin Clinched It With Just 7 Seconds Left

Oshawa Legionnaires faded from the O.H.A. Intermediate "A" race on Tuesday night when they bowed out gallantly and with colors flying, as they dropped a 5-3 decision on Kingston's ice in the 5th and deciding game of their group semi-final series.

Kingston Locos advanced to the group finals against "Petes," final series to start this week-end, and judging by the high-class brand of hockey being displayed by these two teams in their playoff games of recent days, the winner of the Lakeshore Inter. "A" group should be favored to capture the O.H.A. Provincial title in that series.

Close for Two Periods

It was a hectic tussle for two periods. Bill Mortimer opened the scoring against his former Oshawa mates but "Buck" Davies came back to tie the count, on a pass from "Junior" McMullan. About a half-minute later, "Spud" Murphy drew a minor penalty but the Legionnaires "killed" off the two minutes without damage, despite Kingston's valiant efforts to break the tie.

A record crowd of 2600 fans was on hand to see the crucial battle and maintained enthusiastic acclaim of the spectacular hockey displayed throughout the entire sixty minutes.

In the second stanza, Joey Catlin scored on a three-way play, to put "Locos" out in front 2-1. It proved the only goal of the middle frame. Frank White missed on a glorious chance to tie up the score, when he went right in on Glynn Udall, all alone. Stranded with a broken stick, Udall made a desperate sweep at the puck and White just failed to lift the puck into the net.

Catlin Collects

It was Joey Catlin, speedy left-winger for the Limestone City team that brought victory to Locos and a berth in the group finals. He moved into high-gear in the third period, to leave his check "Andy" McMullan behind on two successive thrusts. He took a pass from Partis for the goal that started the tide's turn and then he popped off a three-way play to make it 4-1.

The gallant Oshawa crew fought back grimly and finally Regina Tisdall scored on a three-way play with Furey and Davies, to make it 4-2.

This one came at the 14-minute mark. With only 40 seconds left to play, and Oshawa forcing the Kingston team back into their own end and back on their heels too, as they hammered away at Udall's citadel, "Buck" Davies finally tallied on passes from White and Peters, to make it 4-3.

By this time the Kingston team and fans were frantic with anxiety. Legionnaires thronged to the attack again, in quest of the tying goal. Udall made a spectacular save as Peters fired from a tough angle and then Mortimer broke up the ice, passed to Catlin and Kingston's "big gun" moved in on "Rube" Waddell to clinch the victory with his 4th goal of the night, making it 5-3, with only 7 seconds left to play.

Both Teams Sensational

Although Joey Catlin, with his four goals out of the Kingston's total of five, was of course the outstanding star of the night, both teams, individually and collectively, played in sensational fashion.

"Gar" Peters did a sensational job of checking Johnny Carr-Harris, Kingston prolific scoring right-winger. At centre, Jack Tisdall and Frank White held their own with Kingston's ace pivot men, Partis and Murphy.

Frank White was one of Oshawa's best but not far ahead of Furey, and Tisdall, while "Buck" Davies stood out as the fastest man on the ice, when he really turned on his speed. He was Oshawa's best on the attack and while he scored two of Oshawa's three goals, he was robbed on at least four other great bids. Cliff Hinton, on defense, was another standout for Oshawa, while "Rube" Waddell was brilliant in the nets, turning in his best game of the season in a vain effort to bring victory to Oshawa.

Played at terrific clip, the game was nevertheless quite clean with only two minor penalties being meted out, both to Oshawa, and neither had any bearing on the goal-scoring.

KINGSTON — Goal, Udall; defense, Mortimer, McNaught; centre, Partis; wings, Catlin, Carr-Harris; subs, Watts, Nicholson, MacGregor, Aitken, Murphy, Lay.

OSHAWA — Goal, Waddell; defense, Hinton, Murphy; centre, White; wings, A. McMullan, Davies; subs, Furrel, Tisdall, J. McMullan, Fraser, Peters, Reagan.

Officials—Ken Holmeshaw, Toronto referee; Speedy St. Louis, Belleville, linesman.

First Period
1—Kingston, Mortimer 7.50
2—Oshaw, Davies (J. McMullan, Furrey) 15.29
Penalty—F. Murphy.

Second Period
3—Kingston, Catlin (Mortimer, McNaught) 9.00
No penalties.

Third Period
4—Kingston, Catlin (Partis) 3.35
5—Kingston, Catlin (Partis, Carr-Harris) 13.15
6—Oshawa, Tisdall (Furrey, Davies) 14.22
7—Oshawa, Tisdall (White, Peters) 19.20
8—Kingston, Catlin (Mortimer) 19.53
Penalty—Hinton.

1946: When hockey season ended, Cliff continued his Kingston visits whenever he could get there from his job at General Motors in Oshawa. Cliff especially enjoyed spending time with Dodie, going to dances, and swimming at 'Elevator Bay' on the Lake Ontario shore of the Auld farm property. They were soon engaged to be married. *See **Appendix D Pg 280** for Auld Property information.*

1946: These summertime photos from Dodie's collection had to be included in this book! The dog with Cliff is likely a spaniel belonging to Isabelle Forsythe or her boyfriend, Jack Sudds, who are on the left behind Cliff in the photos below. Isabelle and her brother Joe Forsythe, standing headless? with arms spread, were Dodie's niece and nephew; daughter and son of her sister Helen and Neil Forsythe.

Cliff was visiting from Oshawa and enjoying time with Dodie and her family at the Auld farm and on the wharf at Elevator Bay. Dodie was on right, peeking out behind Cliff's left shoulder. These and the two lower photos on page 105 were likely taken by Joe's girlfriend, June Stanton. Those three fun loving couples were married within the year after these photos were taken.

Marriage and Starting a Family 1946-1948

Wedding Bells for Cliff and Dorothy 10 September 1946	109
General Motors Employment at Oshawa	110
1st Daughter, Judith Anne Hinton, 8 June 1947	111
Cliff's Mother Phyllis, Year in UK (Sept 1946-Oct 1947)	114

Wedding Bells at Oshawa

Clifford and Dorothy were married on September 10, 1946, at Oshawa, Ontario Canada

Wedding Attendants were Cliff's friend Alex Reid and Dodie's sister Betty Auld

Author's note: I discovered this early 1947 photo in my mother's collection and have appreciated it as happy newlyweds enjoying the post war energy of downtown Toronto.

I believe they are walking on Yonge St, with one of 9 United Cigar stores in the background (from the Toronto Directory 1947). Mom's sister Betty likely took the photo. Perhaps they were on their way to a movie; 'The Best Years of Our Lives' released December 1946 or 'It's a Wonderful Life' released January 1947.

Mom and Dad were expecting me, their first child. Dad was still working at General Motors in Oshawa and travelling as a sales representative. From my recollection of Mom's stories, I believe they had a small apartment above a store in Toronto.

On their July 7 application for my June 8 birth certificate my mother listed her address as Leaside, Toronto and my father listed his as Oshawa, Ontario, and he signed as the informant living at 17 Quebec Ave. It was likely his registered address because he worked from Oshawa General Motors although he spent whatever time he could with Dorothy at their apartment in Leaside Toronto. When my father was away on business my mother must have missed him but had good family support. She likely spent time nearby with her sister Betty who had recently moved into a flat in their eldest sister Violet Stephens' home at 26 Glengrove Ave.

1947: On June 8, Cliff, and Dodie's first child, Judith Anne, was born at the Grace Salvation Army Hospital at 650 Church St. Toronto.

In the photo below, Dodie is holding baby Judy near the clothesline by the back door at 26 Glengrove Ave.

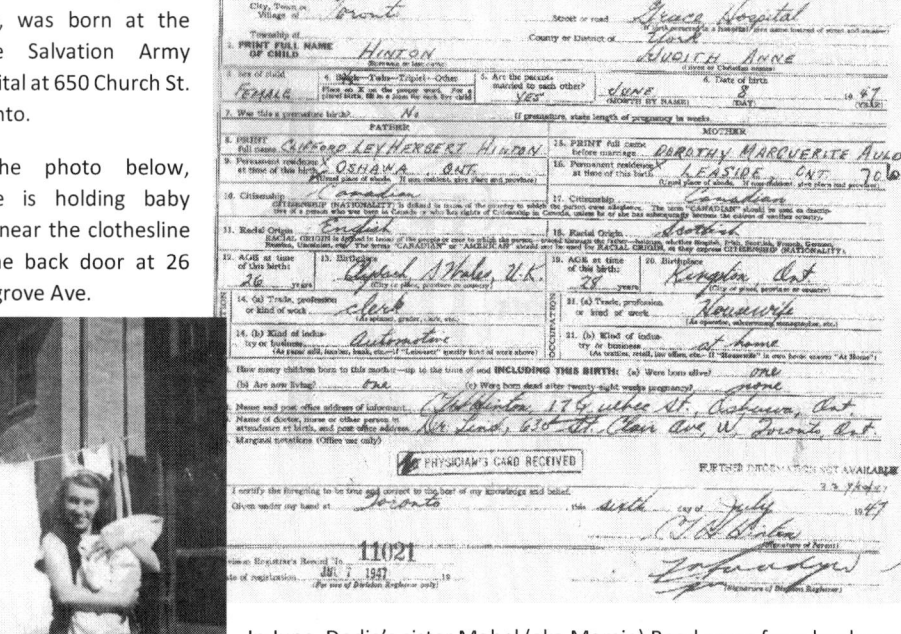

In June, Dodie's sister Mabel (aka Mamie) Read came from her home on the Auld farm in Kingston to visit her sister Violet Stephens and to meet her niece Judy, 13 days old.

In the photos below, Judy is held by her Aunty Vi left, her mother Dodie centre, and her Aunt Mamie at right in the backyard of 26 Glengrove Ave. Her Aunt Betty likely took the photos.

See **Appendix Pg282** for 26 Glengrove Ave house information.

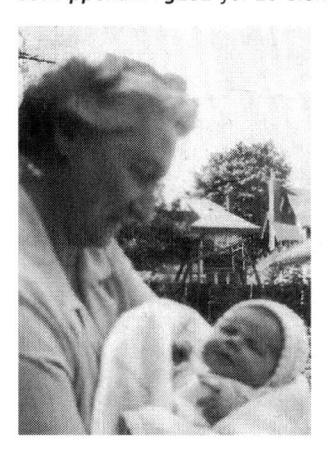

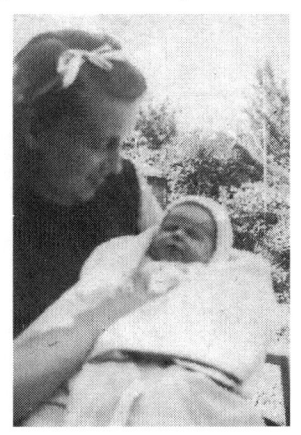

1947: In July, when Judy was 5 weeks old, Betty took some photos while they were enjoying a summer day, again in the backyard at the Stephens' house where they often visited while living in Toronto.

Cliff and Dodie often visited Dodie's sister Betty Auld who worked at Smith Mfg. and was rooming at their elder sister Violet Stephens' Toronto home. In the photo below, Cliff is feeding Judy on the front porch at 26 Glengrove Ave.

112

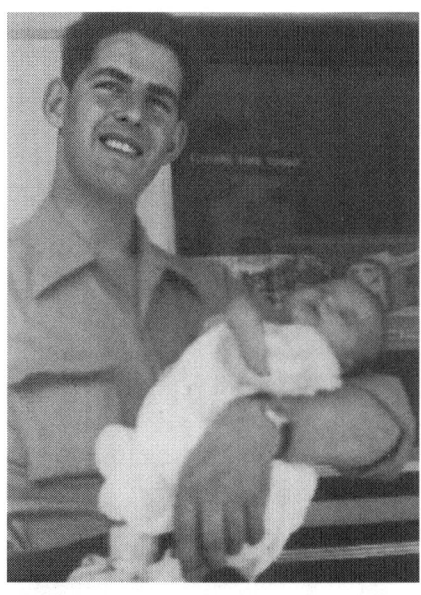

1947: In July, Dodie and Cliff took photos of each other with Judy, by the door to their small apartment over a store in Leaside.

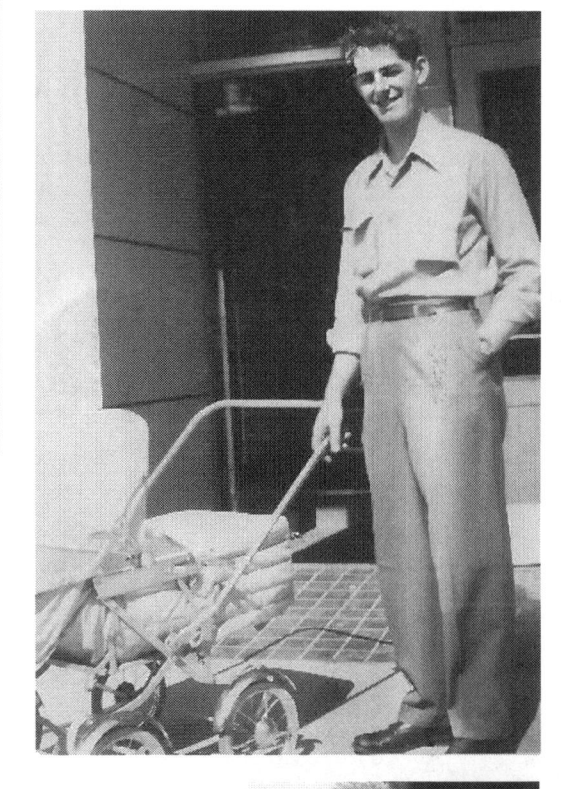

The photo at right, is of Dodie with Judy at the Auld family farm. In August, "Scotty drove us to Grampa Auld's at Kingston" when Judy was 8 weeks old. Cliff's childhood friend, Alex Reid, was that 'Scotty'. *(see **Pg 133** for this quote from Judy's baby book)*

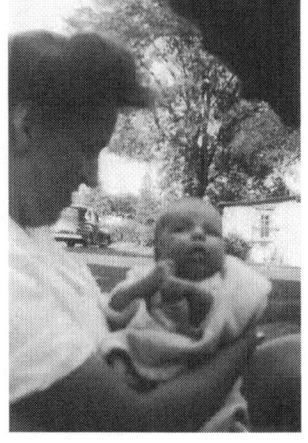

113

Phyllis Hinton's Trip to the UK 1946-47

1946: Phyllis was eager to visit her family back in England and Wales. Both she and her mother Martha Brinn had become widows when John Brinn died in February 1938 and Melville Hinton died in August 1939. Sadly, they were also both grieving the 1944 deaths of Phyllis's brother Fred Hoad in February, her son Hugh Hinton in August and her nephew Jack Hoad in October of 1944. So, when the war ended, Cliff's brother Doug made his mother's travel arrangements through his government connections, and she sailed from New York City aboard the troopship, *John Ericsson*. Passenger lists below, document that she arrived at Plymouth, September 14, and stayed with her mother at 10 Hamilton Terrace, Pembroke, Wales. The Atlantic crossing would have taken 8 days, so she must have left Oshawa on her preplanned trip, well before September 10, the day her son Clifford and Dorothy were married at Oshawa. They surely had her blessings and could not wait until her 1947 return.

The *MS Kungsholm* which had been built in 1928 for the Swedish American Line, was requisitioned during WWII by the US Government as troopship **MS John Ericsson**.

QR code is Wikipedia link for MS Kungsholm (1928)

Phyllis aboard the *John Ericsson*.

Phyllis Hinton's Trip to the UK 1946-47

1947: Phyllis spent a wonderful year with her mother and visited her many nieces and nephews in Wales. She also did some travelling and visiting with friends and family in England.

Phyllis enjoyed having her picture taken in Welsh costume and likely her mother Martha's hat or similar. See **Pg 116** for Martha's photo.

In July, Phyllis enjoyed scenic views of the Bosherston Pools at Stackpole, south of Pembroke Wales.

Cliff's mother returned to Canada in late October 1947, aboard the ocean liner, *Aquitania* which had also been used as a troopship during WWII. Phyllis had left her home in Oshawa, shortly before the wedding of Clifford and Dorothy Auld. So now back in Oshawa, she would have been eager to see her son and new daughter in law, as well as to meet her first grandbaby, already 4 months old. Cliff and Dodie had given their daughter the same name as Phyllis's favourite 8-year-old grandniece Judith Anne Jones.

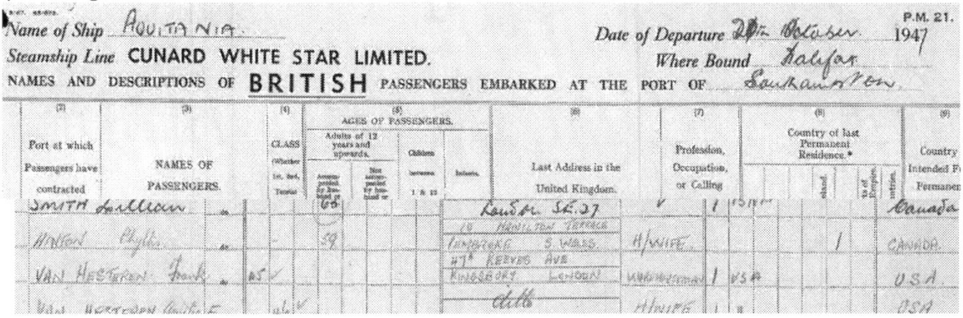

115

1947: Phyllis was happy to share the treasures she was bringing with her from Wales; her childhood recital chair, her mother's bible, an 1890 photo of Martha in Welsh costume, a christening gown worn by Phyllis and her sons and likely other treasured memorabilia. These are the items I knew of.

This little recital folding chair belonged to Cliff's mother Phyllis. I think it was given to her as a young girl by her grandfather John Davies Sr. when she lived with him from about 1898 to 1902 at her Uncle John Davies Jr. home in Pembroke Wales.

We have for sale a charming late Victorian or Edwardian Arts and Crafts country oak folding child's chair dating to somewhere around 1900.

This rather attractive and decorative dark oak child's folding chair consisting of a back with a shaped upper rail, two further square cut cross rails joined by four perpendicular dowel rods all coupled to lateral square cut supports which extend down to form the front legs. The solid oak seat is in turn supported by a fourth dowel rod rail in the back and also by an extension of both back square cut legs. The back and seat are decorated with a total of 11 brass studs.

Phyllis gave the chair to Cliff and Dodie for their daughters, and it can be seen **(Pg 167)** by the Christmas tree in the 1953 photograph. (The chair is now at my home) Researching for the chair in antique collections, I found the same one described above dating about 1900.

Phyllis also brought the baby christening gown which had been worn in Wales by her and her sons when they were baptised. Judith Anne was already age 1, too old to wear the dress when she was baptised. It was used for Susan's baptism on 13 March 1949. Then it was likely given to Doug and Doris for their children's' baptisms.

Phyllis was given her mother Martha's family bible. It included a Family Register which Phyllis updated. Doug and Doris Hinton added their entries, and they passed it to Roy and Norah Hoad for additional information. *(My cousin Libby (Hoad) Clarke shared it with me.)*

Phyllis also kept this 1890 photo of Martha (Davies) Hoad in Welsh costume. Phyllis wore her mother's hat in a July 1947 photo of her in Welsh costume when she was visiting Martha and family at Pembroke, Wales. *See previous page.*

1947: In October, when Phyllis was home from her year in the UK, Dodie brought Judy, 4 months old, by train from a visit at Kingston to meet her grandmother and Uncle Doug at their Oshawa apartment. It seems that Cliff was away on business and so was not with them. From Oshawa, Dodie and Judy took a bus to Toronto to visit Betty who took these photos below of Judy with her mother Dodie and her Aunt Violet. *(See Judy's baby book on* **Pg133**)

In December, Cliff, Dodie, Judy, and Betty travelled to Kingston to spend Christmas at the Auld farm. Behind Cliff with Judy, is Mary (daughter of Dodie's sister Mamie) and Don Laturney's house newly built by Grandpa Thomas Auld. Below are Helen, Dodie and Betty are with 5-month-old Judy.

1947/48: Cliff (Row 2, 2nd from right) as a Sales Manager for General Motors Products.

1947/48: Cliff (Row 2, 2nd from right) at a Trade show for GM Products.

General Motors Promotion Move to North Bay, Ontario, Canada 1948-1951

606 Cassels St, North Bay, Ontario	121
Easter Weekend Trip to Toronto and Oshawa	121
1948 Letter From UK, Granny Martha Brinn	123
1948 Letter From UK, Cousin Grace Jones	124
1948 Letter from Kingston Ont., Father-In-Law Thomas F Auld	125
Phyllis Marries Rev Frank Wootton, 11 June 1948	126
Family at Cobourg and Colborne, Ontario	127
Family at Auld Farm in Kingston, Ontario	129
1949 Letter from UK, Granny Martha Brinn	134
2nd Daughter, Susan Elizabeth Hinton, 7 February 1949	135
General Motors 1949, Sales Manager	138
1949 Family at Toronto, Colborne, Cobourg and Kingston	139
Summer 1950 at North Bay, Ontario	139
Summer 1950 at Kingston, Ontario	143
General Motors 1950, Sales Manager	147
Winter 1950-51 at North Bay, Ontario	149
Winning Friends and Influencing People	151

1948: The Hinton Family Moved to North Bay

1948: Cliff began work as sales manager for General Motors Products and they moved to a rental house at 606 Cassels St in North Bay. At Easter they visited family in Toronto while Cliff was there for business. These photos were taken April 23-25 at 26 Glengrove Ave. Dodie and Betty had Judy out on the sunny second floor back deck off Betty's suite at the Stephen's Glengrove home. See **Appendix Pg 282.**

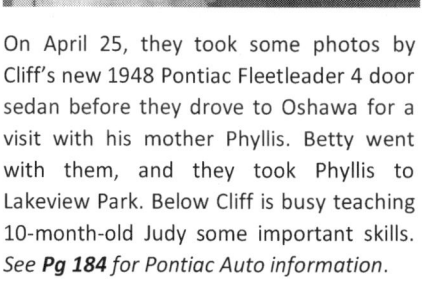

On April 25, they took some photos by Cliff's new 1948 Pontiac Fleetleader 4 door sedan before they drove to Oshawa for a visit with his mother Phyllis. Betty went with them, and they took Phyllis to Lakeview Park. Below Cliff is busy teaching 10-month-old Judy some important skills. See **Pg 184** for Pontiac Auto information.

121

1948: These photos were taken on April 25 at Lakeview Park in Oshawa on the shore of Lake Ontario. Notice Cliff in his double-breasted suit with the wide lapels, Judy in her knitted sweater coat and Dodie in her fashionable duster coat that she sewed for herself to wear on this beautiful spring day.

Cliff took this photo of Phyllis, Betty, and Dodie with Judy. Judy is standing at the bumper of Cliff's Pontiac. Parking posts in the background are also on **Pg 160.**

1948: The following is a transcription of a letter sent to Dorothy at 606 Cassells St in North Bay when Judy was 10 months old. Cliff's Granny, Martha Brinn (1860-1950) age 88, is replying to a letter that Dorothy had written to her about Cliff's busy sales job and living in North Bay. His dimpled chin mentioned in the letter can be seen at right in Cliff's 1947 portrait. Clues in this letter suggest Cliff likely visited his Granny in 1943 during his wartime posting in England.

April 27, 1948

10 Hamilton Terrace, Pembroke, South Wales

Dear Dorothy

At last, I am going to try to write you a few lines trusting they will find you and Cliff and baby well. How I would love to see you all.

Yes, dear it is nice for you to be settled in your own home and now you will feel much better you have made friends with the people, and it is nice of the minister to call on you. Hope you will be able to go to chapel or church when you can. You must take Judy with you. She will get used to going after a while. Hope Cliff is home with you on Sundays. I know just how you feel being so far from your home and all the people strange to you.

Pleased to say I keep well but I do miss Phyllis. I had hoped she would have come back to me when Douglas was married. Now she is getting married herself so I must give up all thoughts of seeing her again, and Douglas, well he seems to have upset all his plans. They should have talked over their religion affairs long before the time. I don't like the idea of him living in the flat by himself. Still, he is old enough to know what he is doing.

I am pleased Cliff is married. Give him my love and a big X. Hope he is looking after you and his daughter. I am sure he is a proud father and I pray God will bless you both and the dear baby. I am longing to see the snaps of her. Your mother tells me she got Cliff's dimple. Pity you are so far away from your home. I am here alone but I got lots of nice friends. Mind take care of yourself. Good night. God bless you.

Your Loving Granny,

M Brinn

See **Appendix C Pg 245** for Martha Brinn's original handwritten letter.

1948: The following letter was written in mid May by Cliff's step cousin Grace (Brinn) Jones (1912-2003). Her father was Phyllis's closest stepbrother Sydney Lloyd Brinn (1887-1952). Grace was 6 in 1922, when her Aunty Phyllis and her three boys emigrated from Wales to Canada. Grace and her husband David Jones had one daughter Judith Ann born Feb 4, 1939, who would be 9 when this letter was written. It is likely that Cliff visited the Jones family in 1943 when Judith Ann was 4 years old. Cliff and Dodie likely named their first daughter after Grace and David's daughter. That would please Cliff's mother who was very fond of her great niece.

12 Prendergast St., Llanelly, Wales

Dear Dorothy and Cliff,

What a lovely surprise I had, having a letter from you! it was very sweet of you to write to me, and I do hope I shall hear from you again soon. So glad to know you like the woolly set, and that it fits little Judith. I only went by guess as regards the size, and after taking quite a while to reach you, I was beginning to think maybe it would be too small. Babies seem to grow so quickly, don't they?

Aunty Phyllis told me all about Judith Ann and she certainly seems very proud of her too. I guess Cliff is thrilled too now he's a daddy??

I do hope you will write again Dorothy, tell me about yourselves? I'd love to hear from you. Has Aunty been staying with you lately? I'm wondering if she's married yet. I haven't heard for a while, maybe she is rather busy though. There's always lots to do at these times. Well, what's it like in Canada these days" we have been enjoying some lovely sunshine here for the last two weeks, hot tropical weather. We went to the beach quite a lot, Judith is very fond of the water. She's got quite a lovely tan now: the sun has been so strong. Anyway, the weather has now changed, it's bitterly cold again, and the rain has been falling. How long it's going to last, I don't know. Once the rain starts in Wales it never knows when to stop. I expect Aunty has been telling you all about us here in England. We had a lovely summer while she was over, and I had a nice holiday at Grams while she was there.

The last time I saw Aunty, I was only about six years old. It's a long time, but I'm still as fond of her as my mother tells me I was when I was six. I was sorry to see her go back in a way.

Well dear, I'm afraid I haven't much to tell you in this letter, more news as we go along, I expect. I've just been getting Judith back to school after the Whit Holiday (May 16 was Whit Sunday); am I glad too! But she is fond of school, so there's no trouble about her going.

So now I'll say cheerio to you both, write again soon won't you. My love to little Judith and to you both.

Yours Sincerely

Grace   XXX

See **Appendix C Pg 248** for Grace Jones' original handwritten letter.

1948: In June, Dodie's father replied to her letter sent a while earlier from North Bay. He spelled her name 'Dody', his spelling of Dodie, her shortened given name, Dorothy. He talks of all the work he is doing on the farm, his new tractor, and of his leg injury. He hopes his upcoming plans to attend the Auld and Wallace family reunions at Stratford and Guelph don't "gang agley" which is a Scottish term meaning "go wrong". He also talks of Cliff's mother's, "Ma Hinton's", upcoming marriage and Judy's 1st birthday coming soon. It appears that Cliff, Dodie, and Judy will be staying at Vi's when they come down from North Bay on June 10th for the June 11th Wootton wedding at Oshawa.

Auldsville, Kingston

June 6, 1948

Dear Dody,

Poor little dear, haven't had a letter from home for so long over a month was it, well that is too bad. That is why I'm taking pity on you or maybe I'm inflicting myself on you. However, you will have to put up with it till I get through this time. I hear you are coming to Toronto on the 10 th, well the chances are I will be there at that time also if things don't (gang agley) which I hope they don't.

I had a bad leg all last week, it seems I hit my shin against something harder than the bone, and about a week after it got infected something like I had in my face last year. Last Sunday I went to Dr Bennett, and he advised me to put hot applications to it so I was in bed for a couple of days, it is a little sore yet but the pain is almost gone. I got my potatoes all in a week ago last Friday. Gordon helped me for a day and a half. The ones I put in the last of April are up and I have some of them hoed but I still have 21 rows to hoe before I can get away. At least I'll try to.

Mrs. Heagy wrote last week and said they were having their reunion on the 12th of June so I'll have to be in Toronto before that as I have to go to Stratford first and see the crowd there, and as the reunion is at Guelph this year it will be on my way back, and I want to stay at Cobourg a day or two. Perhaps Violet will be able to go with me to Guelph. I don't suppose you can go, and Mabel can't get away this year.

Rather a surprise Ma Hinton getting married was it, or did you know it was coming. Well according to what you say, he is to be congratulated and I hope they will be happy.

You were asking how I liked the tractor. I think it is just dandy. It never thinks the day is long and feed it, oil it and water it and it just goes on and on and does the work a lot quicker than old dobbin. And look at the time I save. Well times do change don't they.

Well, I guess Judy is going to have an anniversary soon so I'm sending her a card and I suppose I'll be seeing you at Vi's sometime this week.

Hoping Cliff and you and Judy are keeping well,

Dad

See **Appendix C Pg 252** for Thomas Auld's original handwritten letter.

Cliff's Mother Phyllis Marries Rev Frank Morris Wootton

1948: Rev FM Wootton became pastor at Northminster United Church in 1936 when he, his wife Harriett and their daughter Helen moved next door to the Hinton family on Jones Ave.

```
Woolley, Albt E (Dorothy B), h 180 Nassau
Woolworth, F W Co Ltd, F E Bartlett mgr, 18 King w
Woon, Ella (wid Arthur), h 102 Mary
Wootton, Frank M, Rev (Harriett), pastor Northminster United Ch,
    h 28 Jones av
Wootton, Helen A, 28 Jones av
Workman, Lloyd C (Mary), acct Genl Mtrs, h 32 Brock w
Worner, Minna (wid Wm), 195 Simcoe n
Worobec, Sophie, dry gds 607 Albert, res 30 Jackson
```

```
JONES AV, w from
    Simcoe n, 1 n Ross-
    land rd (E.Whitby)
12 R A Wallace
16 K C Watson*
20 F C Fox
24 H M Hinton*
28 Rev F M Wootton*
32 D C McArthur*
```

The neighbours became friends and the Hintons got to know the extended Wootton family then living in Oshawa and Whitby. When Melville Hinton died in August 1939, Rev. Frank M. Wootton officiated at his funeral. About 1940 Rev.Frank Wootton moved to a church in Picton and the Hinton and Wootton families remained friends. Frank's wife Harriet became very ill with senility in 1942 and died 23 May 1947 at Cobourg Hospital. After Phyllis returned in October 1947, from her year in Wales, she and Frank decided to be married. Following their marriage at Oshawa on 11 June 1948, they moved to a two bedroom house on Church St in Colborne where he was minister for a short time at Colborne United Church. He retired soon after and died there on 20 February 1952. Frank Morris Wootton is buried with his first wife Harriet at Glenwood Cemetery in Picton, Ontario. *See Pg 160*

Cliff's mother Phyllis continued to live for 22 more years at Colborne until she died 25 October 1974 and was buried with Cliff's father at Mount Lawn Cemetery in Whitby.

Rev. Frank and Phyllis Wootton with Judy, Dodie, Kate, Walter and Linda Hoad.

1948: June 29, on their way to Colborne for Judy's Baptism, Cliff, Dodie and Judy stopped at Cobourg for a short visit with Dodie's sister Grace McNab and her family. This photo is of Judy's cousin Agnes holding Judy. Cliff Hinton's 1948 4-door Pontiac Fleetleader sedan is parked on Blake Street. *See **Pg 184** for auto information.* At right, Judy, at one year old, is almost walking. Below, Cliff is with Dodie and Judy at the McNab home.

Judy got lots of attentiion from her Aunt Grace, Uncle Jack and cousins Jean Grace and Agnes during their stay at 183 Blake Street. *See **Appendix D Pg 288** for house plan.*

1948: On June 30, Cliff took Dodie's sister Grace and niece Agnes with them for the baptism at the Wootton home on Church St. in Colborne. Judy wanted to walk in this photo with Cliff, her Grandma and Grandpa Wootton, and her Aunt Grace McNab posing with Mrs. Turpin by her house next to the Wootton home. Judy had fun on the grass with her Grandma and cousin Agnes McNab watching.

See **Appendix D on Pg 283** for Wootton home floor plans..

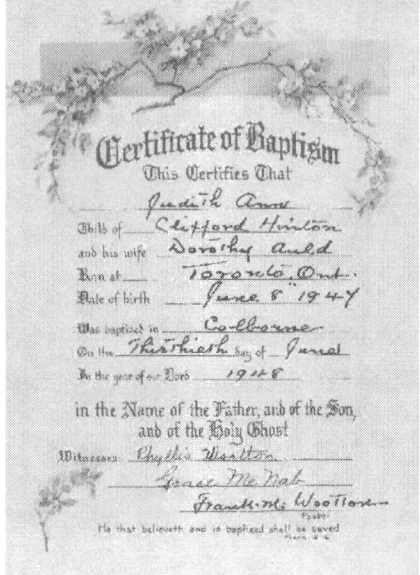

On this occasion, Judy was baptised by her grandpa Rev Frank Wootton.

1948: During July, Cliff, Dodie and Judy enjoyed their first summer in North Bay. Dodie and Judy made new friends in the neighbourhood while Cliff was busy with his General Motors business meetings and travels. When he had summer holidays, he went fishing with a friend at nearby Lake Nipissing. Is that a long neck beer bottle in his hand? Nice catch! Trout?

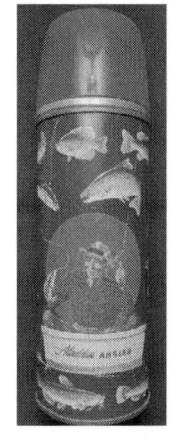

At left is a photo of his 'Aladdin Angler' fishing thermos which I still have with his war medals, postcards of Italy and war time cigarette case. *See **Appendix B Pg 230 and 234** for Cliff's collection.*

Celebration at Kingston for Thomas Forrest Auld

On 1 August 1948, the family came together to celebrate Grandpa Auld's 75rd birthday. Thomas, born in Scotland on 21 Aug 1875, was really 73. The confusion came with his 1889 arrival as an orphan in Canada. He married Mary Moncur in 1894 and by 1919 they had 10 children. On this happy occasion, family group photos were taken. Here is Thomas Forrest Auld surrounded by his eight daughters; top left in order from eldest Vi, Mabel, Grace, Helen, Thelma, Lillian, Betty and Dodie. Cliff was such a lucky brother in law!

129

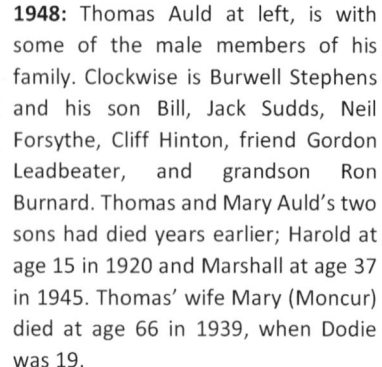

1948: Thomas Auld at left, is with some of the male members of his family. Clockwise is Burwell Stephens and his son Bill, Jack Sudds, Neil Forsythe, Cliff Hinton, friend Gordon Leadbeater, and grandson Ron Burnard. Thomas and Mary Auld's two sons had died years earlier; Harold at age 15 in 1920 and Marshall at age 37 in 1945. Thomas' wife Mary (Moncur) died at age 66 in 1939, when Dodie was 19.

Thomas Auld is at centre, with his youngest daughter Dorothy, a favourite son-in-law Clifford Hinton and a very busy 13 month old granddaughter Judith Anne aka Judy.

In September, below, Cliff and his family were back again on another trip from North Bay and this time they were able to visit family at Toronto, Colborne and Kingston. Judy was walking and on the go with cousin Ron Burnard at Vi and Burwell Stephen's Toronto home.

1948: In September, after stopping in Colborne, Cliff and his family contined on to Kingston, taking Cliff's recently married mother Phyllis Wootton with them. Phyllis would enjoy her frequent visits with the Auld family at Kingston. Phyllis stood by the laneway holding Judy.

At the Kingston farm, Judy, at 15 months, enjoyed running around and riding with Grandpa Auld on his new tractor. In these photos he watched her as she ran down the lane and across his front yard.

See **Appendix D Pg 280** for Auld Farm.

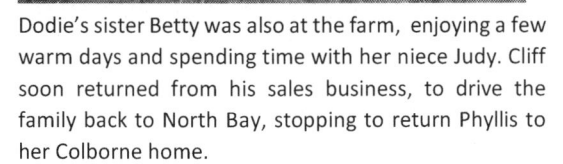

Dodie's sister Betty was also at the farm, enjoying a few warm days and spending time with her niece Judy. Cliff soon returned from his sales business, to drive the family back to North Bay, stopping to return Phyllis to her Colborne home.

By their Church St house, Rev Wootton greeted Phyllis and the Hinton family on their return from Kingston.

1948: Duing the autumn months, while Cliff was travelling, Dodie and Judy enjoyed quiet days in their rented house at 606 Cassels St.

On walks in their North Bay neighbourhood, they would visit friends on Second Ave. where Judy would have playtime with Richard Pelletier.

Judy, in buggy and standing below, is wearing her new suit that her Aunt Betty had knitted for her.

At Christmas, Cliff drove Dodie and Judy to Kingston. They stopped for an overnight visit with Betty and the Stephens family at 26 Glengrove Ave in Toronto (photo left).

"*On Christmas Eve (they) travelled (Hwy 2) from Toronto, stopping at Oshawa, Cobourg, Colborne and Picton and crossed on the Picton Ferry.*" They enjoyed a very happy Christmas at the Auld farmhouse. "*Santa brought her (Judy) a doll carriage, a doll, carpet sweeper, and rocker and she got a lot of other things.*" (See **Pg 133** for these quotes from Judy's baby book)

132

1948 Summer, Dodie wrote in Judy's baby book.

Going Places!

To the park   May 1948.
 "   "   zoo
 "   "   circus
 "   "   beach   August 1948

8 weeks old   By motor to   Scotty drove us to Grandpa Auld's at Kingston
4½ months "   train   from Kingston to Oshawa to meet Grandma Hinton
    "   "   bus   from Oshawa to Toronto to Auntie Vi's & Auntie Betty
           "   boat   "

1948 Christmas, Dodie wrote in Judy's baby book.

The First Christmas

Judy's first Christmas was spent at Grandpa's in Kingston. She was just over six months old and sat in her high-chair at the Christmas tree to open the presents. She liked the tree lights and the wrapping from the presents. And did better than anyone else in receiving presents.

The Second Christmas

Her second Christmas was also spent in Kingston. She travelled from North Bay by car. Christmas Eve travelled from Toronto stopping at Oshawa, Cobourg, Colborne and Picton and crossed on the Picton Ferry. Santa brought her a doll carriage, doll, diaper soaper and rocker and she got a _lot_ of other things.

The Third Christmas

1949: Below is a transcription of a letter sent to Dorothy when Judy was 18 months old. Cliff's Granny, Martha Brinn (1860-1950) age 89, is replying to a Christmas letter, photograph of Judith Anne at age one and gift of chocolates that Dorothy and Cliff had sent to her for Christmas 1948. There is mention of a second Hinton baby (Susan Elizabeth) expected soon. "Cliff will tell you about the girls" in this letter, is evidence that in 1943 Cliff visited his relatives in Wales.

See **Appendix C Pg 255** for original letter.

Air mail letter sent to Mrs. C Hinton,
606 Cassells Street, North Bay, Ont., Canada

January 1949

10 Hamilton Terrace, Pembroke, S. Wales

Dear Dorothy,

The lovely photo of baby Judith came Xmas day. How lovely of her. She looks just the same as Cliff looked when he first went to Canada and just the age. Thank you for sending it to me. All the friends say she is a lovely girl. I am so pleased to know your mother will be with Cliff and baby while you are in Hospital. Cliff will be quite a family man with 2 children. Mind take care of yourself.

Please to say I keep well. Madeline came home for Christmas. She is so bright and full of life. She is in the Land Army. Margaret is nursing in Hospital in London. Cliff will tell you about the girls. I'd love to see baby and hear her trying to talk. I go back over the time when the 3 boys were her age. Now they are all so far from me.

Thank you for the nice big box of chocolates. You are too good to me. My dear, I feel ashamed to write to you. my eyes are really bad. It is a job to get new glasses. So please excuse this badly written letter. Thank Cliff for his letter. He is a dear boy. Give him a big X for me.

The weather is cold and such a lot of fog and rain. Hope dears you all spent a happy Xmas. Did Father Christmas bring you all a lot of gifts?

Will close trusting you are all well. Good night. God bless you all.

Your loving Granny
M Brinn   XXXXXXXXXX

1949: Cliff's mother Phyllis, (above left) came to stay for some time with Cliff and Judy while Dodie was giving birth to their second daughter Susan Elizabeth on February 7 at St Josephs Hospital, North Bay. Dodie's sister Violet (middle with Judy) also came to see baby Susan and to spend time with the family. She may have accompanied Phyllis at least one way on the train or bus.

On March 13, Susan Elizabeth was Baptised by Rev A.E. Armstrong at St Andrew's United Church. She wore the long christening dress that Phyllis brought from Wales in 1948. It was the one her daddy and Phyllis, now 'Grandma Wootton' had worn at their baptisms many years before (1887, 1921) in Wales. Cliff's brothers Douglas and Hugh also likely wore the dress at their baptisms (1918, 1919) . Susan was the first of Phyllis's grandchildren to wear it.

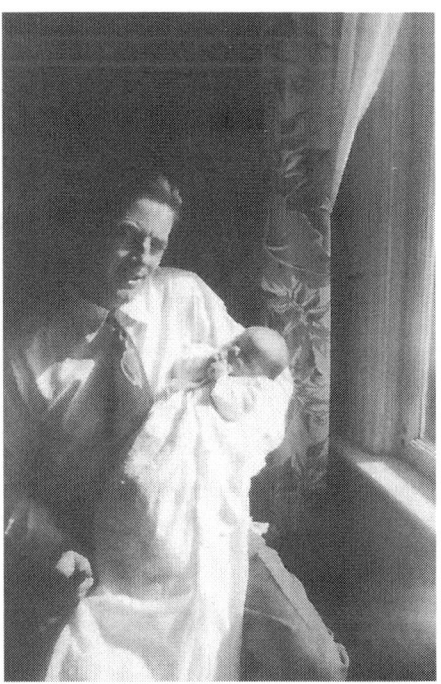

1949 Spring, Dodie Wrote in Susan's Baby Book.

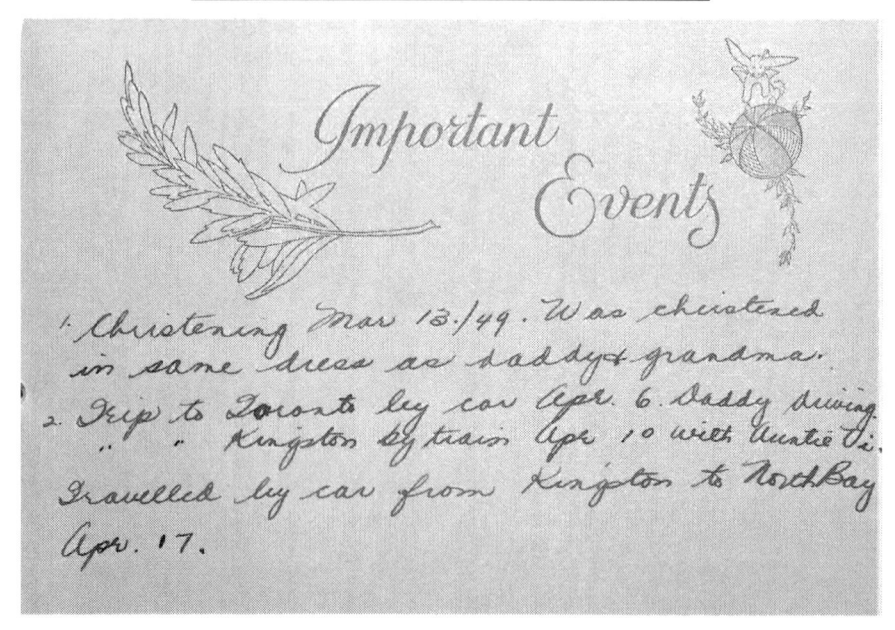

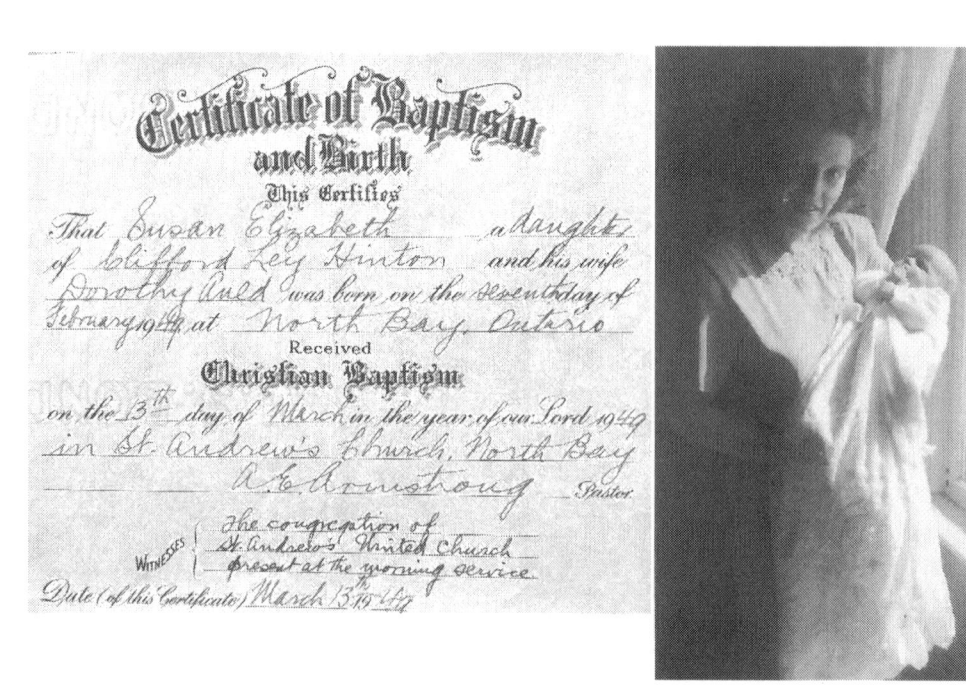

Important Events

1. Christening Mar 13./49. Was christened in same dress as daddy & grandma.
2. Trip to Toronto by car Apr. 6. Daddy driving
   " " Kingston by train Apr 10 with Auntie Vi.
   Travelled by car from Kingston to North Bay Apr. 17.

Certificate of Baptism and Birth

This Certifies

That Susan Elizabeth a daughter of Clifford Ley Hinton and his wife Dorothy Auld was born on the seventh day of February 1949 at North Bay, Ontario

Received

Christian Baptism

on the 13th day of March in the year of our Lord 1949 in St. Andrew's Church, North Bay

A. E. Armstrong, Pastor

WITNESSES: The congregation of St. Andrew's United Church present at the morning service

Date (of this Certificate) March 13th 1949

1949: On April 6, at almost 2 months old, Susan was ready to travel and to meet more relatives. Cliff drove them to Toronto to visit with family at 26 Glengrove Ave (at left) while he was busy with General Motors sales meetings. When Cliff was in Toronto, or Oshawa he often brought his wife and daughters with him for visits with family.

On April 10, Dodie's sister Violet went with Dodie and her girls to Kingston by train. *See Susan's baby book on previous Pg 136..*

Judy had fun with her cousin Carolyn Sudds (below) as they ran on the laneway by the drive shed where Grandpa Auld kept his new tractor.

On April 17 Cliff collected Dodie, Judy and Susan at Kingston and drove them back to North Bay.

1949: Cliff (Row 3, 4th from right) as a Sales Manager for General Motors Products.

1949: Cliff (Row 2, far left) representing GM Products at an executive meeting.

1949: On May 15, Cliff and his girls had another opportunity for a trip, in Cliff's 1948 Pontiac sedan, to 26 Glengrove Ave., Toronto, for Dodie's 30th birthday. *See **Pg 184** for Cliff's autos.*

Susan, 3 months, watched while Dodie and Cliff had a serious talk with Judy, nearly 2, in her knitted sweater.

After Cliff left for work, Betty, Dodie, and Judy walked with Susan in her carriage to a nearby park where they took some more photographs. Notice Susan's knitted clothes and pompom blanket.

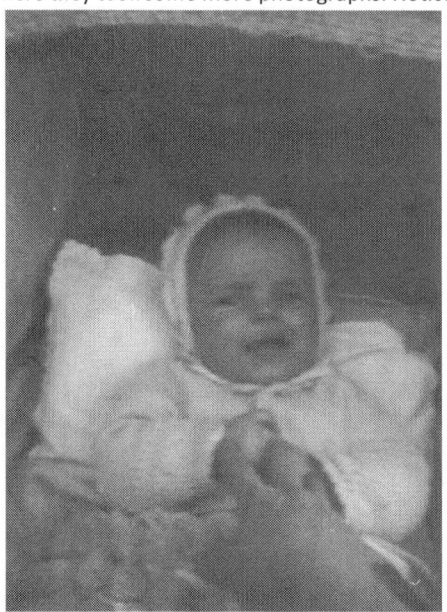

Watching her Aunt Betty take photos of the family, Judy squatted down, like Betty would often do to take pictures of the little ones.

In the photos below, Susan is with her with her Aunt Betty at left and with her mother Dodie who is again wearing her fashionable duster coat in the photos above and below right.

1949: On June 11, Cliff's family made a stop at Toronto and then at Colborne on their drive from North Bay to Kingston for a weeklong visit with family.

Above left, Susan is with her sister Judy on a lounger at 26 Glengrove Ave. Above right is Cliff with Linda Hoad age 5, Judy age 2, Dodie, and Susan 5 months old at the Wootton's Church Street home in Colborne.

Dodie, Judy, and Susan spent a week visiting with family at the Auld farm. Susan and her cousin Garry Sudds enjoyed some time together in their buggy parked on the driveway by the Auld house. Behind the buggy one can almost see the old water pump beside the maple tree and the new Laturney home which was built by Grandpa Auld in 1947.

Once again, Judy is mirroring her Aunt Betty as she takes Judy's photo by the garden where she has been picking raspberries. Up the drive is the barn and the Icehouse, converted in 1941. Grandpa wrote that Cliff helped him renovate it in 1951. See **Pg 157** and **Appendix C Pg 280**

1949: At the weekend, Cliff brought Grandma to the Auld farm. Here she is with Susan at 4 months and Judy age 2, on the steps of the Laturney house.

Also photographed are Judy with Helen, Mamie and Betty at top, Dodie centre and Susan with Lillian. (4 of Dodie's 7 sisters).

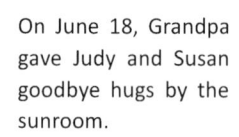

On June 18, Grandpa gave Judy and Susan goodbye hugs by the sunroom.

Dodie, Cliff, and their girls said 'goodbye' and had a photo taken by their new 1949 Pontiac Chieftain 2 door sedan before they left to take Phyllis to Colborne and then drive home to North Bay. See **Pg 184** for *auto information.*

There are no photos or information about the events of late summer and autumn of 1949, except a wedding portrait (**Pg 73**) of Cliff's brother Douglas Hinton and Doris Hele who were married at Oshawa, on 27 September 1949. It is probable that Cliff, Dodie, Judy and Susan spent Christmas with family at Kingston. There were no photos, but Aunt Betty said they taught 2 ½ year old Judy to recite "The Night Before Christmas" in a highchair while they were all there that Christmas.

1950: Cliff continued his frequent General Motors sales trips around Ontario so while he was away in June, Cliff's Aunty Kate and Uncle Walter drove Phyllis to North Bay. Dodie showed them around North Bay, and they stopped at the North Bay Harbour to take some photos.

Notice the busy Cassells Street views in these photos of Judy at age 3 and Susan on-the-go at 16 months.

Phyllis always enjoyed time with her granddaughters and was pleased to be there for Judy's 3rd birthday. For the party, Phyllis wore her favourite dress, pearls, and sensible shoes; her long hair in it's usual updo! Judy and Susan had leaves they picked from the garden while waiting for party friends to arrive.

1950: This photo from Phyllis's collection, on which she has written 'Judy' and 'Susan', was taken at Judy's 3rd birthday party. On the top step, beside Judy (wearing a hair bow), are friends Richard Pelletier and his sister who lived around the corner at 418 Second Ave W. Their parents Evelyn and Raymond Pelletier became good friends with Dodie and Cliff. Notice Susan's playpen behind them on the porch. It seems that soon after this the Hintons moved from 606 Cassells St. to a cottage on Lake Nipissing and then to a house nearby, on Third Ave, North Bay.

By mid June, Grandpa Frank Wootton and his brother Percy drove to North Bay to see the Hinton family and to collect Grandma Phyllis Wootton from the Lake Nipissing cottage where the Hinton family was staying. Percy and Frank laid on the beach while Grandma played in the sand with Susan and Judy.

144

While they were at the cottage, Cliff took his girls for a swim in the chilly waters of Lake Nipissing.

Another Summer at Kingston

1950: At the end of June, the Hinton family drove to Kingston so, while Cliff was working, Dodie and the girls could spend summertime at Grandpa Auld's farm. Neil and Helen Forsythe greeted them when they arrived, and Cliff parked his Pontiac on the grass by the sunroom. Judy and Susan had fun for a few weeks with cousins Carolyn and Garry Sudds. Behind them in the photo below is the Laturney house that grandpa built in 1947.
See **Appendix D Pg 280** *for map of Auld Farm.*

1950: In July, Cliff returned to get his girls. Susan sat and Judy stood by his car parked on the front lawn at the Auld farm. They joined friends Edna (in swimsuit) and Joe Acton, son Peter (in bib shorts), daughter Kathy (with tube) and their Acton cousins for a swim and picnic. Cliff must have taken the photos. Notice the vintage cars and his 1949 Pontiac Chieftain with a towel over the window, for Susan's nap. See **Pg 184** for auto information.

1950: Cliff (Row 3, 2nd from right) as a Sales Manager for General Motors Products.

Cliff had moved his family to North Bay in 1948 when he became a regional sales representative for General Motors Products. GM products may have included automotive and household appliances. His region was largely spread out in central Ontario, and he would have been travelling to various towns and cities as well as attending meetings in Oshawa. By 1950 he was promoted to regional sales manager. The photo below was taken outdoors by the General Motors Canada offices on Ritson Rd., likely early in the summer of 1950.

Summer at North Bay

1950: A benefit of living in North Bay was the proximity to lakeside cottages. Cliff, Dodie, Judy, and Susan spent time at their friends' Lake Nipissing cottage. They played on the beach and went for a ride in their motorboat. Without life Jackets!

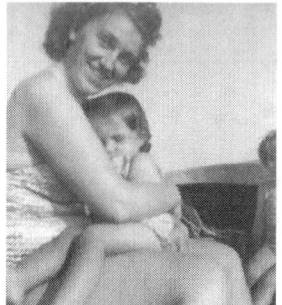

148

Another Winter at North Bay

1950: The Hinton family moved to a larger house at 241 Third Ave in North Bay. In December Dodie's eldest sister Violet came from Toronto to spend some time while Cliff was away on one of his many business trips for General Motors. When Cliff returned, they were ready to drive his sister-in-law to Toronto and to spend Christmas at Kingston. Vi likely took the family photo of the Hintons on the front steps of their Third Ave home. (thanks to my *cousin Ron Sudds who did photo enhancement)*

1951: Judy and Susan enjoyed playing outside in the great amount of snow that fell in North Bay that winter. Susan had her second birthday at this house and surely had a wonderful time at her party with her sister and friends. Dodie always had a talent for great parties!

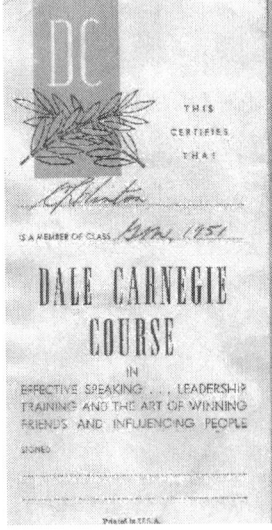

Move to Oshawa

1951: That Winter, Cliff took a Dale Carnegie course with a GM automotive sales group in preparation for his move to Oshawa in a promoted sales management position with the General Motors Service division. Cliff celebrated his 30th birthday on March 11, 1951.

GENERAL MOTORS PRODUCTS
OF CANADA, LIMITED
UNITED MOTORS SERVICE DIVISION

L. HINTON

Winning Friends and Influencing People

What many people remembered most about my father was his charming personality. As the third son in his busy family, he was able to develop his charms: watching and learning from his older brothers, staying under the radar, and using his winning smile to get away with mostly harmless mischief. He was also a good listener and a team player, using his excellent social skills to get ahead in all aspects of his life. His winsome personality was witnessed by the Auld family when he set his eyes on Dorothy and was appreciated by his employers and co-workers when he took on leadership roles in his career in automotive sales and services. He had natural success in following *Dale Carnegie's rules* outlined in the list below where he marked 4 of them for special attention.

Fundamental Technique in Handling People

1. Don't criticize, condemn, complain.
2. Give honest, sincere appreciation.
3. Arouse in the other person an eager want.

Six Ways to Make People Like You

1. Become genuinely interested in other people.
2. Smile.
3. Remember that a man's name is to him the sweetest and most important sound in the English language.
4. Be a good listener. Encourage others to talk about themselves.
5. Talk in terms of the other man's interest.
6. Make the other person feel important—and do it sincerely.

Nine Ways to Change People Without Giving Offense or Arousing Resentment

1. Begin with praise and honest appreciation.
2. Call attention to people's mistakes indirectly.
3. Talk about your own mistakes before criticizing the other person.
4. Ask questions instead of giving direct orders.
5. Let the other man save his face.
6. Praise the slightest improvement. Be "hearty in your approbation and lavish in your praise."
7. Give the other person a fine reputation to live up to.
8. Use encouragement. Make the fault seem easy to correct.
9. Make the other person happy about doing the thing you suggest.

Twelve Ways to Win People to Your Way of Thinking

1. The only way to get the best of an argument is to avoid it.
2. Show respect for the other man's opinions. Never tell a man he is wrong.
3. If you are wrong, admit it quickly and emphatically.
4. Begin in a friendly way.
5. Get the other person saying "yes, yes" immediately.
6. Let the other man do a great deal of the talking.
7. Let the other man feel that the idea is his.
8. Try honestly to see things from the other person's point of view.
9. Be sympathetic with the other person's ideas and desires.
10. Appeal to the nobler motives.
11. Dramatize your ideas.
12. Throw down a challenge.

Seven Rules for Making Your Home Life Happier

1. Don't nag.
2. Don't try to make your partner over.
3. Don't criticize.
4. Give honest appreciation.
5. Pay little attentions.
6. Be courteous.
7. Read a good book on the sexual side of marriage.

Return to Oshawa, Ontario, Canada 1951-1953

Summer 1951, at Kingston and Grandpa's letter	155
General Motors, Sales Manager 1951	159
Death of Stepfather, Rev Frank Wootton (1872-1952)	160
Summer 1952, at Kingston, Ontario	161
3rd Daughter, Deborah Jane Hinton, 28 September 1952	162
338 Colborne St, Oshawa and Toronto Weekend	163

1951: By Spring, Cliff and Dodie were happy to be back in Oshawa closer to their friends and family. They lived with good friends Alex (Scotty) and Pat Reid at 634 Grierson St while Cliff and Dodie found a two-bedroom flat in a house at 338 Colborne St E. In June, they drove to Colborne and then took the Wootton grandparents on to Kingston with them.

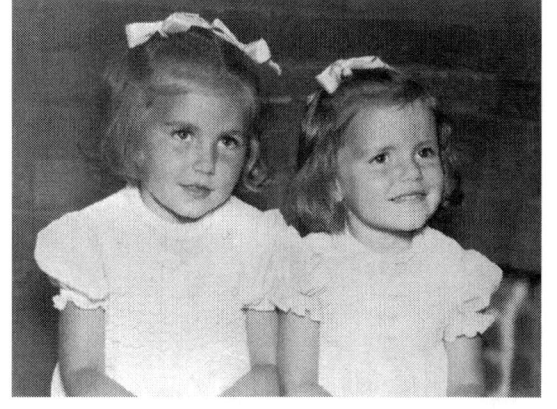

In these photos cousins Peggy Laturney (baby) and Carolyn Sudds were sitting by the Auld house with Phyllis, Susan, and Judy. Below Susan and Judy were sitting with Grandpa Wootton.

This portrait of Judy and Susan was taken in front of the Auld farmhouse fireplace. For many years Cliff carried this favourite photo in his wallet. Dodie, Judy, and Susan enjoyed a few weeks at Kingston while Cliff was working. He joined them in July for a two-week holiday and to help Grandpa Auld on the farm. See **Pg 157** and **Appendix C Pg 259** Grandpa Auld's 1951 letter.

While at Kingston, Cliff and Dodie drove to Syracuse for a short holiday, leaving Susan and Judy in the care of the aunts and uncles who lived at the Auld property. On their trip to home in Oshawa, they stopped at Colborne and went to the beach. Judy and Susan wore new sunhats and played with sand toys that Cliff and Dodie bought for them in Syracuse.

155

1951: In late summer, the Hintons drove to Toronto, stopping at 26 Glengrove Ave and at 24 Norway Ave where they saw Cliff's Uncle Walter Hoad and Aunty Kate who drove with them to Colborne to visit her sister-in-law, Phyllis.

1951: Now in his hometown, Cliff resumed his love of sports by playing hockey with an Oshawa General Motors adult leisure team and by coaching an Oshawa Bantam Baseball team.

1951 OSHAWA WHOLESALE BANTAM BASEBALL TEAM

Back Row: — Left to Right — Cliff Hinton (Coach), Larry Steffen, Joe Victor, Don Badour, Ross Aselstine (Commissioner), Ron Proctor, Ron Norman (Captain), Dave Weldon, Frank Kelemen (Coach)

Front Row: — Left to Right — Lorne Jeffs, Bruce Harding, Jim Milton, Jim Read, Orvil McCaughey, Jack Germond, Al Fleming.

Front Centre: — Frank Locke (Bat Boy)

1951: In November, Grandpa Auld, age 76, sent a letter to Vancouver telling Dodie's sister Thelma and family about recent family news. He mentions having his helpful son-in-law Cliff at the farm for a few weeks in the summer and tells other news about Cliff's family. It is wonderful to hear Grandpa's 'voice', his humour, and his industriousness in this letter. Cliff and Dodie were planning to build a house in Oshawa near Park Rd and John St where lots were being developed. Their plans changed with the expectation of a new baby in September 1952, Cliff's new work at Kralinator Ltd., and their 1953 move to Preston.   See **Appendix C Pg 259** for Grandpa Thomas Auld's handwritten letter.

Mr. and Mrs. A. F. Burnard
1120 W 22nd Ave
Pemberton Heights
North Vancouver, B. C.

Auldsville
R.R. 7 Kingston   *Nov 4, 1951*

Dear Thelma, Alex, and Ronnie,

Now hang on to your hearts, this may not happen again for another blue moon or until I have another spasm. In fact, I did not intend to write you tonight. I intended to write to Violet, and we were just eating a little snack about 10:30 and Violet rang up to say that Ruth and her and the baby were coming tomorrow night, (it seems Bill is away for a week) so they could get away all right. So that ruled out a letter to Violet, but I considered you might not take it amiss if I dropped you a line.

According to Helen you must have heard I have been busy getting a house fixed for the Sudds family. Well, I started along about July 15th at the house. I had a lot to do it. I had let Burke put up a stairway in it and then along in June when I was up at the reunion at Stratford and Toronto, they had a falling out with Mary Margaret. It wasn't Mary's fault. She was baby sitting for Jack and Isabel, and Frankie and Elsie were keeping her company. Isabel had left 50 cents on the table for Mary. I should say two 25 cent pieces. Well Frankie and Elsie picked up the money and told their parents that they got it for minding the children. Well, you know what Helen is like in anything like that. She told them what had happened, and she says you should have seen the way he carried on and he gave Frankie an awful licking and said they had better get out before they were accused of something else. Well of course I didn't hear about it till I came home, and in the meantime, he had ripped up all his garden stuff packed it all in boxes and had it all ready to move. He got a house in Odessa. I think he is there yet, but he was back trying to get rooms with Mrs. Bertram, in which he didn't succeed. Well, he finally moved about the middle of July and ever since then what with the potatoes and tearing the house apart I have been pretty busy.

I tore out the stairway and then I took in the cement porch on the east side and built the stairway right up the east side. I took out the dividing wall on the porch side and put it all in the living room. I insulated all the new part and even insulated the whole of the roof. I had to put in about half a new floor upstairs and made one bedroom downstairs instead of two. Clifford had two weeks holidays and he helped me quite a lot. The result is you would hardly know it for the same house.

Well, I worked along at it till I had to get at my potatoes. I think I got them out in two weeks time. I did not have so many this year but of course I did not put in as many, but they are twice the price they were last year so that helps a lot.

Well, I finally got the house, so it was liveable and about three weeks ago I started to tear down the Thompson cottage. I had the kitchen and sun parlor on the front part down and Violet happened to come down. She wanted to buy the cottage and move it up just east of the barn. So, I sold it to her, and I have to finish taking it down. I would have had it down last week, but we had a snowstorm Friday so I can't do anything till it clears up. When Violet comes down, she will likely be helping me to finish it up. She says she wants someplace when she comes down that she can call her own, so that will be another house to build in the spring. Cliff and Dodie are going to build in the spring also, so I don't think I'll be very idle next year.

I am also getting a road built across the marsh on the west side of the railway. I want to put the whole of the back field in another subdivision. There are about 12 acres there and if I can sell the lots it will mean about 35 or 40 lots. I had the surveyor look it over and he thought I had a good proposition. Of course, the road across will cost one over a thousand dollars, but it seems to be the only way of making anything out of that back field.

I suppose the girls keep you informed about the family news. Mabel was up to Grace's for a week before Dodie left. Cliff has got a house in Oshawa for the winter, or perhaps until he gets his own built. I guess likely you know all that already.

Well, I finally lost my job at the light house. They found out I was over 65 and of course that is the governments rule to retire employees. But why didn't they fire me before they hired me. I was over 67 then but of course there was a war on then and they couldn't get anyone else who would take it. No one in particular is taking my place. They intend to run it from Prescott. I'm not finding any fault. I am applying for the old age pension. I sent word to Mai Russell to try and get my birth certificate about two months ago. As I didn't hear from them, I applied to the Sunlife Insurance Co for an affidavit of an Insurance I had taken out 51 years ago. I got that yesterday, so I'm all set now.

I think I have given you all my news or what have you. Thank Ronnie for writing to Grandpa and when I get money enough, I'll come and maybe stay longer than you want me to. I won't have much to do after I get the house down. I'm still building bookcases. I wish you were nearer so I could give you one.

Dad and Grandpa

PS I suppose you knew we got in an oil furnace last year and oh boy does it work nice. So, I'll have nothing to do and lots of time to do it in.

I notice when I told you about Burke building the stairway, it was not satisfactory. It took up too much of the living room. Now the room at it's widest is 16 ft and the front door now faces the south, or the waterfront and it is 18 ft in length, so it really looks nice.

1951: Cliff (Row 3 center) as a Sales Manager for General Motors.

This is likely an executive and sales management group working out of the offices at General Motors Canada Ltd on Ritson Rd in Oshawa. The photo was taken outside by the front entrance.

1952 Rev Frank Morrison Wootton (1872-1952) Obituary

1952: Sadly, Phyllis was widowed again on February 20, when Rev Frank Morrison Wootton died at age 78 in Colborne. He was buried with his first wife Harriet at the Glenwood Cemetery in Picton, Ontario. Over the next years, Phyllis remained friends with her 5 Wootton stepchildren and their families, Morris Wootton, Edith Sifton, Helen Lush, Jean Mahaffy, and Ruth Blakely.

In April, with exciting news about a baby expected in September, the Hinton family was at Colborne with Phyllis for Easter Sunday. Cliff looks dapper in his bowtie, with daughters Susan and Judy in hand.

Rev. F. M. Wootton Dies Known in Owen Sound

A United Church Minister, Rev. F. M. Wootton, well known in Owen Sound, died in Colborne on Feb. 20, at the age of 78. He served with the former Methodist Church, and later the United in Winnipeg, Moosejaw, Stratford, Brantford, Hamilton, Peterborough and other cities. He was active in church work up to the last.

Mr. Wootton's first wife, Harriet Louise Frost, daughter of Alfred Frost, Grey County Crown Attorney the marriage taking place in Owen Sound in 1899. She died a number of years ago, and Mr. Wootton was married to Phyllis Hinton of Oshawa in 1948.

Also surviving are a son, Alfred Wootton, Whitby, and four daughters, Mrs. C. H. Sifton of Cobourg, Mrs. G. Lush of Hamilton, Mrs. F. J. Mahaffy of Montreal and Mrs. Clelan Blakey of Picton.

In May, when Dodie was 5 months pregnant, Aunt Betty visited the Hintons at Oshawa for Dodie's 33rd birthday. It looks like they were at Lakeview Park for a picnic lunch. See **Pg 122** for parking lot posts clue.

160

1952: In July, the Hintons were at Kingston in time for Peggy Laturney's 2nd birthday. Grandpa Auld's brother-in law, Uncle Bob Charles, was visiting from Glasgow Scotland. He is seated below with Gary, Peggy, Judy, Susan, and Carolyn in front.

Group photos below L-R, are of Don and Mary Laturney, Uncle Bob Charles, Aunt Mamie, Belle and Bill Charles, Grandpa Tom Auld with Cliff, tallest at top. Dodie replaces Mary in back left of lower left photo. In front are Peggy with Uncle Bob, Carolyn, Judy with Belle Charles, and Susan in front of Bill Charles.

1952: A third daughter, Deborah Jane, was born on September 28 at Oshawa General Hospital. Judy started going by taxi to afternoon Kindergarten at Ritson Road P.S. and Cliff was busy travelling as a salesman for General Motors. Susan was at home with Dodie and baby Deborah. They enjoyed the sunny kitchen of the second-floor flat, with a south window view to Colborne St. While Judy was at school, Susan helped her mother with cake baking and minding her sister Deborah. Their flat had a living room and bedroom overlooking the back yard. Susan and Judy shared a small bedroom next to the kitchen, tucked beside the stairway at the front of the house. That winter Judy and Susan spent too much time in that cozy room, with the shades drawn, while recovering from measles infections which Judy brought home from school. Deborah and their mother may have had mild cases of measles and they all later had mumps. See **Pg 167**.

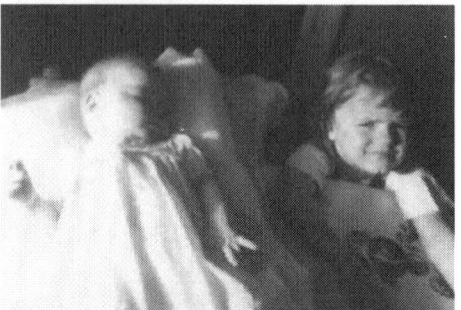

See **Appendix C Pg 284** for house info.

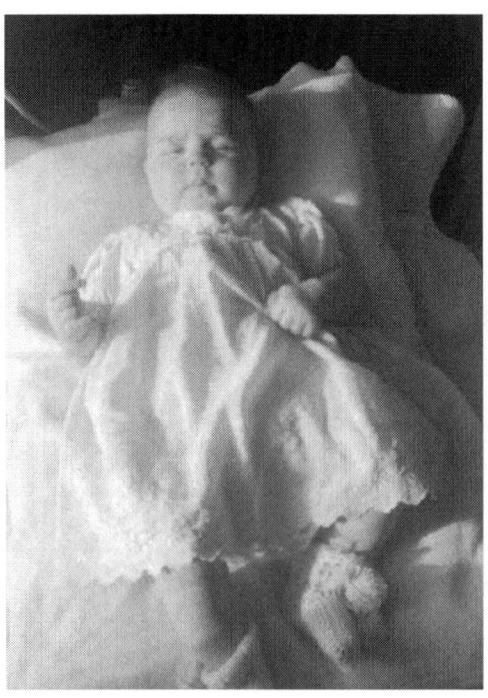

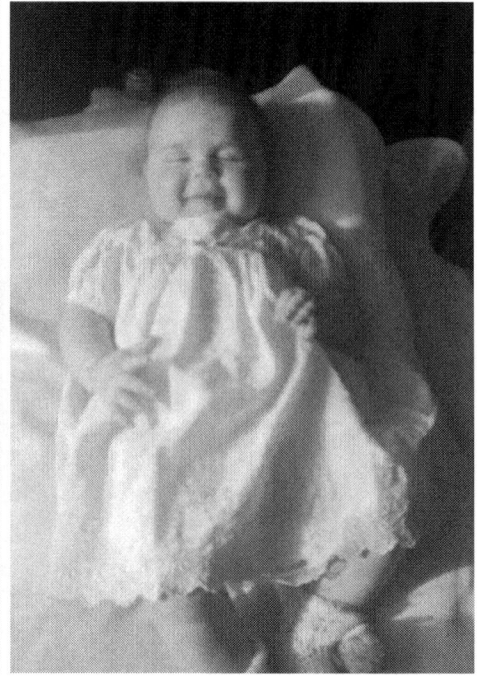

1952: In late November, Cliff, Dodie and their three young daughters had a weekend visit with Dodie's sister Betty Auld at her new apartment #209 at 2175 Avenue Rd near to the new and expanding 401 Hwy in Toronto. Betty had a sofa bed and modern swivel chairs (which were later reupholstered at 3 Breadner Dr, *Pg 193,* and are now at Susan's home). She also had the modern stereo cabinet now at Deborah's home. With their mother and their Aunt Betty, they shopped for new winter outfits at a plaza nearby on Wilson Rd. They especially enjoyed watching cartoons on Betty's new TV. They also watched the Toronto Eaton's Santa Claus Parade in black and white, the first year it was televised! On the new CBC network!

Judy and Susan were on the front steps of their home at 338 Colborne St. in Oshawa, and in the driveway by Cliff's 1949 Pontiac Chieftain sedan, wearing their new coats, hats, and matching pants. Susan's was rose wool with brown velvet trim and Judy's was blue wool with royal blue velvet trim.

By December, Deborah was 2 months old. Susan and Judy had new matching snowsuits, knitted hats and mitts ready for winter play at their Oshawa home.

Career Move to Preston, Ontario, Canada 1953-1957

Kralinator Limited, Assistant Sales Manager	167
124 Laurel St, Preston	167
Trips to Colborne	168
Christmas 1954, at Preston	173
Mother's Day 1955, at Colborne	174
Death of Father-In-Law, Thomas Forrest Auld (1875-1956)	176
Labour Day 1956, Weekend with Family at Montreal	179
Kralinator Limited, Promotion to Project Sales Manager	181
New Puppy "Pete" at Christmas 1956	182
Cliff's Automobiles 1948-1957	184

Move to Preston

1953: Cliff was recruited from his sales position at General Motors Products to be the assistant sales manager in the Domestic Sales Division at Kralinator Ltd in Preston (Cambridge since 1973). Instead of building a new house in Oshawa, he and Dodie purchased their first home ownership, a house in Preston for their family.

New Kralinator Sales Appointments

JOHN J. LISCOMBE   CLIFFORD L. HINTON

C. N. Fouse, President of Kralinator Limited, Preston, Ont., has announced two new staff appointments. John J. Liscombe has been named sales manager, and Clifford L. Hinton assistant sales manager, of the Domestic Sales Division. They will be responsible for the national promotion and merchandising of Kralinator Oil Filters and Replacement Cartridges.

In April, Cliff's mother Phyllis joined the Hinton family for their move from Oshawa to Preston and to help them settle into their home which they had purchased at 124 Laurel Street. Dodie had complications from the mumps she caught from Judy and Susan. She had an allergic reaction to penicillin and needed doctor's care. 7-month-old Deborah may have also had a mild mumps infection.

See **Appendix C Pg 286** for floorplans.

167

1953: By Mother's Day, May 10, Dodie and her girls had recovered from the mumps, and they visited Cliff's mother Phyllis at her home in Colborne.

By June, the Hinton family was happily settled in their new neighbourhood. Judy had her 6th birthday and finished her kindergarten year at Preston Central PS. Cliff enjoyed success in his position with Kralinator Ltd. His work involved a lot of travel in his 1949 Pontiac 2-door Chieftain. He would soon get a new 1953 4-door Chieftain sedan. *See **Pg 184** for Cliff's autos.* Dodie and the girls were happy when they could have him at home with them on weekends.

In August, the Hinton family spent time at the Auld Farm in Kingston. They met Helen Lindsay, granddaughter of Bob Charles, who was there visiting her cousins. She had moved from Glasgow Scotland to work at a printing company in Toronto and she shared an apartment with Dodie's sister Betty Auld. At right is a photo of Helen with the Hinton girls in the garden at their grandma Phyllis Wootton's house in Colborne.

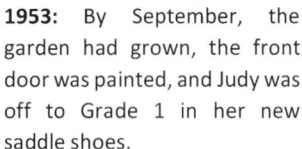

1953: By September, the garden had grown, the front door was painted, and Judy was off to Grade 1 in her new saddle shoes.

Christmas was mostly a happy time at their Preston home. It seems that Susan may have decided against joining her two sisters for their photo above. Maybe she was not impressed with sister Deborah sitting in her chair! Deborah has 'Elly' and Judy has 'Betty Grable'. Susan's 'Gina Lollobrigida' is lying alone by the tree. Cliff had fun naming the dolls for his favourites! Note the abandoned child-size folding chair at the right edge of the photo. (Phyllis brought it from Wales in 1947) *See **Pg 116***.

It had been a very good year for Cliff in his new position as assistant sales manager with Kralinator Limited. Several colleagues became close friends, such as Bruce Hodge in middle row, far left and Dick Liscombe in front, far left. Cliff in commanding pose is at far right in middle row.

169

1954: The 1 ½ story house at 124 Laurel St was the perfect home for the Hinton family. It had two upstairs bedrooms and a small main floor bedroom, perfect for guests and the sewing machine. When Cliff was on the road and the girls were to bed, Dodie spent evenings sewing cushion covers, window drapes and clothes for herself and her daughters. Susan and Judy proudly wore their 'Mom made' suits with new Easter accessories to Sunday School with next door friends Susan and Mary Balfour. See **Appendix C Pg 286** *for floorplans.*

On Easter Sunday, Cliff drove his family to Colborne in his new 1953 Pontiac Chieftain 8-cylinder, 4 door sedan (was it blue?).

In this after church photo, Phyllis seems to be smiling with amusement when Deborah was swinging her Easter basket. Then with hats and jackets off Susan swung her basket too.

1954: By June, Dodie's new drapes were up, the front door and porch railing were painted, a concrete pad was poured behind the drive, and Cliff had built a stone-wall garden under the living room window. Enjoying life in Preston, their daughters had new friends and even on the coldest winter days, stayed outside playing until the streetlights came on. Building blanket forts over the clothesline, riding new bikes and fun the sand box became favourite spring and summer activities. *See **Appendix C Pg 286** for house plans.*

In July, the Hintons drove to Colborne to visit with Grandma Wootton and Cliff's 3-year-old niece Dale Hinton who was staying with her 'Granny' for a few days. They had fun in the yard with neighbours Kathleen and Reed. Later Cliff drove the family to nearby Presqu'ile Park at Brighton for some time at the beach. While Phyllis and Dodie sat with Deborah, Susan and her cousin Dale enjoyed playing in the sand and surf. Judy could only splash her feet as she was still healing from stitches after a fall off her bike when she rode too quickly up the narrow walkway around their Preston house.

1954: In September, Susan, age 5, started Kindergarten and Judy, age 7, was in grade 2 at Preston Central PS. Deborah had her 2nd birthday on September 28. Dodie used her sewing talents to make her daughters' party dresses and the Little Dutch Girl Hallowe'en costumes for Susan and Judy.

Their Aunt Betty enjoyed her visits to Preston. Here she is sitting in the sun on the concrete patio by the porch at the back door to the kitchen. Dodie is behind her, likely hanging clothes with pegs on the pulley clothesline that extended from the porch to a backyard post. See **Appendix C Pg 286** *for house plans.*

Dodie sewed a new winter coat with a velvet collar and covered buttons for Judy. Susan had grown into Judy's blue coat. Dodie also made their plaid wool pants. Judy and Susan stood with next door neighbours Susan and Mary Balfour for a photo in their winter outfits.

172

1954: It was a very happy Christmas, having Clifford's mother, Phyllis Wootton, staying with them for the holidays. She slept on a day bed in the main floor sewing room. *See house plan in **Appendix C Pg 286.***

These photos were taken on December 26, when Dodie's sister Betty Auld and cousin Helen Lindsay drove out to Preston from their Toronto apartment to visit the Hinton family and Grandma Wootton on 'boxing day'. Susan had a new rocking chair and was pleased to be in the Christmas tree photo this year! The three sisters are holding new dolls that Santa left for them.

See photo above on the book cover.

1955: It was a beautiful day at 124 Laurel St, on Easter Sunday, when Cliff's daughters wore new dresses sewn by their mother Dodie. Deborah's was a cotton dress with a smocked bodice. Susan's and Judy's were made of organza with Peter Pan collars and waistline sashes. They also had new hats and gloves which they wore to Sunday School at Preston United Church.

In May, Cliff drove his family to Colborne to visit his mother on Mother's Day. Dodie and her daughters wore dresses that she sewed on her 'new' machine. Dodie's Singer peddle machine had been converted to electric! Judy and Susan enjoyed cutting paper dolls and clothes with little tabs from Eaton's catalogues. Following their mother's example they made paper patterns, and using Dodie's fabric scraps, they cut and sewed simple clothes for the fashion dolls they got for Christmas. Cliff was always proud of his girls and very interested in their activities. That Fall he encouraged Susan and Judy to take skating lessons.

1955: Deborah had her 3rd birthday on September 28. Susan age 6 was in grade 1. Judy age 8 was in grade 3 and joined the 4th, Preston Brownies. Susan and Judy enjoyed learning to figure skate with their neighbourhood friends and although Cliff's expertise was hockey skating, they were very happy when he assisted at some of their figure skating lessons. For Christmas they got new skates from Santa and beautifully made velvet skating dresses with knitted accessories.

1956: Deborah was still too young to skate, but she was eager to play outside in her snowsuit and angora hat and mittens. Her sisters and their Laurel St. friends had fun sledding on the backyard hill.

1956: In April, Cliff drove his family to Colborne for Easter Sunday services at the United Church. Phyllis had her great niece Linda Hoad, age 12, visiting her.

1956 May 22, Family Group for Funeral of Thomas Forrest Auld.

1956: On May 19, just 4 days after his youngest daughter Dodie's 37th birthday, and after a short illness in hospital, Cliff's father-in-law, Thomas Forrest Auld, died at age 81. Cliff and Dodie left their three daughters with Grandma Wootton at Colborne on their way to join the Auld family at Kingston for the May 22nd funeral at Queen St United Church. Grandpa Auld was buried at Cataraqui Cemetery with his wife Mary who died in 1939.

L-R is Lillian Auld, Bill Charles, Ruth Stephens, Cliff and Dodie Hinton, J Grace McNab, Jack McNab, Bob Charles, Grace McNab, Betty Auld, Agnes McNab, Isobel Sudds, Helen Forsythe, Vi Stephens, Mable Read, Mary Laturney, Delbert Sudds, Jack Sudds and in front is Garry and Carolyn Sudds, Allan Stephens, Jean Reddy with Jimmy, Peggy, Don and David Laturney.

1956: In June, Dodie's sister Thelma Burnard and her son Ron came from Vancouver to be with the family who were still mourning their father's death. The photo at left is of his eight daughters from eldest at right, Violet, Mabel, Grace, Helen, Thelma, Lillian, Betty, to youngest at left, Dodie. Below right is another photo of the 8 sisters, missing their father but happy to be together at the Auld home.

L-R is Jim and Jimmy Reddy, Neil Forsythe, Jean Reddy, Betty Auld, Ron Burnard, Mable Read, Cliff Hinton, Thelma Burnard, Grace McNab, Bill Stephens, Lillian Auld, Don Laturney, Vi Stephens, Mary Laturney, Dodie Hinton, Burwell Stephens, and in front is Susan Hinton, Judy Hinton, Peggy Laturney, Allan Stephens, and Deborah Hinton.

1956: In August, some of the family got together again to see Ron and Thelma Burnard before they returned to Vancouver. Uncle Bob Charles had come to spend time with some of his Auld cousins who were also there for these photos that were taken with Cliff's mother in the backyard at her Colborne home. Unfortunately, Cliff is not in these photos as he was in Calgary on a business trip.

In the two photos above, Dodie at left, switched places with her sister Vi who is behind Ron Burnard. Next is Betty Auld, Phyllis Wootton, Judy Hinton, Mabel Read, Deborah Hinton, Bob Charles, Lillian Auld, Susan Hinton, and Thelma Burnard.

THOMAS F. AULD
The funeral of Thomas F. Auld, 81, RR 7, Cobourg, who died at Kingston General Hospital, took place from Queen Street United Church to Cataraqui Cemetery. The service was conducted by Rev. H. M. Servage.
Pall-bearers were J. Henderson, L. Day, V. Fraser, G. L. Leadbeater, L. Bertrim, and J. G. McNab.
Mr. Auld, who had lived in Kingston for over 66 years, was born in Leith, Scotland, the son of Peter and Margaret (Forrest) Auld. He was a dairyman until he retired eight years ago.
Surviving are eight daughters, Mrs. C. B. Stephens (Violet), Toronto; Mrs. L. A. Read (Mabel), Kingston; Mrs. J. G. McNab (Grace), Cobourg; Mrs. H. N. Forsythe (Helen), Kingston; Mrs. A. F. Burnard (Thelma), Vancouver; Mrs. C. L. Hinton (Dorothy), Preston; Miss Lillian Auld, Kingston and Miss Bette Auld, Toronto; 12 grandchildren and seven great-grandchildren.

This old black & white photograph c1950 shows a typical working view of a MASSEY HARRIS "PONY" in the field of Mr. Thomas F. Auld's farm on the old Front Rd near the former Kingston Elevators.

The Obituary, at left, was in the Cobourg newspaper mistaking his home as Cobourg. The other details are accurate. Grandpa's tractor photo was in a later issue of the Kingston Whig Standard Newspaper.

1956: When Cliff returned from Calgary, he took his family on a 400-mile road trip in his 1955 Pontiac, to spend Labour Day weekend at his brother Doug Hinton's home in Ville St Laurent, Montreal. They likely drove Cliff's mother with them or drove her back to Colborne. Cliff's mother Phyllis may have already been visiting her son Doug, his wife Doris, Robert almost 2 and Dale on her 6th birthday. She wore her beautiful new skirt for the occasion as she helped grandson Bobby away from Cliff's 1955 Pontiac. Below she is dancing with Cliff and looks very happy to have him there with his wife Dorothy, Deborah almost 4, Susan age 7, and Judy age 9.

The cousins had fun playing together in the yard and in the unfinished basement where the girls had beds set up for the weekend visit. I remember hearing the adults upstairs talking of current events and Doug's controversial DEW (Distant Early Warning) project.

*See next **Pg 180** for a link to information about DEW.*

Distant Early Warning (DEW) Line

You can read about this in a 2007 article at:
http://www.journal.forces.gc.ca/vo8/no2/doc/lajeunes-eng.pdf.

A completed DEW Line radome, circa 1956

THE DISTANT EARLY WARNING LINE AND THE CANADIAN BATTLE FOR PUBLIC PERCEPTION

by Adam Lajeunesse

Introduction

In December 1954, construction began on the Distant Early Warning (DEW) Line, an integrated chain of 63 radar and communication centres stretching 3000 miles from Western Alaska across the Canadian Arctic to Greenland.[1] This predominantly-American defence project, designed to detect Russian bomber incursions into North American airspace, was the largest technological undertaking the Canadian Arctic had yet witnessed. The DEW Line was only one in a series of defence projects that Canada and the United States had jointly embarked upon in the Far North since the Second World War. However, the sheer magnitude and unprecedented expense of the project, coupled with Canada's inability and disinclination to contribute to it, was widely seen as presenting a greater challenge to Canadian Arctic sovereignty than anything that had happened earlier in the region. The source of Canadian anxiety over Arctic sovereignty was the lack of any substantial physical Canadian presence there. While there were few serious fears of an official American usurpation of Canadian territory, there were serious concerns for loss of *de facto* control over that territory. It was reasoned that a large, unilateral American construction project in the North would inevitably result in the United States military exercising effective control over the region. The Americans would administer the territory, would guard it, would observe from it, and, given the local demographics, would effectively populate the region. While Canada might retain legal title to the land, this assertion of *de facto* control by a foreign state would have fundamentally undercut the image of Canadian sovereignty in the North, both domestically and internationally. To avoid the impression that any abdication of sovereignty had taken place, and to avoid actually investing heavily in the DEW Line itself, the Canadian government's principal aim in dealing with the construction and operation of the Line became one of maximizing the *perception* of Canadian control and influence. Canadian policy focused upon the pursuit of *appearance* over *substance*, with the promotion of an idea rather than the pursuit of its physical embodiment becoming its primary objective. It was this battle for perception that became the driving force and the ultimate end-state of Canadian policy with respect to the DEW Line, from its inception to its manning during the 1950s.

Adam Lajeunesse is an MA student in History, currently studying Arctic sovereignty and security at the University of Calgary. His thesis examines Canadian-American relations in the Canadian Arctic throughout the Cold War period.

Summer 2007 • Canadian Military Journal   51

1956: Susan and Judy put on happy faces in their new permed hairdos and matching outfits. They were ready for the first day of school that year at Preston Public School, Susan in grade 2 and Judy in grade 4.

Susan and Judy were enrolled in the 4th Preston Brownie pack. Dodie often took the girls to Sunday School at St Paul's United Church where Judy joined the Explorers group.

Deborah had her 4th birthday September 28.

Cliff, at age 35, enjoyed great success as a project sales manager for Kralinator Ltd. He travelled throughout Ontario and attended tradeshows and meetings across Canada and in the USA.

For his travels, Cliff had bought himself a 1955 Pontiac 4 door sedan. *See **Pg 184** for Cliff's autos.*

1955 Pontiac 4 door Sedan. Finished in Sea Foam Green and Ivory. Equipped with 8 cylinder motor, directional signals, window washers, back-up lights, air conditioning heater. O.K. Guaranteed at .. $1895

1956: In December, Cliff returned late one evening from a business trip bringing home a new puppy for the family. It was a terrier and dalmatian mix, with a dark patch over one eye. The girls agreed with their dad to name him Pete. Cliff boarded off an area in the basement; a kennel for Pete while he was still a puppy. The only photo of Pete was taken in January 1957, with Deborah carrying him up the sidewalk beside the house and Cliff's 1955 Pontiac in the driveway.

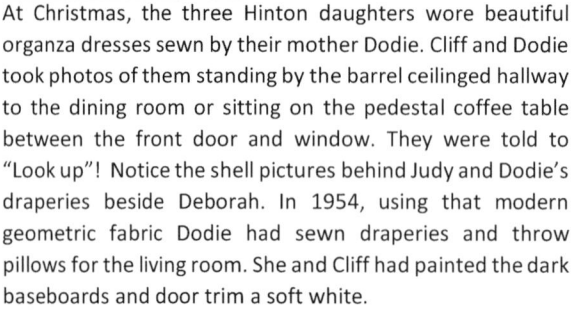

At Christmas, the three Hinton daughters wore beautiful organza dresses sewn by their mother Dodie. Cliff and Dodie took photos of them standing by the barrel ceilinged hallway to the dining room or sitting on the pedestal coffee table between the front door and window. They were told to "Look up"! Notice the shell pictures behind Judy and Dodie's draperies beside Deborah. In 1954, using that modern geometric fabric Dodie had sewn draperies and throw pillows for the living room. She and Cliff had painted the dark baseboards and door trim a soft white.

182

1957: Deborah enjoyed her winter at home while her sisters were at school. She played in the snow with her Preston friends and helped to look after their dog Pete.

Cliff must have been home that January day with his 1955 Pontiac in the driveway and Pete outside. He always shovelled the walkways when he was home. But Cliff was too soon again packing his ironed shirts, neckties, and bowties into his bag, saying goodbye to Dodie and his daughters, and leaving on another business trip.

Dodie took photos of Cliff, Susan, and Judy with the snow shovel beside Cliff's 1955 seafoam green Pontiac sedan.

The cars that Cliff owned after WWII, during the years 1946 to 1957 were all built at the Oshawa General Motors Plant. These QR codes are from *ClassicCarCatalogue.com*.

1946 Chevrolet Fleetmaster 2 door sport coupe with 6-cylinder engine **(Pg 94)**

1948 Pontiac Fleetleader 4 door sedan with 6-cylinder engine **(Pg 121, 122, 127, 139)**

1949 Pontiac Chieftain 2 door sedan with 8-cylinder engine *(Pg 142, 146, 156, 163, 168)*

1953 Pontiac Chieftain 4 door sedan with 8-cylinder engine *(Pg 168,170)*

Cliff sold his 1953 Pontiac Chieftain and bought a 1955 Pontiac Chieftain 4 door sedan with a V8 engine. The 1955 car may have been pre-owned, and he may have purchased it early in 1956. *See photos* **Pgs. 179, 181, 182 and 183**. Sadly, Cliff lost his life, in a head on collision, at the wheel of this automobile on an icy road near Windsor Ontario.

A Father Gone Too Soon
27 February 1957

Accidental Death at Windsor 27 February 1957 — 187

News Clips and Funeral 2 March 1957 — 188

Stager-Pass funeral Home — 190

Remembering the Day My Father Died — 191

Condolences and Support — 192

Gone Too Soon — 196

Life Goes On — 196

Dorothy Marguerite Auld Hinton 1919-2004 — 197

Clifford Ley Herbert Hinton 1921-1957 — 198

1957: On February 7, Judy sent this short note with a drawing to Grandma Wootton. Susan's 8th birthday would have a Valentine theme. At the party the girls made Valentine crafts and enjoyed Dodie's heart shaped birthday cake with pink frosting and cinnamon hearts.

Feb 7th From Judy,
Dear Grandma,
Remember when I said that that I'd give you a picture of someone or something to take home with you? (Here it is)
I think we are going to have fun at Susan's Birthday party this afternoon. Susan was going to have 14 but one got sick with the chickenpox. So now there are only 13.

With Cliff's and Phyllis's birthdays approaching on March 11 and 13, Dodie took her daughters shopping for birthday gifts, including lavender soap for Phyllis and gold cufflinks with ruby stones for Cliff. They were excited about celebrating the upcoming birthdays.

Little did they know that their happy life would soon be disrupted with the accidental death of their cherished father while on a business trip to Windsor Ontario.

DISTRICT MEN HURT
Clifford L. Hinton, 35 Preston, Killed In Head On Car Crash Which Claimed Total Three Lives

Clifford L. Hinton, 35, 124 Laurel street, Preston, was one of three persons who lost their lives, while an additional three were hospitalized with serious injuries, in a head-on two car collision on icy highway No. 3 near Windsor, early last Wednesday morning. Instantly killed also was Mrs. Lillian Johnston, 38, an Essex, Ontario, woman, while on Wednesday night Mrs. Jean Turdell, 24, of Essex, also died of injuries.

Still hospitalized are Norman Johnston of Essex; John L. Liscombe, 38, of Galt, and Walter Staubitz, 55, of Hespeler. Their injuries are serious, but are not considered critical.

Road Icy

The fatal crash occurred 10 miles southeast of Windsor at 12.30 a.m., the highway being covered with ice at the time. The Essex car was proceeding toward Essex and the Preston vehicle toward Windsor. The head-on impact knocked both cars almost clear of the highway on their own sides of the road.

Essex Provincial Police relayed the news of the death of Mr. Hinton to Preston police at 3.15 on Wednesday morning, and the sad news was relayed in turn by police officers to his wife and employer.

To Appointment

Manufacturer's sales representative for Kralinator Ltd., Preston, Mr. Hinton had left Preston with two fellow employees, Liscombe of Galt, sales manager of manufacturer's sales, and Staubitz of Hespeler, tool designer, late on Tuesday afternoon. They were enroute to Windsor on a regular appointment call with Chrysler Corporation.

Native of Wales the late Mr. Hinton came to Canada in his youth and joined the staff of Kralinator Ltd., Preston in December, 1952. Previously he had been employed with General Motors, Oshawa. While resident in Oshawa he was an outstanding performer for the Oshawa Junior OHA hockey team. Joining the Canadian Army in January, 1942, he was discharged in 1945.

He was married to Dorothy Auld, whose family home is in Kingston, on September 10, 1946, at Oshawa.

Survivors

His wife, three daughters, Judith, aged 9, Susan, aged 8, and Deborah, aged four years; his mother, Mrs. Frank Wooten of Colborne, Ont. and a brother, Douglas Hinton, of Montreal, survive.

Rev H. J. Herlihey officiated at funeral service conducted on Saturday afternoon from the H. K. Stager Funeral Home to St. Paul's United church. Numerous beautiful floral tributes, and the many friends in attendance from Preston and distant Ontario points, indicated esteem in which the deceased was held. Interment was in Preston Park Lawn cemetery.

The pallbearers were Alex Reid, Alfred Brisbois and Paul Mutrie, of Oshawa, Clayton Johnston, Lloyd Balfour, Nevin and Bruce Fouse and A. Jansen, all of Preston.

The Preston Times article on Wednesday, March 6, 1957

The Preston REPORTER

TWO MEN INJURED
Preston Man Dies In Head-On Crash

A resident of Preston for the past four years, Clifford L. Hinton, 35, was killed early today in a two-car collision on icy highway No. 3 near Windsor. Mrs. Lillian Johnson, 38, an Essex, Ont., woman who was a passenger in the other automobile, also died as a result of the accident.

Four others were hospitalized. John (Cracky) Liscombe, 37, of Galt, and Walter Staubitz, 55, of Hespeler, are in Metropolitan hospital at Windsor. They were in the automobile heading toward Windsor where the trio were bound on business for Kralinator Ltd., Preston, by whom they are employed.

Liscombe's injuries are reported to consist of broken ribs and shock. Staubitz suffered scalp lacerations, a possible skull fracture and a compound fracture of the leg. His condition was regarded as fairly serious.

TWO OTHERS HURT

Norman Johnson, husband of the dead woman, suffered lacerations and shock. Mrs. Jean Trudell of Essex, a passenger in the Johnson car, suffered a possible fracture of the skull and is considered in serious condition.

Details of the accidents are vague as police were unable to question the injured. Drivers of the cars had not been determined.

The crash occurred 10 miles southeast of Windsor at 12.30 this morning. The highway was covered with ice at the time.

Police said the Essex car apparently was heading toward that town while the other vehicle was bound for Windsor. Both autos were knocked almost clear of the highway on their own sides of the road.

Tragic news of the death of Clifford L. Hinton, of Preston, was relayed by Essex Provincial Police to the Preston Police department at 3.15 a.m. today, and lo-

cal officers conveyed the word to his wife and employers.

BUSINESS TRIP

The late Mr. Hinton, who was manufacturer's sales representative for Kralinator Ltd., Preston, had left Preston with two fellow employees, Jack Liscombe, of Galt, sales manager of manufacturer's sales, and Walter Staubitz, of Hespeler, tool designer, late on Tuesday afternoon for Windsor. They were on a regular appointment call with Chrysler Corporation.

Born in Wales, the deceased came to Canada in his youth, and before becoming associated with Kralinator Ltd., Preston, in December of 1952, had been employed with General Motors at Oshawa.

A veteran of World War II, the late Mr. Hinton joined the Canadian Army in January, 1942, and was discharged in 1945.

He was a former outstanding player on the Oshawa Junior OHA hockey team.

On September 10, 1946, he was married at Oshawa to Dorothy Auld, whose family home is in Kingston. They resided at 124 Laurel street, Preston.

Surviving are his wife; three daughters, Judith, aged 9; Susan, aged 8, and Deborah, aged four years; his mother, Mrs. Frank Wooten, of Colborne, Ont., and a brother, Douglas Hinton, of Montreal.

The late Mr. Hinton will be resting at the H. K. Stager Funeral home from Thursday noon. Complete funeral arrangements have not been completed.

CLIFFORD HINTON
... Dies in Crash

JACK LISCOMBE
... Injured

The Preston Reporter article on Wednesday, February 27, 1957.

Local newspapers in Preston, Oshawa, Windsor, Toronto, and Kingston told of the tragedy and of the funeral arrangements. Apparently, Cliff was resting in an open casket at the Stager Funeral Home from Thursday noon until Saturday at 1:00. The funeral was at 2:30 on Saturday March 2, 1957.

HINTON, Clifford L. H.—Suddenly as the result of a car accident near Windsor, on Wednesday, February 27th, 1957, Clifford L. H. Hinton, beloved husband of Dorothy Auld, and dear father of Judith, Susan and Deborah, son of Mrs. Frank Wootton, of Colborne, Ont., and the late H. M. Hinton of Oshawa, and brother of Douglas Hinton, of Montreal, P.Q., in his 36th year. The funeral will be held at St. Paul's United Church, Preston, on Saturday, March 2nd, at 2.30 p.m. Resting at the H. K. Stager Funeral Home until Saturday at 1 p.m., then at the church, where the casket will remain open until time of service. Interment in Park Lawn Cemetery, Preston.
F28-1h

CLIFFORD HINTON

Funeral service for Clifford L.H. Hinton, 35, of Preston, who died suddenly as the result of a tragic head-on two car accident near Windsor early on Wednesday morning, will be conducted in Preston on Saturday afternoon at 2.30

The late Mr. Hinton is resting at the H.K. Stager Funeral Home until Saturday at 1 p.m., then at the St. Paul's United church where the casket will remain open until time of service. Interment will be in Park Lawn cemetery, Preston.

There were over 50 floral tributes, as many cards of condolence and a great many friends, family and business associates attending Cliff's funeral on March 2. After Cliff's death Phyllis and Dodie received many letters of condolence. Cliff was admired and loved by many people in many places. Dodie replied to all of them and kept them in a memory box. Seven of these are included here and in Appendix C Pg 264-276.

CLIFFORD L. HINTON

Funeral service for Clifford L. Hinton, 35, of 124 Laurel street, Preston, who died in an early morning head-on two-car crash last Wednesday morning near Windsor, was conducted on Saturday afternoon from the H. K. Stager funeral home to St. Paul's United church. Two Essex women were also killed and two district and one Essex man confined to hospital with serious injuries, aftermath of the tragic crash.

Rev. H. J. Herlihey officiated at the largely attended service, which included friends of the deceased from many outside points. Numerous beautiful floral tributes further bespoke the esteem in which the late Mr. Hinton was held. Interment was in Park Lawn cemetery, Preston.

The pallbearers were Clayton Johnston, Lloyd Balfour, Nevin Fouse, Bruce Fouse, A. Jansen, all of Preston, Alex Reid, Alfred Brisbois and Paul Mutrie, all of Oshawa.

The Kingston Whig Standard, Friday March 1

HINTON—Accidentally in Windsor on Wednesday, February 27, 1957, Clifford L. Hinton, beloved husband of Dorothy Auld (formerly of Kingston), and dear father of Judy, Susan and Debbie. Funeral from his late residence, Preston, Ont., 2:30 Saturday afternoon.

MRS. CLIFFORD L. HINTON and family wish to thank their many friends and neighbours for kindness and sympathy shown during their recent bereavement; the many beautiful floral tributes and the loan of cars.
M5-1h

Stager-Pass Ltd.

FUNERAL HOME · 566 QUEEN STREET · TELEPHONE OLive 3-2941

PRESTON, ONTARIO

FUNERAL OF THE LATE CLIFFORD L HINTON.

Feb. 27th-Mar. 2nd 1957

TO FUNERAL SERVICE	$475.00
MOTOR TO WINDSOR	45.00
AMBULANCE SERVICE IN WINDSOR	15.00
Toronto and Oshawa Paper Notices	8.25
	$543.25
3% Discount $475.00	14.25
	$529.00

MAR 1957 PAID STAGER-PASS LTD.

March 26th, 1957

Received Payment
in full with Thanks
W W Stager

Remembering the Day My Father Died

For most of my life memories of that fateful February day were somewhat forgotten but since writing this book my recollections have been revived. I remember being awakened, before sunrise, to the mournful cries of my mother after police knocked at our door to deliver the life changing news of her husband's fatal automobile accident. It must have been police, at mom's request, who called to inform neighbours and relatives so that Dodie would have support on that difficult Wednesday morning. I think our neighbour Hazel Balfour arrived next. Then our youngest and eldest aunts, Betty and Vi, came quickly from Toronto. Our mother was very shaken and sad, maybe in shock!

I think Susan and I went to school that day, as usual with Susan Balfour, knowing that our dad was in an accident but unclear about his condition. After school Aunt Vi told us in a very stoic manner that our father had died and that our mother would be needing us to be good girls. Of course we were always good girls! I now know she had good intentions but at the time I felt that Aunt Vi was interfering and it should have been our mother who told us. I'd lost my father and they were keeping my mother from us. For a short while it seemed we also lost our mother to her grief!

Somehow Aunt Mamie arrived from Kingston and with Aunt Betty was comforting her sister Dodie. Uncle Doug arrived from Montreal to help make arrangements for Stager-Pass Funeral services. I can't be sure how Grandma Wootton was informed and supported with the heartbreaking death of her youngest son. That evening, feeling sad in our bedroom, I heard adult discussion downstairs, so different from our usually quiet home. I think it was suggested that we girls go to stay with other relatives and I remember feeling that our wonderful, competent mother was being undermined by some bossy relatives, trying to take over! Being protective of mom, I must have voiced my concerns. I remember thinking that I was being ingnored or told that my uncle and aunts knew better.

It was mom's sisters Betty and Mamie who encouraged her to make some decisions for herself and her daughters. That is why we sisters weren't sent away, and although we don't remember being at the funeral or the burial on Saturday, we remember 'saying goodbye' to our father lying in an open casket at the funeral home. I remember the strong scent of abundant flowers and thinking that I was not looking at my real father. It gave me hope that he actually was somewhere else and would return to us like he always had when he travelled.

In the next weeks and months, I enjoyed the company of friends at school, at Brownie and Explorer meetings, at Riverside Park for safe biking competitions, and during a July week at Five Oaks United Church Camp (*that's me in the photo*). I remember feeling a little strange while enjoying our traditional summer weeks at Kingson. I remember feeling fatherless, detached from normalcy, with secret wishes for my dad's return.

Those feelings soon enough passed and, in a distant perspective, I was correct in thinking my dad would somehow come back to me. Now I see his features, mannerisms and interests appearing in his 9 grandchildren and in his 19 great grandchildren. He lives on in them.

Condolence Letters

Dodie's friend Edna Acton was shocked by the news of Cliff's sudden accidental death. She tried to convey her condolances to her dear friend Dodie. See **Appendix C Pg 264.**

Dodie dear, March 1st, 1957, Kingston, Ontario

It is very hard for me to write you this letter. I know there is very little I can say to make things easier, my heart is just aching for you. I was never so shocked in my life and I can't imagine what you must be feeling. I'm only sorry I can't be near enough to be of some help to you at this time.

It must be hard to understand why these things happen, knowing Cliff was not a careless man. I'm sure he would never want to leave you with such a responsibility. Yours is no easy task and if there is any way Joe and I can help you and the children please let us do that much for you. I know that is poor consolation at this time but we mean it from the bottom of our hearts, my poor Dodie.

Many people have asked about you and I'm sure they all send you deepest sympathy. Please let us know what your intentions are and maybe we can help. May the Lord rest his soul and help you now when you need it so badly.

Try and think of all the good things you two had and I'm sure you will have some awfully good memories. They are a far cry from what you had together but you sure had a fine man. Some people never have one like him in all their lives. God bless him. Please offer my sympathy to Cliff's mother. I'm sure like yourself her heart is heavy with sorrow!

Please write to us when you feel you can. Your children must be very sad. They have indeed suffered a loss early in their lives. They have a wonderful mother, thank God.

God bless you Dodie and remember we are here to help all we can.

Love and our sincerest sympathy,

Edna, Joe and family.

Phyllis's stepdaughter Helen (Wootton) Lush wrote a note to Dorothy. Her husband George Lush had died in 1955 at age 43 early in their 10 year marriage. See **Appendix C Pg 266.**

Dear Dorothy: Saturday - March 2/57

My heart goes out to you today – How well I know what you are going through, I understand. I didn't buy flowers but wish you to use the enclosed for the chidren.

Love, Helen Lush

The daughter of a long time friend of Cliff's mother Phyllis wrote a letter to Dorothy. See **Appendix C Pg 267** for the handwritten letter.

Sunday, Mar 3   Box 262, Fergus, Ont

Dear Mrs. Hinton:-

      Having known Cliff from the time he was 18 months old until young manhood, it was a great shock and sorrow to learn of his tragic accident. It is so difficult to offer sympathy when your whole world is shattered, but I do urge you to turn to Phyllis for comfort. She has suffered and lost so much. She has lost two sons – both suddenly, and the boys' father in a long, slow agony. Surely she will be able to help you from her wide experience and great faith,

      You may recall she planned to visit us the last time she was in Preston, but your kiddies developed a contagious disease, so she thought it best not to come. If she is in Preston now, I do hope she will come here for a few days before returning home. We may be able to make some arrangement regarding transportation. I understand you have 3 small children. They will wring your heart strings just now, but having to do the ordinary, everyday chores for them will help you hold on to your sanity, and in time, they will be a great comfort to you. We are fortunate enough to have 3 girls – Linda, age 12, Marnie, age 7, Elizabeth, age 4.

      I am writing to Phyllis in care of yourself, in the hope she is staying with you for a while. If this is not so, would you be kind enough to send her letter on to her? I would very much like to hear from you when you feel able to write. As a tangible expression of my sympathy, you will find $5.00 enclosed. Use it in whatever way you think best.   Yours sincerely,

                                         Rose (Slade) Mills

Dodie's sister Thelma Burnard sent her a vey heartfelt letter of condolence and support. See **Appendix C Pg 271** for the handwritten letter.

Mar 3, 1957,   1120 W. 22nd St., North Vancouver, BC

Darling Dodie,

      It is truly dreadful to be so far away at a time like this, but believe me dear, we have been right there beside you, both in our thoughts and our prayers. You may remember when mother was so ill, she said that "life is just a test', and I can't help but feel that Cliff has passed his test somewhat sooner than most of us, for he was a perfect husband and daddy. He has given you many glorious memories and three darling little girls, who will be great blessings to you. He has also given you a wonderful mother, who will be such a comfort to you, as I'm sure, you will be to her.

      I was hoping that one of the girls might find time to drop us a note, and when you feel up to it, Dodie, we'd love to hear from you. If there is anything at all that you would like us to do, you know you have only to ask it. Will you give our love to Mrs. Wootton and tell her we have been thinking of her. And now my Darling, all our love to you and the girls and God Bless you all.

                                       Al, Ron and Tim.

Cliff had travelled to Calgary in August of 1956 for automotive business. His host family there sent a note of condolence to Dorothy. See **Appendix C Pg 273** *for the handwritten letter.*

March 5, 1957, 3419 31 St. S.W., Calgary,
Alberta

Dear Mrs. Hinton,
    It was a great shock to us to learn of Cliff's passing and in such a very tragic manner. You have our deepest sympathy.
    During Cliff's visit to Calgary last year, he was at our home, and one evening we went downtown for dinner and spent a long time talking. He told us about you and the children. You are all going to miss him terribly.
    I hope you have relatives or close friends with you to help ease your sorrow. We are thinking of you.

Sincerely,
Joan North

Phyllis's stepson Morris Wootton was in Tampa Florida when he heard the news from his Uncle John Wootton. He and his wife Grace sent this note to Dorothy. See **Appendix Pg 274**

March 5/1957 Tampa Florida

Dear Dorothy
    Our deepest sympathy goes out to you in this time of tragic loss. It is so hard to understand! We have been so shocked since John gave us the news and we too have felt a keen sense of loss in Clifford's passing.
    I am sure that the comfort and sympathy and companionship of loving friends will be of great help to you at this time. The fact that your family needs you and the ever-presence of the Great Healer will all give you strength to carry on.

Love,
Morris and Grace

Park Lawn Cemetery in Preston, Ontario

Clifford Ley Herbert Hinton 1921-1957

Cliff's childhood friend Alex 'Scotty' Reid was deeply saddened by Cliff's sudden death. His wife Pat wrote a letter of condolence and support to her friend Dodie. In early 1951 they had been delighted to have Dodie, Cliff and their daughters, stay a few weeks with them at their home on Grierson St in Oshawa while Cliff and Dodie looked nearby for their own home.
See **Appendix C Pg 275** for the handwritten letter.

634 Grierson St., Oshawa, Ontario
Dearest Dodie, Judy, Susan, Deborah

    I do hope this letter finds you all well. I wanted to write to you sooner but anything I could have said couldn't have helped such as a time like this. As you say there are so many things we do not understand and until something as Tragic as this happens none of us know how we could react to it. Cliff was so well liked, respected by his friends, and loved by those who were close to him.

    You, Mrs. Wootton, and the children have been very close in our thoughts and prayers the past weeks. I do hope it won't be too long before we see you all again and that you will be feeling better. Things won't be the same for you Dodie because we cannot live in the past. You've got something no one can take away from you and that's the Happy Years you and Cliff had together. Now you have yourself and your health to think of so that you can continue to be the best mother in the world to 3 of the loveliest, well behaved little girls that you've been blessed with. A very big challenge to any young woman, but we all know with out a doubt that you will make it.

I've never had to write a letter like this before Dodie. I hope I've put the right things down. I've just said what I feel, and I do hope you will understand me.

I must go now and will write again soon.   All our love, Pat, and family

1957: In June, Alex Reid, his wife Pat and their two daughters came from Oshawa to see Dodie and her daughters and to visit Cliff's grave at Park Lawn Cemetery in Preston.

195

1957: in July, Cliff's good friend and Kralinator colleague Bruce Hodge and his wife Fran came to visit Dodie. They brought their 3 daughters to spend some time with the Hinton sisters. The six girls had a bit of fun cooling off in the wading pool set up on the slab where Cliff had planned to build a garage for his car and trailer. Susan Balfour joined the girls for a photo on the Hinton's front lawn. Her father, Lloyd Balfour, who lived next door in the house pictured below, was a pallbearer at Cliff's funeral. Lloyd's wife Hazel Balfour was good friends with Dodie and like a second mother to the Hinton girls.

Gone Too Soon

For a mere 10 years, my father Clifford was a wonderful husband and an amazing father for his daughters Deborah, Susan and me. He was an excellent provider and had great plans for our futures in Preston. His tragic early death meant he would miss many of our milestones: birthdays, graduations, sports, first jobs, first dates and weddings. I do have vague memories of watching Saturday TV with him, Sky King, The Lone Ranger, Lassie and baseball games. I also remember dinner time discussions. How angry and protective he was when he learned that some young boys were giving me a hard time, chasing me through the wooded path on my way home from school! He had important impacts on our early development and would have been such an amazing grandfather. But life goes on and he would be very proud of our mother Dorothy and the happy life she made possible for us.

Life Goes On

1957: In August, Dodie and her girls spent time in Kingston, enjoying the comfort of family. Judy, Susan, and Deborah were especially happy to see their cousins. Back row Carolyn 9, Susan 8, Judy 10, Peggy 7, and Garry 8 with Deborah who would be 5 in September and Ron Sudds who was sharing his 4th birthday cake. It was likely during that time Dodie finalized plans to move from Preston and to purchase a home in Toronto.

1957: In September, Judy was 10 in Grade 5, Susan was 8 in Grade 3 and Deborah was having her 5th birthday and attending Kindergarten at Preston Public School. Their Preston house was for sale, and they would soon be moving to Etobicoke. Using Cliff's life insurance money, their mother, purchased a newly built house with 3 bedrooms and a suite for Aunt Betty. A great place to build a happy future for Cliff's family!

Dorothy Marguerite Auld Hinton 1919-2004

Our mother was a talented woman who worked at the Bank of Montreal to support us. After she retired at age 65, she earnestly took up sewing and eventually became very active in the Etobicoke Quilter's Guild. She was also a nurturing mother who encouraged her daughters' happy, productive lives. She thoroughly enjoyed spending time with her daughters, their husbands and 9 grandchildren. She barely had time to meet the first 3 of her 19 great grandchildren before she became ill, had a fall, and sadly, died 15 December 2004 at age 85. But that's another story and another book!

Our Wonderful Father, Forever in Our Hearts

Clifford Ley Herbert Hinton 1921-1957

Afterword

Author's Reflections

While the research and construction of this book have been enjoyable and challenging, the difficult part was deciding on a title. My original motivation was to share family history with family and friends. My ongoing effort would be to write a series of books about my ancestors and to portray the essence of their lives. To that end I have decided **A Father Gone Too Soon** will be the title of this book about my father Clifford Ley Herbert Hinton.

During the latter stages of writing his story I found myself marvelling at the fast-moving pace of my father's life and the breadth of experience packed into a short 35 years:

1. Cliff's roots were in the unlikely but fortunate circumstances of his parentage. His parents were each first born children of insecure coupling and their joining together originated from First World War happenstance.
2. Cliff was a third child of parents who, soon after he was born in 1921 at Clydach, Wales, decided to embark on the great adventure of emigration to Canada.
3. Cliff enjoyed a happy fast paced decade growing up in Oshawa, Canada's Motor City, with great schools and exceptional sporting and hockey opportunities.
4. Still a teenager, Cliff suffered the heartbreak of his father's lung cancer illness and early death in 1939.
5. As he was becoming an adult, Cliff took on the responsibilities of work, of supporting his mother, of military service during the Second World War and, sadly out of his control, the loss of his brother.
6. With a positive attitude, Cliff embraced postwar happiness in his favourite hockey sport, while resuming ambitious career building in the automotive industry.
7. Cliff's hockey games and his wartime service connections led to a 'chance' meeting with Dorothy Auld, their whirlwind romance, and their marriage in 1946.
8. While building his career and his family life, Cliff and Dorothy moved about with only 2-3 years each in Toronto, North Bay, and Oshawa before settling in Preston for a mere 4 years until his tragic accidental death in 1957.

Hardly able to relax and enjoy the security of the happy life he had created; unable to nurture his daughters' growing up years, never knowing his grandchildren, not growing old with his cherished wife Dorothy. This is the essence of my father Clifford's life, with so much potential, **A Father Gone Too Soon**.

Appendix A

20 Page Booklet

Memorial Cup Comes to Oshawa

Season 1938-39

Cliff kept this 20-page commemorative booklet,
about people and events important to him.

*

Cliff is named (Pg16) as a defence player with 1938-39 "Canada Bread" championship team in the Oshawa Minor Hockey League known as "The City League".

*

The history of the GM Factory League is given on Pg18.

In 1937-38, when Cliff started employment as a clerk in the auto parts department, he played defence on the Main Office team in the General Motors Interdepartmental Hockey League

*

In 1940-41, Cliff played defence on the Oshawa Junior Bees Team.
A bit about this team and its history before 1939 is given on Pg7.

*

After WWII Cliff played defence on the Oshawa Legionnaires veterans' team.   That was 7 years after this 1938-39 commemorative booklet.

Appendix A   **1938-39 Oshawa Generals wins Canadian Junior Hockey Championship**

In honour of Cliff's love of hockey, these are scans of his copy of the 20-page commemorative Memorial Cup booklet. *Author's note: Thanks to my sister Susan for sharing this booklet and the hockey news clips which I included earlier in this book,* **Pg 53, 57-59, 66-68, 92-104**.

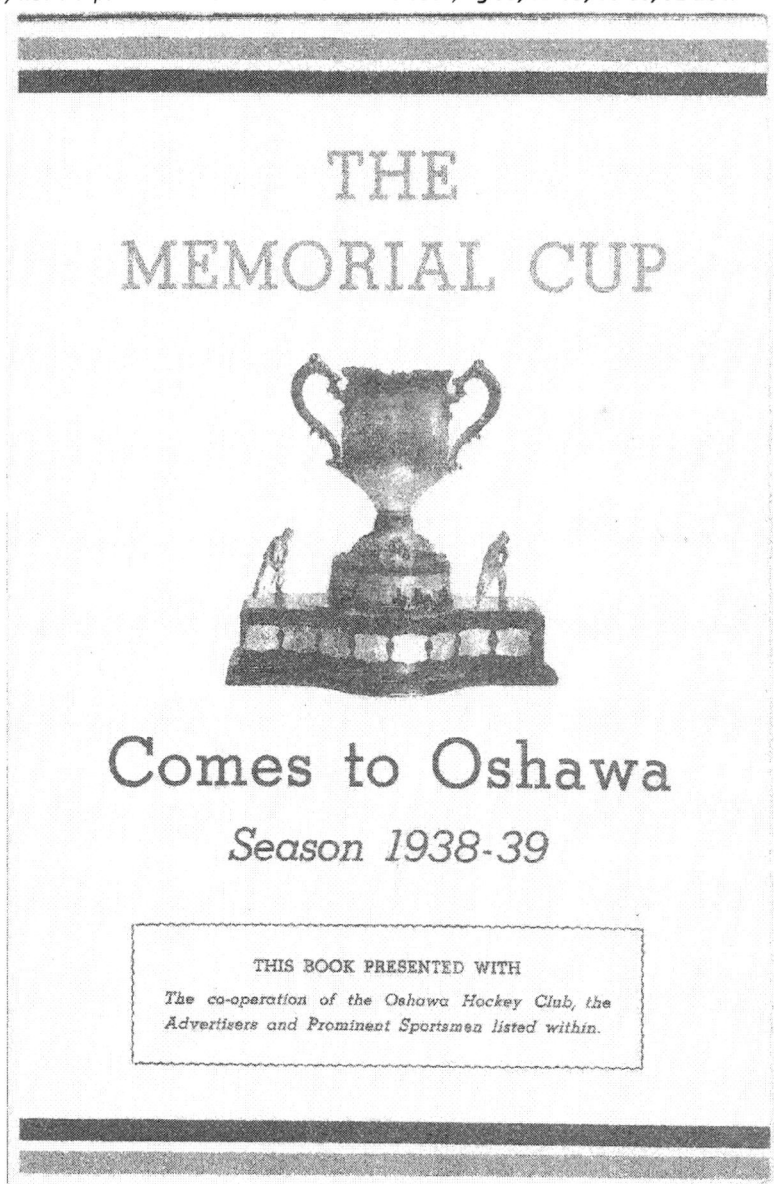

THE MEMORIAL CUP

Comes to Oshawa

Season 1938-39

THIS BOOK PRESENTED WITH
The co-operation of the Oshawa Hockey Club, the Advertisers and Prominent Sportsmen listed within.

Appendix A   **1938-39 Memorial Cup commemorative book**

CONGRATULATIONS
To the Oshawa Generals and Executives

As a small token of our appreciation to the Dominion Junior Champions, we are pleased to donate to each and every member of the club, free Wash and Grease jobs for their cars, for the balance of 1939.

Harry O. Perry
CITIES SERVICE STATION
222 King Street West
Phones 2015, 2266
SERVICE is our middle name

The Home of Seiberling Tires "On Time"

Congratulations

"GENERALS"

A Good Job Well Done

DRINK Coca-Cola

204

Appendix a   **1938-39 Memorial Cup commemorative book**

A MESSAGE FROM THE MAYOR

As Mayor of the City of Oshawa for 1939 I am pleased to honor and extend congratulations to our Junior Hockey Team and those who either sponsored or trained these young Champions.

I would like to say that winning the Memorial Cup is the highest honor any Junior team can receive in Canada. It puts each player in a class by himself and gives him the opportunity of going farther in hockey, even in the professional class if he should choose to do so.

I believe I speak for most citizens and fans when I say we enjoyed every junior game played this season. At this time I would also congratulate our Senior, Junior B, Intermediate, Collegiate and Juvenile teams. They all played good hockey and reached either finals or semi-finals this year.

J. A. Coleman, Mayor.

Appendix A   **1938-39 Memorial Cup commemorative book**

Dear Hockey Fans:—

My sincere thanks for your support all along the road that led us to the Junior Championship of Canada and the Memorial Cup!

It takes not only team spirit but Community spirit as well, to make the most of the playing ability our boys possess.

I believe the loyalty and encouragement of the fans was a factor in our victory and on behalf of the Club I gratefully acknowledge our debt.

Yours for hard, clean, cup-winning hockey.

James B. Highfield
President,
Oshawa Hockey Club.

— 2 —

Appendix A   **1938-39 Memorial Cup commemorative book**

Editor's Introduction

By

Herb Chesebrough

Oshawa Correspondent, The Globe and Mail

Congratulations to the Oshawa Hockey Club who have at last realized their ambition of bringing a Canadian Junior Hockey Championship to the Motor City after many years of disappointment, during which Oshawa has nearly always been represented by a strong entry.

This year's Memorial Cup winners after losing to St. Michael's College in the S.P.A. series went through their section of the Big Eight group with only one loss that to St. Michael's College in Toronto. In the group playoffs the Generals defeated St. Michael's College in the three out of four games of a hard fought series and then swept Native Sons before them with three straight wins to annex the Ontario title. A fast, strong North Bay Trapper squad was defeated in two straight games while Verdun Maple Leafs pulled a major upset in the first game of the Eastern Canada finals by winning the first game in Montreal. Despite Verdun's goaltender Oshawa won the next two games, qualifying to meet Edmonton Roamers, heralded as the Wonder team of the West for the Memorial Cup. After winning the first two games by substantial margins the Generals dropped the third game of the series when Elmer Kreller disorganized the whole team with a magnificent display of checking. The team won their honors in the torrid fourth game of the series when they came from behind twice to win going away by a 4-2 score. Seldom does a team receive the support from fans as this year's champions were given and the victory was celebrated in Oshawa by one of the most happy and noisy welcomes in history.

A grand team and a grand club, the desire of this booklet is to commemorate Oshawa's first Canadian championship with an interesting souvenir and we thank our contributors, who have through unselfish effort made this possible.

These Oshawa Hockey Boosters Congratulate Oshawa Generals

Sam Rotish	Scott Hubbell
Eric A. Leach	Holden & Holden
L. S. Palmer	Noah Matthews
Paddy Gould	Les Baker
Bill McNeill	Soanes Bros.
Joe Jackson	Walter Branch
Bill Burns	Canning Clothiers
Clive File	Jack Jackson

Motor City Bowling Club

— 3 —

Appendix A   **1938-39 Memorial Cup commemorative book**

Real Champions

By Fred Jackson, Sports Editor, Toronto Daily Star

Like other members of the sports scribbling fraternity yours truly has had his share of those priceless, spine-tingling moments when he has been privileged to see championships won and lost and before any more is said or this typewriter is laid to rest for the day we'd like to go on public record as declaring that Oshawa Generals' magnificent display of recent date when "your kids" copped the Memorial cup belongs in the top shelf of "Memory Lane."

We're not quite sure why we're here on this occasion because everybody knows that anybody from 'Hogtown" just hates to see an outside team win anything. At least that is the popular conception, a hangover from bygone days when they tell me such a condition actually existed. Happily these are the days of enlightenment when we can all join hands in admiring a great little hockey machine go through its paces regardless of where the troops pick up their mail.

It seems to me that the best tribute I can pay Oshawa Generals, 1939 junior champions of Canada, is that they are WORTHY of the traditions handed down to them by one of the greatest sports centres in the country. We in Toronto appreciate the splendid spirit that prevails in your city. . . . . the whole-hearted support you give your teams and the general "All-for-one and one-for-all" attitude that is always noticeable. All the world loves a winner but you have shown over a period of years that win, lose or draw you get behind your teams in a manner that more often than not, makes us just a trifle envious.

Win—lose—or draw, we said. Well today it's win and more power to you. Generals proved they have the heart of champions when after taking two games with ridiculous ease they received a rude setback in the third of the Memorial cup tilts and for considerable of the fourth game were in a fair way to inherit a headache. It was when most of the fans were scurrying around looking for aspirin tablets that the gamesters who were wearing the sweaters of a grand club said in so many words, "They can't do that to us" and proceeded to "mow them down" as Charlie McCarthy says.

Keep this down to a couple of hundred words, your committee said when extending the invitation to say "hello" to the champions on behalf of The Star. Well here I am far beyond the limit and many things left unsaid. Our Mr. "Red" Burnett, a chap who has parked close by your bench ever since Tracy Shaw started his masterminding chore, has an assignment in connection with this celebration and maybe we'd better ease off now and let "Red" carry on.

Before we do, however, we'd like to sign off with a toast to Tracy Shaw, a grand coach and a gentleman!

P.S.—On second thought maybe we should have a Royal Commission appointed. You Generals are getting altogether too hot. It was only a few short months ago that another General Motors spot—St. Catharines—won the Mann cup. That fellow Carmichael must have something!

COMPLIMENTS

DOUG. LAURIE

•

BROWN'S SPORTS & CYCLE CO. LIMITED

345 Yonge Street - - - - - Toronto

—4—

Appendix A   **1938-39 Memorial Cup commemorative book**

Meet Tracy Shaw
By Vern DeGeer, Sports Editor, Toronto Globe and Mail

"One of the best-coached junior hockey teams I've seen in many years," was the way Manager Lester Patrick of the New York Rangers described Oshawa Generals after watching Canada's 1938-39 junior champions fashion a 12-4 victory over Edmonton Roamers in the second game of the recent Memorial Cup title series at Toronto Maple Leaf Gardens.

"That boy Billy Taylor is the smartest junior I've seen in 20 years, but don't forget he has a strong supporting cast and my opinion is that much of the club's success must be attributed to the man doing the coaching," Patrick added.

Here you had a rich tribute to Tracy Shaw, the silver-haired Toronto sportsman, who coached Oshawa Generals to a Canadian junior championship by conquering Edmonton Roamers. And the thousands of us who watched the Generals fashion their first Dominion crown, had ample opportunity to observe the smooth bench-directing of the champions at times when strategy was at a premium as a result of the tenacious shadowing of Billy Taylor by Elmer "Bloodhound" Kreller of Edmonton.

TRACY SHAW

Few of our Canadian coaches have come up through the ranks with more impressive records than Oshawa's hockey title leader. He served his apprenticeship with De La Salle juniors, graduated to Aura Lee and marched on with Argonaut seniors as a centre. In baseball he campaigned with St. Andrews, Hillcrests, St. Pats and Leaside. Turning to rugby football, Tracy played for Northview, junior O.R.F.U. champions. He wielded a potent stick for Maitlands in lacrosse.

The guy, we would say, has something.

Congratulations
"GENERALS"

WE ARE PROUD OF YOU

The Dairies of Oshawa

— 5 —

Appendix A   **1938-39 Memorial Cup commemorative book**

From the Gondola --- By Foster Hewitt

Congratulations Oshawa in winning the Memorial Cup this year with one of the greatest junior hockey teams this commentator ever had the privilege of watching in action.

Led by Billy Taylor, possibly the greatest ice general to ever perform at Maple Leaf Gardens, the team packed exceptional scoring power. Taylor himself was magnificent, reminding one of a smooth-working quarter back on a championship football team, rallying his team mates and calling every play before the opposition anticipated it.

Winnipeg Monarchs rank as one of the best junior teams the writer can remember watching in action, but Oshawa this season compared with them through the medium of their tremendous scoring punch. The Generals exhibition in the first two games of the Cup series exceeded the expectations of even the most optimistic. Edmonton after the first ten minutes of these games, failed to withstand the Oshawa pressure, and never say die spirit, that goes for real champions.

One of the most remarkable features of the Oshawa team however to one who has watched almost all their games on Garden ice, was the splendid showing of Les Colvin and Dinny McManus, the two Oshawa netminders. Although these two boys alternated in goal neither of them was guilty of an off night in the nets, yet the mental strain they were under was enough to make any goaltender blow up. A really wonderful team, packed with power and dependable performers in every position making them worthy winners of the highest honors.

He Shoots! He Scores!

Orv. Smith bangs home one of the Oshawa goals in the second game of the final series as Jud McAtee looks on watched by Dave Farmer. Billy Drever is the baffled net minder.

— 6 —

Appendix A   **1938-39 Memorial Cup commemorative book**

The Oshawa GM-Men

The GM-Men, Oshawa's representatives in the O.H.A. Senior group this year, became the first Oshawa Senior team to play off for the Ontario Senior Championship. The team was one of the league's biggest drawing cards and featured a first string forward line of Lex Chisholm, Winkie Smith and Cliff Maundrell that compared with any in the league. Proof of their scoring potency is shown by the fact that Chisholm, who later turned professional with Toronto Maple Leafs, led the league in scoring, while Smith and Maundrell finished well up in the statistical records. The team's second line was composed of Roy Covert, Jerry Cooper, Doc Dafoe and Regina Tisdall. Defense duties were capably taken care of by Doc. Rowden (the league's highest scoring defenseman), Doug Maundrell, Captain Scotty McAlpine and Bill "Squeak" Morrison. Earl "Peg" Hurst had a grand season in the nets, while Jack McEwan took part in early season games as did Bill Hastie, Bill Tribble again officiated as manager while the ever-popular Geordie Easton was trainer. The team finished second behind the powerful Goodyears, whom they tied three times in league contests, defeated St. Catharines' Chiefs in the Ontario semi-finals and were eliminated by Goodyears in a thrilling championship series.

Oshawa Coca-Colas

No hockey record would ever be complete without a story about the Oshawa Coca-Colas. This gallant band of puckchasers made up of players who have made hockey history at one time or another, devote their time and ability endeavoring to win the O.H.A. Intermediate B title. Scan this line-up and see if it does not bring to your mind stirring hockey battles of not long ago. Goal, Mac McQuaig (with Oshawa Intermediates for many years). Defense, Josh March (brother of the famous "Mush" March of Chicago), Benny Benham (hails from the west), Dud Everett (a member of the old Tandy league), Dan McTavish (with Generals last year). Forwards—Red Krantz (Centre on the Generals second line last year), Walt Hooper (a Junior B star of the Tigers), Doug Rowden (always a fighter with the "Cokes"), Glad Clarridge (on the great Junior team that lost to Sudbury), Army Armstrong (a former Oshawa senior), Pete Goodchild (with the juniors against the great St. Mikes' team of Metz, Kelly and Jackson), Buzz Bennett (a factory league star). Coach, Carl Houck (starred on Oshawa teams for many years). Manager, Ab Hambly (always a sport booster in Oshawa).

Oshawa Junior Bees

Too little credit has been handed out to Coach Frank Black's Junior Bees, a grand little team that many hockey followers believe would have been crowned Ontario champions but for illness and injuries. The Bees defeated Peterboro Colts in a best of five series for their group championship and then proceeded to eliminate Kingston Frontenacs, last year's title holders. The team won the right to enter the Provincial round robin series with Niagara Falls, Kitchener and Runnymede by upsetting the powerful Barrie Colts in straight games. In the round robin series the kids lost out by a single point, having entered the series deprived of Scotty Reid, a member of last year's Memorial Cup finalists who was ill with pneumonia while Wally Wilson, high scoring centre was far from his best owing to a bad leg.

The personnel of the team included Wally Wilson, Gar Peters, Mickey McMaster, Scotty Reid, Porky York, Maxie Yourth, Andy McMullen, Tommy Murphy, Ian Fraser, John Kitchen, "Oatsey" Phillips, E. Salter, Jim Daniels and Don Morris.

Congratulations "Generals"

You have done a fine job in bringing such high honors
to our city

GORDON DAVIS

DAVIS' SUNOCO STATION

Appendix A   **1938-39 Memorial Cup commemorative book**

Billy The Kid
By Elmer J. Ross, Oshawa Correspondent, The Toronto Daily Star

It is doubtful if there has ever been a player to pull on an Oshawa hockey sweater that has been a greater favourite with hockey fans and officials alike, than "Billy" Taylor, Captain of this year's edition of the Generals.

To this writer falls the task of bringing to Oshawa hockey fans the intimate inside story of the Blond Bomber of the junior ice lanes. Last year Bill hit the headlines of sportdom when he led a grand little team to the Memorial Cup finals only to go out after a great series with St. Boniface Seals but the thrilling sight of Billy the Kid wig-wagging his way down centre ice to hold the spotlight with Walter Stanowski of the Seals will linger long with the record crowds that witnessed the series.

This year Bill started out with an almost entirely new team. Two boys who he had never played with before, Nick Knott and Roy Sawyer, were soon hitting the headlines . . . prolific scoring aces who learned to take Taylor's deft passes with almost monotonous regularity to blaze a trail as one of the highest scoring junior front lines since Conacher and Jackson were cashing in on the passing ability of Eddie Convey of the famous Toronto Marlboros. When Sawyer ran into his unfortunate accident it was Norm McAtee who replaced him and once again Taylor displayed his amazing ability to fit in with any player and the line worked as strong as before.

BILLY TAYLOR

Billy was born in Winnipeg, but left the West when he was only eight months old. His next stop was St. Catharines where he resided until he came to Toronto at the age of seven. His love for hockey appeared while he was attending separate schools. He first turned out with St. Clare's minor bantams and after one year with that club transferred his allegiance to St. James' bantams and then back to St. Clare's minor bantams.

"How did you come to become associated with the Leafs as their mascot?" we asked Taylor.

"That happened one night while I was playing for St. Clare's. We went up to Wexford to play an exhibition game. On the program with us were Toronto Marlboros. Frank Selke was in charge of the Marlboros. The next year I went to the Marlboro bantams and Selke got me the job of mascot with the Leafs. I then played with Marlboro bantams and Maple Leaf minor bantams in the Toronto Hockey League.

"Where did you get your first real hockey tuition and from whom?" we asked Taylor.

"I really got my first schooling in the fundamentals of hockey from Father S. Casson at St. James' separate school. I then went to De La Salle College where I played under the Brothers there. Then I played my first O.H.A. hockey when I went to St. Michael's College. Jerry Laflamme polished up my hockey considerably and also taught me lots of little tricks. I played for St. Mikes for two years. We went to the Junior B finals in 1936 and we won the title in 1937."

Bill's next jump was to Toronto British Consols juniors in the Big Seven Group and it was Bill's club that knocked Oshawa Juniors out of the running that year.

The rest of Bill's hockey history is well known to Oshawa hockey fans. He came to Oshawa last year and from there on he has rapidly skyrocketted to stardom.

Although many in this city might not be aware of it, Bill is just as good a son as he is a hockey player. Last year after the Memorial Cup finals Bill dug into his pockets and sent his mother away on a trip. Mrs. Taylor originally came from Scotland and one of her fondest dreams was to make one more visit to her homeland. So Bill made his mother's dreams become a reality.

And so Oshawa hockey fans we have given you Billy Taylor, fine hockey player, good son and a real gentleman. What more could any hockey fan ask for?

— 8 —

Appendix A   **1938-39 Memorial Cup commemorative book**

Officers of
The Oshawa Hockey Club
Season 1938-39

Hon. Presidents
R. S. McLaughlin   H. J. Carmichael   G. W. McLaughlin

President
J. B. Highfield

Vice-Presidents
Dr. S. J. Phillips   C. E. McTavish   J. L. Beaton

Secretary
N. K. Hezzelwood

Treasurer
S. E. McTavish

Immediate Past President
C. F. Cannon

Executive Committee

F. M. Black	C. D. Lyons
J. F. Carnwith	C. C. McGibbon
J. J. English	W. Pearson
H. Hall	D. W. Rowden
Dr. W. J. Langmaid	F. V. Skinner
M. Leyden	W. Tribble
E. A. Lovell	J. N. Willson
O. H. Luke	L. C. Workman

— 9 —

Appendix A   **1938-39 Memorial Cup commemorative book**

OSHAWA GENERALS
CANADIAN JUNIOR HOCKEY CHAMPIONS
1938 - 39

BACK ROW (left to right)— Sammy Johnson, Trainer; Matt Leyden, Manager; Tracy Shaw, Coach; C. E. McTavish, Vice-President; Neil Hezzelwood, Secretary; Stewart McTavish, Treasurer; W. Pearson, Executive.

MIDDLE ROW (left to right)— Joe Delmonte, Defense; Don Daniels, Defense; Jimmy Drummond, Defense; George Ritchie, Defense; Gerry Kinsella, Right Wing; Nick Knott, Left Wing; Orville Smith, Centre; Jud McAtee, Left Wing.

FRONT ROW (left to right)— Dinny McManus, Goal; Norm McAtee, Centre; Billy Taylor (Captain), Centre; J. D. Highfield, President; Roy Sawyer, Right Wing; Gar Peters, Centre; Les Colvin, Goal; Stated, Harry Frame, Stickboy.

Appendix A   **1938-39 Memorial Cup commemorative book**

Thumbnail Sketches of the Oshawa Generals
CANADIAN JUNIOR HOCKEY CHAMPIONS 1938-39

BILLY TAYLOR, captain and centre ice star of team for past two years and best known junior puck chaser in the Dominion. Starred on Toronto junior teams before becoming Oshawa's favorite player. On the Toronto Maple Leaf negotiation list. Graduates from junior ranks this year.

NORM McATEE, centre and left wing, hails from Stratford, and member of famous hockey family. Relentless checker and smooth playmaker. Was one of the team's stars in final game. Only 18 years of age; has two years of junior hockey left.

ORVILLE SMITH, centre, brother of Nakina and Carl "Winkie" Smith. A Northern Ontario boy, gained prominence with St. Michael's juniors. One of the team's hardest workers and considered by some the best junior in Canada during a ganging attack. Still has a year in the age limit ranks.

ROY SAWYER, right wing, learned his hockey under Harold Luke in the Oshawa city league and starred with Whitby juniors last season. The team's second highest scorer, he was unfortunate to break a bone in his left ankle in the Verdun series. Still has a year of junior hockey left and a great prospect.

NICK KNOTT, left wing, member of last season's Kingston Junior Bee champions. A big rangy youth with a powerful skating stride and a hard shot, is being closely watched by Toronto Maple Leafs. Still has a year of junior left with a brilliant hockey future ahead.

JUD McATEE, left winger and brother of Norm McAtee. A strong skater and checker, possessed with possibly the team's hardest shot. First gained hockey prominence in Stratford and appears destined for professional ranks on the season's display. Still has a year left in junior.

GERRY KINSELLA, right wing, an Ottawa boy who first attracted attention by his scoring feats with Perth Blue Wings last year. A splendid skater and always a scoring threat, added considerable punch to the team's second line. His last season in junior ranks.

JIMMY DRUMMOND, right defense, a big blond, fast skating bodychecker, who starred for Toronto Marlboros last year. One of the team's spark plugs, enjoyed a brilliant season. On the Toronto Maple Leaf's list, he appears headed for stardom in monied ranks. His last year of junior hockey.

DON DANIELS, right defense, called by some the best defensive player in junior hockey. An Oshawa boy who learned his hockey in the city league; he has starred in two Memorial Cup finals. The heaviest player on the team, still has a year in junior ranks and with past experience should continue to greater achievements.

GEORGE RITCHIE, defense or right wing. Gained prominence with Toronto Marlboros last season, and one of the most versatile players with this year's team. A fast skater who never stops trying, should be a standout next year, being still eligible for junior hockey.

GAR PETERS, centre, an Oshawa boy who played Junior Bee hockey this winter and juvenile last year. Did grand job of stepping into breach caused by injury to Sawyer and next season should become one of Ontario's better known junior stars.

(Continued on page 20)

— 12 —

Appendix A   **1938-39 Memorial Cup commemorative book**

Close Harmony Paid Dividends

By Ed Fitkin, Sports Writer, Toronto Globe and Mail

As the fellow eating his morning grapefruit once remarked: "There's more to this than meets the eye!" And there was more to Oshawa's winning the Memorial Cup than the rather prosaic fact that they outscored Edmonton Roamers in three out of four games.

We think you can place the finger on the team spirit of the Generals in analyzing the main contributing factors toward their success in bringing Oshawa its first Dominion championship. We did not hear of a single instance where friction raised its ugly head during the season. Over a campaign that stretched from November to April, that's really something.

The boys respected Tracy Shaw's judgment. They played hockey for him—and him only. No one tried to tell Tracy how to run his team, and that's another noteworthy feature. Interference is something any good coach resents.

The players worked together as a unit. There were no petty jealousies, no envy because one or two of the boys got more publicity than the others. Usually the other fellows dismissed this with a shrug and an ungrudging: "Boy, they deserve it."

Typical of the "All-for-one and one-for-all" spirit of the Generals was the way the rival goalies, Dinny McManus and Les Colvin, teamed up all season. They took turns in the net throughout the campaign and were the best of pals.

We liked the scene in the Oshawa dressing room after the Memorial Cup had been won. Dinny McManus yelled: "Who said we were a one-man team?" And Billy Taylor, to whom the remark was kiddingly directed, was one of the noisiest participants in the cheer that followed.

We fraternized with the players all season in the role of hockey reporter. In fact, we have a sneaking suspicion we became something of a mascot in the playoffs.

They're a great bunch, the Generals, on and off the ice. We had a lot of fun with them, and we're glad for the sake of Bill Taylor, Jim Drummond, Gerry Kinsella and Les Colvin that the team captured the Memorial Cup. Next year, these four must step up to higher company.

We're going to miss Taylor because we were usually pretty lucky in tossing for drinks (cokes, y'know) after the games. Why the night Bill scored five goals against Edmonton, he had to buy us a large 'un. And they say he's lucky!

Not only the players but also the "Brain Trust" deserve all the plaudits you Oshawa fans are heaping on their shoulders. You couldn't meet a finer bunch of fellows than Tracy Shaw, Matt Leyden, Harold Luke, Stew McTavish, Neil Hezzelwood and Trainer Sammy Johnson.

No finer aggregation ever gained possession of junior hockey's greatest award!

WE SALUTE THE OSHAWA GENERALS

Champions Every One

Compliments of the Members of

THE SERGEANTS' MESS

Ontario Regiment (Tank)

CONGRATULATIONS "GENERALS"

THE GLOBE CAFE

13 KING ST. E.   -   -   -   -   -   OSHAWA

—18—

Appendix A   **1938-39 Memorial Cup commemorative book**

The Championship Trail
By
"Red" Burnett
The Toronto Daily Star

It is with pleasure I contribute these few words to your booklet in honor of a great team of junior hockey players. Any club that can come from behind like the Generals and carry on with their star right winger on the sidelines deserves to be called GREAT.

My association with junior hockey goes back quite a way, although not as far as that of Harold Luke. I can safely say that the Generals of the 1938-39 season rank with most of the junior clubs which have taken the much coveted Memorial Cup and rate well up on hockey's honor list.

They stepped out against an Edmonton team with a reputation of being a standout force and whipped them three games to one, which leaves no doubt as to their superiority. The series had a little of everything. Taylor stole the show the first two games. Kreller, of Roamers, took the headlines in the third game and then in the fourth and best match of all two unsung heroes of many an Oshawa victory—meaning the McAtee boys—took top honors. It was a fitting climax to a fine season.

Last year's finals probably had more thrills and with a few breaks Oshawa might have taken that set of games from St. Boniface Seals, who were crowned Canadian champions after five stirring struggles. The year before that Winnipeg Monarchs, one of the most polished junior clubs this writer has ever had the pleasure of watching, whipped a bruising Copper Cliff team to take the honors.

In 1936 West Toronto Nationals, a powerful club with little crowd appeal, won the title with ease. That squad had Roy Conacher, Johnny Crawford, Red Heron. Oshawa's Carl Gamble, Bobby Laurent and several other standouts on its roster and in my opinion was one of the most powerful teen-aged clubs Toronto has ever produced.

The season before that Oshawa won the O.H.A. junior title only to lose it in the committee room. The Canadian finals were played in the West and of course we did not have the pleasure of watching them. In 1934 Oshawa was again very prominent owing to the fact that its lads gave the great St. Michael's team their toughest series until they had to go all out to whip Edmonton in the Canadian finals.

Before that Newmarket with Howie Peterson, an Oshawa boy, and Pep Kelly, who played for Oshawa the year previous, won the Canadian crown despite a number of injuries. It seems that whenever we get mixed up in Junior hockey some one from Oshawa is always around.

Before that if you'll remember Nakina Smith, who later played senior in Oshawa, led Sudbury Wolves to the north country's first Canadian junior crown.

We could keep going down the list but won't. Instead we'd like to say that in our opinion Owen Sound's famed 60-minute club of 1929 which won the Memorial Cup was one of the gamest crews we ever watched. Marlboros champions in 1930 probably had the most power with Charlie Conacher and Harvey Jackson patrolling the wing lines.

That's as far back as we can go . . . sorry folks!

In closing I'd like to add the hope that Oshawa's team sticks together next year. If they do, there is no reason why they can't repeat their great work of the past season.

Well done Tracy Shaw and your Generals.

CONGRATULATIONS OSHAWA GENERALS
On Winning the Memorial Cup

The Grand Cafe

BETTER FOOD — EXCELLENT SERVICE

14½ KING ST. E. (Upstairs)   -   -   -   OSHAWA

— 14 —

Appendix A   **1938-39 Memorial Cup commemorative book**

Did You Know?
By
O.H.A. "Harold" Luke

THAT Don Daniels, Roy Sawyer and Gar Peters all commenced their hockey careers with Kinsmen Midgets in the Oshawa City League. Les Colvin is also a league graduate.

* * * *

THAT The Oshawa Hockey Club took charge of all O.H.A. hockey in Oshawa in November 1929 at the request of the O.H.A. From 1925-29 The Shamrock Hockey Club controlled Junior hockey in Oshawa through the Oshawa A.A.A. while the Oshawa City Hockey Club handled the Intermediate hockey.

* * * *

THAT among the players on the Shamrock roster transferred to the Oshawa Hockey Club were How Peterson, Vic Burr, Ray Gunn, Eddie Drinkle, Horace Little, Don Black, H. Robinson, C. Ames, G. Bates, R. Clary and Glenn Mundy. Matt Leyden and the writer were appointed a committee of two to carry out the transfer in a regular manner.

* * * *

THAT Walt Fair of Oshawa Juniors of 1912-13 season was rated as one of the best and was selected to play for the O.H.A. all star junior team that season. At that time an all-star team always was selected to play the Ontario Junior Champions as a grand finale.

* * * *

THAT Bob McCully, now with New Haven Eagles, while playing with Oshawa Juniors in 1931-2 set a scoring record never equalled on local ice when he rifled 9 goals past a bewildered Willowdale netminder besides drawing down an assist.

* * * *

THAT the largest paid attendance to ever witness a hockey game in Oshawa was on February 26th, 1931 when St. Mikes played Oshawa Juniors. The cash customers totalled 4,334.

* * * *

THAT Joe Jackson of Cedardale fame, still loves to talk of the palmy days when Aubrey "Dit" Clapper of Boston Bruins was starring on his South Oshawa team in the Oshawa Church League.

* * * *

THAT Donald Walker "Doc" Rowden, possibly the greatest Junior hockey player ever developed in the Oshawa Church League signed his first O.H.A. certificate with Oshawa Shamrocks in 1925, playing his first game at Bowmanville on December 30th of the same year.

* * * *

THAT Oshawa Juniors and St. Boniface Seals drew over 56,000 paid customers to the Memorial Cup finals of last year. The largest crowd to ever attend a hockey game in Canada, 15,659, wended their way through the turnstiles at the fifth game. Neil Hezzelwood and the writer still hold an unused ticket each for that memorable game.

CONGRATULATIONS
TO THE MEMORIAL CUP CHAMPIONS

DIAMOND TAXI
47 KING STREET WEST

"*Champions in Taxi Service*"

Phone 651   Phone 651

Appendix A   **1938-39 Memorial Cup commemorative book**

Oshawa's Future Hockey Stars

By W. H. "Bill" Campbell

The Oshawa Minor Hockey League known as "The City League" was organized in 1934 following a proposal by Bill Hancock then coach of Oshawa hockey teams. Through the co-operation of Les McLaughlin, of McLaughlin Coal, Lou Beaton of Beaton's Dairy, Wm. Jack of Canada Bread and Oshawa's three service clubs Kiwanis, Rotary and Kinsmen, the venture was successfully launched.

The Oshawa arena co-operated by allowing the teams that were completely outfitted, use of the arena on Thursday evenings. The first executive comprised S. E. McTavish, president, Lloyd Workman, vice-president and the writer as secretary-treasurer. The present president is Walter Branch and most of the men originally associated with the league still hold office. The league is comprised of six teams, McLaughlin Coal, Beaton's Dairy, Canada Bread, Rotary, Kiwanis and Kinsmen split into juvenile and midget sections. The winning midget team receive the Jack Worrall Memorial Cup while the C. E. McTavish trophy goes to the winning juvenile team.

The juvenile winner also enters the O.J.H.A. playoffs and as a tribute to the calibre of hockey played Beaton's Dairy reached the finals in 1937, McLaughlin Coal won the all Provincial title in 1938 while this year Canada Bread were defeated in the semi-finals by Waterloo McPhails who won the Ontario title. Members of the Canada Bread championship team this season included: Goal—Jakie Nash. Defense—Cliff Hinton, Gord Wilson, Frank Keleman, Butch Suddard, Jack Wetherup. Forwards—Sam Stark, Louie Lott, Norm McBrien, Buck Davies, Lyle McIntyre, Doug Furey. Coach—Joe Patterson. Manager—Bill Jack.

The season is annually brought to a close with a banquet at which all teams are present, when the cups are presented and individual crests given to each player of the winning teams. A real breeding ground, the league has developed many of Oshawa's hockey stars besides instilling into the youths the value of clean sportsmanship and good living.

Well Done "GENERALS"
A CHAMPION EVERY YEAR

•

McLAUGHLIN COAL JUVENILES
All Ontario Juvenile Champions 1937-38

•

OSHAWA "GENERALS"
All Canada Junior Champions 1938-39

•

McLaughlin Coal and Supplies Ltd.
OSHAWA   -   ONTARIO

—16—

Appendix A   **1938-39 Memorial Cup commemorative book**

Mostly About Elmer

By Albert G. Turner

Oshawa Correspondent, The Toronto Telegram

ELMER KRELLER

The Edmonton Roamers will be remembered as the team that went down before Oshawa's Generals, but the name of Elmer Kreller will live forever in the memories of hockey fans across the dominion. He will be remembered most by our own Billy Taylor to whom he stuck closer than a carbon copy in the third game of that memorable series.

With Billy Taylor he skyrocketed into the public eye as Taylor and Trailer, the tandem team of hockey history.

Labeled "Bloodhound," "Shadow," "Gumshoe," "Pinkerton Ace," "Sherlock" or what have you, Elmer stuck so close to Billy Taylor throughout that third game that some of the fans wondered if they hadn't stopped for one too many on the way in. Although it was denied, we still think there was foundation to the rumor that Elmer doffed the red flannels so he could stick closer to the Oshawa ace.

In spite of the fact Billy and Elmer hadn't tried skating together before the game, it wasn't very often he was out of step with Taylor. Admitted he did zig a couple of times when Billy zagged, but he was always around like a tin can tied on the tail of a Whippet.

In the final game Taylor spoiled the whole effect by doing a Kreller on Agar, with the final result being Billy skating around between the two Edmonton centre men like the ham in a sandwich.

Now that it's all over, Elmer is forgiven and has been taken to the heart of the Oshawa fans. They all realize he had a hard job to do, but he made a game try. Several of the Oshawa supporters were keenly disappointed when Elmer didn't come back to Oshawa with Billy for the rousing reception after the final game.

There is still one little point that will have to be straightened away, however, and we think we even have a solution for that. Billy, as top point getter of the Oshawa team, has won for himself a new suit donated by Dunn's Tailors and we humbly submit that if it is a two-pant suit, Elmer should at least get the extra pair of pants.

BILLY TAYLOR

Winner of the Suit of Clothes donated to the Highest Point Scorer

by

LES EAGLESON

Manager of

"DUNN'S TAILORS"

—17—

Appendix A   **1938-39 Memorial Cup commemorative book**

The GM Factory League Hockey
By Ed. Franklin

I think 'twas sometime between October, 1935, and January, 1936, that two arc welders in the Body Room of General Motors, we'll call them Bill Spiff and Jack Jock, were chatting over their noon lunch. Bill turned to Jack and said "Jack, you know that little undersized runt that works at the bench in the far corner?" "You mean the chap with no teeth" asked Jack. "Yes," said Bill, "That's the chap. Well, they say he is a perfect whizz on skates. In fact, he used to play centre for the Big Town Snooters in 1919. Billy Taylor is supposed to be the only one that ever equalled him when it comes to playmaking." "Pouff" said Jack, with as much contempt as he could muster with a mouthful of fried caviar (these boys really were class) "In our department, we have several chaps that used to play hockey right here in Oshawa. You know that bird with the bald spot on top of his head? He was so good that . . . ." and it went on until the starting whistle blew. And right there, the seeds of interdepartmental hockey competition were sown.

It was soon after that (as the crow flies) that Bob Joyce, then bull of the woods in those parts, started the organization of the G.M. Interdepartmental Hockey League. Trophies were donated by the Factory Manager (the Highfield Trophy for the annual winner,) Mike's place (small individual cups for the members of the winning team, and Palm Billiards (cups for the high scorer and best goaltender.)

Truck and Commercial were first winners of the Trophy, nosing out the Stockrooms in the finals. But the advent of the Main Office into the League (they were barred the first year) brought a new champion to the front, as the officers proceeded to kick the opposition around shamelessly to win the title twice in a row, winning out over the Stockrooms, in 1938, and Glass and Trim Pirates just a month ago. The office team, composed of hockey veterans, is a shining example of what Factory League Hockey is intended for—to provide a recreational outlet for those employees who wish to play hockey but who, through age or ability, are unable to play in regulation O.H.A. competition.

CONGRATULATIONS

... Oshawa Generals ...
True Sportsmen - Grand Champions

•

DIXON COAL CO., LIMITED

Congratulations

to the boys who brought honor to Oshawa by winning the Memorial Cup

Every boy not only a good player but the makings of a good man.

MIKE'S PLACE

— 18 —

Appendix A   **1938-39 Memorial Cup commemorative book**

Final Game Goal-Getters

Norm McAtee   —   Jim Drummond   —   Jud McAtee

NORM McATEE, JIMMY DRUMMOND and JUD McATEE, who scored the four goals of the final game that gave Oshawa the Memorial Cup. After Drummond scored Oshawa's first goal things looked bad so the McAtee boys ended the series with a great last period display, Norm garnering two goals while Jud rifled home one to make sure the McAtee family was well represented in the honors.

**CONGRATULATIONS TO THE
OSHAWA GENERALS**
DOMINION JUNIOR HOCKEY CHAMPIONS

TOD'S BREAD
Manufacturers of
"BUTTER-NUT" BAKERY PRODUCTS
"The Standard of Comparison" — in Oshawa for nearly 50 years
PHONE 500

Appendix A   **1938-39 Memorial Cup commemorative book**

Memorial Cup Champions

Records of the Memorial Cup playdowns since its inauguration in 1919 show that the Western teams hold an edge over their Eastern rivals, as they have won the title 11 times to nine victories for the East.

1919—U.T.S. of Toronto defeated Regina Pats 14 to 3 and 15 to 5.
1920—Toronto Canoe Club defeated Fort William 16 to 1 in a single game.
1921—Winnipeg Falcons defeated Stratford Midgets 11 to 9 on the round.
1922—Fort William defeated Regina Pats 8 to 7 on the round.
1923—University of Manitoba defeated Kitchener 7 to 3 and 7 to 3.
1924—Owen Sound Greys defeated Calgary 7 to 5 on the round.
1925—Regina Pats defeated Aura Lee, Toronto, 2 to 1 and 5 to 2.

A best-of-three series was inaugurated in 1926:
1926—Calgary defeated Kingston 2 to 4, 3 to 2 and 3 to 2.
1927—Owen Sound Greys defeated Port Arthur 5 to 4 and 5 to 3.
1928—Regina Monarchs defeated Ottawa Gunners 4 to 3, 1 to 2 and 7 to 1.
1929—Toronto Marlboros defeated Winnipeg Elmwoods 4 to 2 and 4 to 2.
1930—Regina Pats defeated West Toronto 3 to 1 and 3 to 2.
1931—Winnipeg Elmwoods defeated Ottawa Primroses 1 to 2, 2 to 1 and 3 to 0.
1932—Sudbury Wolves defeated Winnipeg Monarchs 2 to 4, 2 to 1 and 1 to 0.
1933—Newmarket defeated Regina Pats 2 to 1 and 2 to 1.
1934—St. Michael's College defeated Edmonton 5 to 0 and 6 to 4.
1935—Winnipeg Monarchs defeated Sudbury Wolves 7 to 6, 2 to 7 and 4 to 1.
1936—West Toronto defeated Saskatoon Wesleys 5 to 1 and 4 to 2.

The years 1937 and 1938 were a five-game series:
1937—Winnipeg Monarchs defeated Copper Cliff Redmen 3 to 4, 6 to 5, 2 to 1 and 7 to 0.
1938—St. Boniface Seals defeated Oshawa Generals 2 to 3, 4 to 0, 2 to 4, 6 to 4 and 7 to 1.
1939—Oshawa Generals defeated Edmonton Roamers 9 to 4, 12 to 4, 1 to 4 and 4 to 2.

THUMBNAIL SKETCHES (Continued)

LES COLVIN, goal tender, been with Generals for past three years after learning hockey in the Oshawa city league. Alternated in nets all season and ranks as one of the best junior netminders in the Dominion. His last year in junior hockey, but should have little trouble making senior ranks.

DINNY McMANUS, goal tender, a Perth boy who starred with the Blue Wings last season. Alternated with Colvin in nets all season, his style of play being exceedingly popular with the fans. One of best age limit citadel defenders in the business, he still has another year in junior hockey ahead of him.

JOE DELMONTE, defense or right wing. A Northern Ontario boy who starred with Oshawa's last season's Juvenile champions. A fast skater with a hard shot, Delmonte showed promise of developing into a star player. Still eligible for junior ranks.

SAMMY JOHNSON, trainer. Been connected with junior hockey for many years, and the players' best friend. A grand conditioner, in his own quiet way helps keep harmony and contributes immeasurably to the team's success.

MATT LEYDEN, manager, has looked after managerial duties of Oshawa junior teams for many years. A quiet young man who commands the respect of the players and keeps friction within club ranks to the minimum.

BUDDY TAYLOR, youthful mascot of the team, who proudly displays the number 17 in between periods when the teams are resting. A junior brother of Captain Bill, Buddy hopes to some day fill Billy's shoes.

HARRY TRESISE, stick boy, a redhead with an infectious smile. Harry proved himself a conscientious, trustworthy helper. Plays hockey himself in the city league, and waiting for the day when he becomes a member of the Generals.

— 20 —

Appendix A   **1938-39 Memorial Cup commemorative book**

In a Class by Themselves

Oshawa's Smart Juniors
and
Kinloch's Smart Clothes

Congratulations to the players and management of the Oshawa Generals on winning the highest honours in Junior hockey—
THE MEMORIAL TROPHY

Kinloch's
LIMITED
OSHAWA

RAY HALLERAN   FLOYD MEDLAND
DON KINLOCH

"GM MEN"   "OUR JUVENILES"

TWO OF A KIND
AND BOTH CHAMPIONS

Oshawa "Generals"

"Canada Bread"

"INTERMEDIATES"   "JUNIOR BEES"

224

Appendix B
WWII RCOC Army Records
for
Clifford Ley Herbert Hinton
March 1942 to January 1946

20 March 1942 Occupational History Form	223
20 March 1942 Attestation Paper	224
22 February 1943 Personnel Selection Record	225
2 July 1945 Supplement to Personnel Selection Record	226
Photos of Cliff's Army Service Tags and Cigarette Case	226
8 January 1946 Confidential Report 2 pages	227
10 January 1946 Active Army Discharge Certificate	229
10 January 1946 Canadian Army Awards	230

Author's note: I applied in June 2017 to Library and Archives Canada for copies of the personnel records for my father, Clifford Ley Herbert Hinton, Service Number B-9203. I received the records in August 2018 and have included some of them in this Appendix.

Appendix B   **1943-1946 Clifford's WWII records**

OCCUPATIONAL HISTORY FORM

THIS FORM IS TO BE COMPLETED FOR EACH MEMBER OF THE ARMED FORCES. THE INFORMATION SOUGHT IS FOR THE USE OF GENERAL ADVISORY COMMITTEE ON DEMOBILIZATION AND REHABILITATION, A COMMITTEE SET UP BY THE GOVERNMENT OF CANADA TO STUDY PLANS FOR ESTABLISHING IN INDUSTRIAL LIFE THE MEMBERS OF THE ARMED FORCES, AFTER DISCHARGE. ACCURACY AND COMPLETENESS IN ANSWERING WILL BE OF MUCH HELP TO THE COMMITTEE.

PLEASE READ CAREFULLY THE INSTRUCTIONS GIVEN ON THE INSIDE OF COVER BEFORE COMPLETING FORM

Section A — GENERAL INFORMATION

1. (a) Print name in full: HINTON, Clifford Loy Herbert   (b) Reg'l B-9203
2. (a) Arm of service: CDC/CA   (b) Unit: 2 Detachment   (c) Rank: Private
3. (a) Date of birth: Mar. 11/21.   (b) Have you any dependents? Yes   (c) Place of residence: 108 Arlington Ave., Oshawa, Ont.
4. (a) Place of enlistment: Toronto, Ontario, CANADA   (b) Date of enlistment: 20-3-42

Section B — EDUCATION AND TRAINING

5. (a) State age on finally leaving school: 16   (b) Were you attending school or college up to the time of enlistment? No
6. State definitely highest standing reached at public, technical or high school (for instance—"4 years, Public School", "two years, High School", "Junior Matriculation", or "4 years technical course in printing", etc.): 4 yrs. High School.
7. If you attended a university, give name of university and standing or degree secured: N.A.
8. (a) Did you ever enter upon a trade apprenticeship? NO   (b) If so, for what occupation? N.A.   (c) Did you finish it? N.A.   (d) If you did not finish it, how long did you serve at it? N.A.
9. (a) What languages do you speak fluently? English   (b) What languages do you read well? English

Section C — EMPLOYMENT CONDITION AT TIME OF ENLISTMENT

10. (a) State whether you were WORKING or NOT WORKING at time of enlistment. (Enter here only "Working" or "Not Working", as case may be; particulars are asked for below): Working   (b) At time of enlistment of what trade union or professional society were you a member? None

Section D — PARTICULARS CONCERNING THOSE WHO WERE UNEMPLOYED AT TIME OF ENLISTMENT

QUESTIONS 11 TO 17 REFER ONLY TO THOSE WHO ANSWER "NOT WORKING" IN QUESTION 10 (a)

11. Had you ever been employed fairly regularly since leaving school? N.A.
12. (a) If answer to 11 be "Yes", state exact trade or occupation at which you actually worked: N.A.   (b) State how long you had worked at this trade or occupation: N.A.
13. If answer to 11 be "No", state exact trade or occupation for which you feel qualified: N.A.
14. If you had been employed after leaving school, state when you last worked fairly regularly before enlistment: N.A.
15. Give details of last employer, if any: Name: N.A.   Address: N.A.
16. Nature of employer's business (for instance, "farmer", or "building contractor", or "boot factory", or "iron foundry", or "retail store", etc.): N.A.
17. (a) If your last employment was in a business of your own, state nature and address of business: N.A.   (b) Date of discontinuing it: N.A.

Section E — PARTICULARS CONCERNING THOSE WHO WERE EMPLOYED AT TIME OF ENLISTMENT

QUESTIONS 18 TO 23 REFER ONLY TO THOSE WHO ANSWER "WORKING" IN QUESTION 10 (a). PLEASE READ THESE QUESTIONS AND REPLY TO THOSE APPLYING TO YOU AT TIME OF ENLISTMENT

IF YOU WERE AN EMPLOYEE WORKING FOR AN EMPLOYER UP TO THE TIME OF ENLISTMENT, PLEASE ANSWER QUESTIONS 18 TO 21

18. Name of employer: General Motors Limited   Address: Oshawa, Ont.
19. Nature of employer's business (for instance, "farmer", or "building contractor", or "boot factory", or "iron foundry", or "retail store", etc.): MOTOR ENG'L.
20. (a) Your specific occupation: Clerk   (b) Number of years' experience at this occupation with any employer: 5 yrs.
21. (a) Did your employer promise definitely to give you employment on discharge? Yes   (b) Did your employer refuse to promise you employment on discharge? No   (c) Do you wish to return to your former employment? No

IF YOU WERE WORKING ON YOUR OWN UP TO THE TIME OF ENLISTMENT, THAT IS TO SAY, OPERATING A FARM, A STORE, AN AGENCY, OR IN PROFESSIONAL PRACTICE, OR AS A PARTNER IN ANY SUCH LINE, PLEASE ANSWER QUESTIONS 22 AND 23

22. (a) State nature of business, or professional practice: N.A.   (b) Where was it located? N.A.
23. (a) Number of years engaged in this business: N.A.   (b) Have you made, or will you make plans to return to the same or a similar business on discharge? N.A.

Section F — PARTICULARS OF FARMING EXPERIENCE

24. (a) Do you wish to engage in farming after the war? NO   (b) Do you feel competent to operate a farm? NO   (c) If so, in what kind of farming? NONE
25. (a) Were you born on a farm? NO   (b) How many years' actual farming experience have you had? NO   (c) In what provinces did you have experience? NONE

Section G — MISCELLANEOUS

26. Have you made any arrangements other than indicated above, for re-establishment in civil life after discharge? No
27. If so, state nature of your plans (for example, do you plan to return to school, or have you been assured of a job, etc.): N.A.
28. State any employment preference or ambition you may have, other than indicated elsewhere in this form: No

DATE: March 20, 1942.   SIGNATURE: Clifford Hinton

Enlistment at Toronto Ontario Canada

20 March 1942

Occupational History Form

Appendix B   **1943-1946 Clifford's WWII records**

Enlistment at Toronto Ontario Canada

20 March 1942

Attestation Paper

FINGERPRINTED AUG 10 1942

ORIGINAL / DUPLICATE / TRIPLICATE

M.F.M. 2
A.P.O. 271

(To be completed in triplicate. Copy designation to be shown by striking out terms not applicable.)

Unit No. 2 Detchm at, ___ CA. (A.F.) Regimental Number XXXXX B-9300

ACTIVE FORMATIONS AND UNITS OF THE CANADIAN ARMY
ATTESTATION PAPER

1. Surname .... HINTON
2. Christian Names .... Clifford Ley Herbert.
3. Present address .... 105 Arlington Ave., Oshawa Ont.
4. Date of birth .... 11 Mar 1921.
5. Place of birth **Wales** (Country) .... Clydach, (County or Province) (Town or Township)
6. Religion (state denomination) .... United Church
7. Trade or Calling .... Clerk.
8. Married, Widower or Single .... Single.
9. Name of next of kin .... Phyllis Hinton.
10. Relationship .... Mother.
11. Address of next of kin .... 105 Arlington Ave, Oshawa Ont.
12. Do you belong to, or have you served in a Reserve Formation or Unit of The Canadian Army? No.
  (If Yes, Give Unit and Dates of Service)
13. Have you served in (a) an Active Formation or Unit of The Canadian Army? No.
  (If Yes, Give Regimental No. and Unit) (Yes or No)
  (b) Any other Naval, Military, or Air Force? No.
  (Yes or No) (If Yes, specify Unit and Period of Service)
14. Did you serve during the Great War 1914-1918? No.
  (If Yes, specify Regimental No., Unit and Dates of Service)

DECLARATION TO BE MADE BY MAN ON ATTESTATION

I, Clifford Ley Herbert Hinton, do solemnly declare that the above particulars are true, and I hereby engage to serve in any Active Formation or Unit of The Canadian Army so long as an emergency, i.e. war, invasion, riot or insurrection, exists, and for the period of demobilization after said emergency ceases to exist, and in any event for a period of not less than one year, provided ...

Date March __, 1942.

OATH TO BE TAKEN BY MAN ON ATTESTATION

I, Clifford Ley Herbert Hinton, do sincerely promise and swear (or solemnly declare) that I will be faithful and bear true allegiance to His Majesty ...

CERTIFICATE OF MAGISTRATE, JUSTICE OF THE PEACE OR ATTESTING OFFICER

The Recruit above-named was cautioned by me that if he made any false answers to any of the above questions he would be liable to be punished as provided by law.
The above questions and answers were then read to the recruit in my presence.
I have taken care that he understands each question, and that his answer to each question has been duly entered as replied to, and the said recruit has made and signed the declaration and taken the oath before me,

at .... this XXXX day of March 19 42.

(Signature of Magistrate, Justice or Attesting Officer, Officer or Rank and Unit or appointment.

N.B. ATTENTION IS DRAWN TO THE FACT THAT ANY PERSON MAKING A FALSE ANSWER TO ANY OF THE ABOVE QUESTIONS IS LIABLE TO A PENALTY OF SIX MONTHS' IMPRISONMENT

Appendix B   **1943-1946 Clifford's WWII records**

Personnel Selection Record at Camp Borden Ontario Canada

22 February 1943

RCOC is Royal Canadian Ordnance Corps

DEPARTMENT OF NATIONAL DEFENCE — Ord. Field Park. (Arm or Corps)

This form will accompany the soldier's regimental documents at all times.

(Army) FURTHER INFORMATION AND FOLLOW-UP

Personnel Selection Record — Private. Trade (if Tradesman or Trade Trainee)
Work in Arm (if Non-Tradesman)

I. B 9203   Pte.   HINTON, Clifford Ley Herbert.   A   21   A
   Regt. No.   Rank   Name (surname first)   A or E Age Med. Cat.

   English   none   2 Can. Army Tank Yrd. Fld. Pk.   Feb. 22/43.
   Main Language   Other Language(s)   Place (Unit) Interviewed   Date Interviewed

II. Revised Examination "M"   Camp Borden   Feb. 20/43.   A.M.B.
                                   Place Tested   Date Tested   By Whom

   168   2   Subtests   15 18 19 26 27 12 18 33   Subtotals 52 53 63   English
   Total Group   1 2 3 4 5 6 7 8   1-3 4-5 5-8 English or French
   Other Tests

III. Educational Background

   Finished 3rd year high, matric course at age 16.
   Family troubles necessitated going to work.

IV. Occupational Background

   4 years as Automotive parts clerk at G.M.C.

V. Military Background   Enlisted 18-3-42 at D.D. 2. Had Basic and Advanced
   Training with present unit. Performed duties of storeman for 2 months
   at Barriefield. Expects to be qualified as technical storeman
   overseas.

VI. Other Personal History and Appraisal

   Age 21. Single, Cat. A. Family at Oshawa. Good family
   relations. 2 brothers, one a lieutenant in R.H.L.I. Fair complexion,
   good appearance, pleasant and easy manner. Co-operative personality.
   Impresses favourably.

   Hobby is model building.

   Reads considerably, news, magazines, fiction. Has normal
   sports and recreational history.

   Well above average intelligence, seems normal emotionally
   and history indicates good balance of character. Impresses as stable
   and dependable. Should be considered as good material for promotion.
   His civilian experience is good background for training as technical
   storeman.

                                                "Q" CARD COMPLETE

VII. Recommendations

   R.C.O.C.   Tech. Storeman. Trades Trainee.

                              (Signed) E. M. Greaves Lieut.
                                                    Army Examiner

See reverse side for further information and follow-up

229

Appendix B   **1943-1946 Clifford's WWII records**

DEPARTMENT OF NATIONAL DEFENCE
(ARMY)
SUPPLEMENT TO PERSONNEL SELECTION RECORD
(MFM 196A)

To be attached to MFM 196, and to be initiated only when MFM 196 is completely filled.

B-9203	Pte.	HINTON, Clifford L. H.
Regtl No.	Rank	Surname / First Name

Additional Follow-up:

Interviewed at 4 Repat Depot (UK) 2 Jul 45. CFEF Draft: 104 MD-2. Cat: "A". Age: 24.

MILITARY BACKGROUND: Enlisted 20 Mar 42. Trained in Canada as RCOC rft for 3 months. O/S Jul 42 with 2nd Army Tank Bde as attached Ordnance storeman. Posted to 1st Corp and Army Troops Sub Park as storeman. To CMF with this unit Oct 43 and remained with them right through to NWE as storeman until returned to U.K. in Far East draft. No battle experience. No hospitalization. MFM 6 clear. Qualified storeman T&D Gp "C".

APPRAISAL: A single man with dependent mother. Appears serious minded and dependable. Appears to be in good health. States he feels fine. Volunteered for Pacific more for adventure. Was apparently engaged to an English girl but had a misunderstanding. This has now been patched up and he wants to marry and consequently is not so keen on Far East Force as he was originally. Would like to carry on as a storeman with ordnance if possible. Motivation is fair.

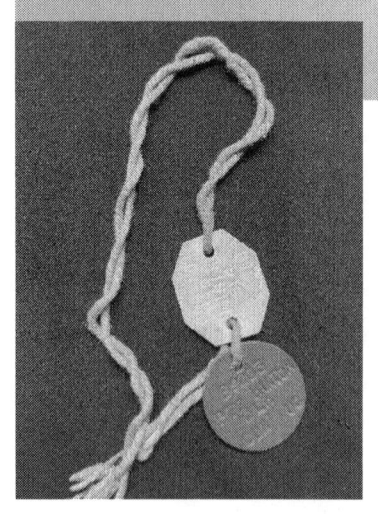

(C H Davis) Maj.

Supplement To Personnel Selection Record at Repatriation Depot   2 July 1945

WWII RCOC service tags

"B9205 PTE HINTON CLH   CDN UC"

Cliff's Cigarette Case

Appendix B   **1943-1946 Clifford's WWII records**

Department of Veteran Affairs, Toronto, Confidential Report Pg1, 8 January 1946

JP   DEPARTMENT OF VETERANS AFFAIRS - W.D. 12   Jan 8, 1946

CONFIDENTIAL   ATTENTION EMPLOYMENT.

1. SURNAME: HINTON   FIRST NAME: Clifford   INITIALS: RANK: Pte.   NUMBER: B-9203   SEX: M
2. DATE OF COMMENCEMENT OF ACTIVE SERVICE: 21 Mar. 42   PLACE: Toronto   YR. OF BIRTH: 1921.
3. SERVICE OUTSIDE CANADA: YES X   IN WHAT SERVICE? army
4. CAUSE OF DISCHARGE: 1029 (5) (c)(i)
5. PRE-ENLISTMENT EDUCATION:-

   Gr. XI Oshawa H.S. Oshawa, Ont. Left at 16 years of age.

6. LANGUAGES:-

   English.

7. OCCUPATIONAL HISTORY:-

   See Below.

8. IMMEDIATE PRE-ENLISTMENT EMPLOYMENT:- (WITH NAME AND ADDRESS OF EMPLOYER)

   Parts clerk-General Motors Co. of Can. Ltd., Oshawa, 5 years.   Ont.

9. SHORT ACCOUNT OF SERVICE, TRAINING AND DUTIES:-

   Total service 3 years 9½ mos.,-o/s 25 mos. saw service as technical storeman Gp. "C" in the RCOC in U.K., Italy and N.W.E. Qualified as a clerk Gp. "C" volunteered for Pacific.

10. EDUCATIONAL COURSES WHILE IN SERVICE:-

    nil.

11. MEDICAL OFFICER'S STATEMENT OF PHYSICAL LIMITATIONS (IF ANY):-

    Fit for normal employment.

Appendix B   **1943-1946 Clifford's WWII records**

Department of Veteran Affairs, Toronto, Confidential Report Pg2, 8 January 1946

12. MARITAL STATUS:- SINGLE   NUMBER OF DEPENDENTS, OTHER THAN WIFE   NONE

13. DISCHARGEE'S OWN STATEMENT OF FUTURE PLANS (IF ANY):-

I have already arranged to return to my former employment in general motors.

14. POST-DISCHARGE MAILING ADDRESS:-

12 Quebec St., Oshawa, Ont.

15. BASIS FOR COUNSELLOR'S RECOMMENDATIONS:-

Hinton's plan to return to his former employment is sound. He has admirably suited to this type of work and in the Army followed a somewhat similar career.

He has a pleasant and alert manner which should serve him well in this type of employment or he could do equally well as an office clerk or a retail sales clerk.

His main problem is a fiancee in England and as soon as he can arrange for her transportation to this country he will use his re-estab. credit in order to buy furniture.

16. ACTION RECOMMENDED:-

Return to former employment as a parts clerk.

17. OTHER POSSIBILITIES SUGGESTED BY COUNSELLOR:-

Seek employment as a clerk office or sales.

18. REFERRED TO:-

N.E.S. Oshawa, Ont.

19. PLACE   DATE   SIGNATURE OF COUNSELLOR: J.W. BERWICK, 8
#2 D.D. Toronto 8 Jan. 46   RANK OR APPOINTMENT CAPT. ARMY COUNSELLOR.

NOTE:- COUNSELLOR WILL CHECK TO SEE THAT THIS FORM HAS BEEN COMPLETED AS REQUIRED.

Appendix B   **1943-1946 Clifford's WWII records**

Active Army Discharge Certificate at Toronto, 10 January 1946

Jan 10, 1946

CANADIAN ARMY (ACTIVE)
DISCHARGE CERTIFICATE

M.F.M. 7 (Paper)
500M—2-45 (6061)
H.Q. 1772-39-1853

This is to Certify that No. B-9203 (Rank) Private

Name (in full) Clifford Loy Herbert PITTS enlisted or was enrolled in the Royal Canadian Ordnance Corps.

the **CANADIAN ARMY (ACTIVE)** at Toronto, Ont. on the 20th day of March 19 43.

She/He served in Canada, United Kingdom, Continental Europe and Central Mediterranean Area.

and is now discharged from the service under Routine Order 1029 (50.1) by reason of TO RETURN TO CIVIL LIFE ON DEMOBILIZATION.

Medals, Decorations, Mentions, awarded in respect of service during this war: 1939-45 Star, Italy Star, France & Germany Star, C.V.S.M. & Clasp.

THE DESCRIPTION OF THIS SOLDIER on the DATE below is as follows:—

Age ... 34 Yrs. 10 Mo.
Height ... 5 ft. 10 Ins.
Complexion ... Pale
Eyes ... Brown
Hair ... Brown

Marks or Scars ... Scar right hypothenar eminence.

Other Active Army Service (This War) ... Nil.

Signature of Soldier

Date of Discharge/ENT
WING
JAN 10 1946
No. 2 DISTRICT DEPOT   TORONTO, ONT.

Issuing Officer
For Officer Commanding, No. 2 District Depot, C.A.
Rank
Date JAN 10 1946 ... 19...

N.B.—As no duplicate of this Certificate will be issued, any person finding same is requested to forward it in an unstamped envelope to the Director of Records (Army), Department of National Defence, Ottawa, Canada.

Appendix B   **1943-1946 Clifford's WWII records**

Canadian Army Awards

AWARDS—CANADIAN ARMY (ACTIVE)			
HINTON, Clifford Ley Herbert	B-9203	Pte.	FILE NO.
SURNAME (IN BLOCK LETTERS) CHRISTIAN NAMES	REG. NO.	RANK ON DISCHARGE	

WAR SERVICE BADGE (CLASS): ELIGIBLE G.S.C No. 610644 (10-1-46) DD 2

CAMPAIGN MEDALS
1939-45 Star
Italy Star
France & Germany Star
CVSM & Clasp
War Medal, 1939-45

548

Briefly noted on Cliff's confidential record at discharge in January 1946 is his intention to have his fiancé come from England to join him. This did not happen, and the reason may have been her reluctance or his change of heart before or after he met Dorothy Auld.

234

Appendix C

Original Handwritten Letters

23 June 1944 To Cliff from his brother Hugh	237
22 August 1944 To his brother Hugh from Cliff	240
27 April 1948 To Dorothy from Granny Martha Brinn	245
May 1948 To Dorothy and Cliff from Grace Jones	248
6 June 1948 To Dorothy from her father Thomas Auld	252
January 1949 to Dorothy from Granny Martha Brinn	255
4 Nov 1951 to Burnard family from Thomas Auld	259
1 March 1957 to Dodie from her friend Edna Acton	264
1 March 1957 to Dorothy from Helen Lush	266
3 March 1957 to Mrs. Hinton from Rose Mills	267
3 March 1957 to Dodie from Thelma Burnard	271
5 March 1957 to Mrs. Hinton from Joan North	273
5 March 1957 to Dorothy from Morris Wootton	274
March 1957 To Dodie from friends Pat and Alex Reid	275

Author's note: These letters were in a memory box held by my mother, Dorothy Hinton since 1957 until she died in 2004.

Appendix C   **1944 June 23 Hugh Hinton's letter to brother Cliff Hinton Pg 1**

23 Jan 1944

Dear Cliff,

You will be surprised to know that I have not seen any action yet. I am afraid everyone back home is thinking of me in the invasion and here I am still in England.

About the only thing of interest that has happened is the robot planes loaded with explosives that the Germans have been sending over. They come in very fast then their motors are cut and they drop to earth apparently exploding

Appendix C   **1944 June 23 Hugh Hinton's letter to brother Cliff Hinton Pg 2**

on impact. Although I have not seen any yet, they have been dropping all around us the last few days. They are not very devastating and the people regard them as a novelty. Their blast effect is great but unless they get a direct hit, the damage is slight.

I received a letter from Jack Davie last week. He tells me Charlie Johnson is in the Army now and that he also may be reboarded and obliged to join up. They certainly are draining the best but of Canada. It is going to be a struggle after the war.

Appendix C   **1944 June 23 Hugh Hinton's letter to brother Cliff Hinton Pg 3**

The war seems to be going well in all parts, and if this continues, Montgomery's prophecy will become a reality. He said the war would be over by Christmas. I hope he is right for I am dying to go home.

There is nothing else I can say Cliff so I shall say goodbye and good luck.

Hugh.

Appendix C   **1944 August 22 Cliff Hinton's letter to brother Hugh Pg 1**

B9203 Pte. Hinton C.
1st Corps, Armer Trps S/P
Can Army Overseas.
C.M.F.

August 22nd,
1944

Dear Hugh:

Please forgive me for not writing sooner. I received your last letter, you wrote June 23rd, quite some time ago. And as usual, I delayed in dropping you a few lines.

I received two airmails from Mother to-day, containing the disheartening news of your injuries. Hugh, I want to tell you how proud I am of you. I am hoping so much that your injuries are slight and that you will be on your feet again soon.

I have read a few reports of your regiment in the papers and my thoughts were with you. I would give anything to have been with you.

Appendix C   **1944 August 22 Cliff Hinton's letter to brother Hugh Pg 2**

Mother seemed quite cheerful in her letters, but she must be worrying about you very much. I was very glad to hear that Doug was able to get home from New York for a few days. Kay & John were very kind to her also. Mother mentioned about the story in the Toronto paper of your exploits during your patrols. You deserve a lot Hugh, for your courage. I know pretty well what you have gone through. It really burns me up to think of the small effort I am turning in. I applied for a transfer to the Combined American & Canadian Special Service Corps, a few weeks ago, without any luck. I like my unit very much, also my work, but at times, such as this, I am

Appendix C   **1944 August 22 Cliff Hinton's letter to brother Hugh Pg 3**

very discontented. I know it's too late to ever think of joining you now, but I want you to know that, my thoughts are always with you and I'm hoping that it will all end soon and we can get to-gether again. I'll have so much to tell you.

You must wonder, Hugh, why I haven't got ahead in the Army. It's not because of my behaviour. I haven't been up for orders since I left Canada. I've had a few chances for promotion, but so far I've felt that the work I have turned in for my unit, is more deserving that what they have ever offered. I know you'll say I have been very foolish, but that is the way I feel.

Appendix C   **1944 August 22 Cliff Hinton's letter to brother Hugh Pg 4**

When I missed out on my commission in leaving Canada a few weeks too soon, I was very disappointed. But now all I'm looking forward to is a speedy finish to this mess we are in.

Well Hugh, it's getting late so I must quit this sheet. Take care of yourself and I hope this letter finds you back on your feet again and happy. I won't fail to write you again in a few days.

All the Best
Your kid brother
Cliff

243

Appendix C   **1944 August 22 Cliff Hinton's letter to brother Hugh, envelope**

Appendix C **1948 April 27, Martha Brinn's letter pg1 sent to 606 Cassells St North Bay**

10 Hamilton Terrace
Pembroke
South Wales

Dear Dorothy
 At last I am going to try to write you a few lines trusting they will find you and Cliff & baby well. how I would love to see you all
 yes dear it is real nice for you to be settled in your own home and now you will feel much better you have made friends with the people and it is nice of the menester to call on you hope you will be able to go to Chapel or Church where you can you must

2

take Judy with you. She will get use to going after a wile. hope Cliff is home with you on Sundays I know just how you feel being so far from your home and all the people strange to you

pleases to say I keep well but I do miss phyllis I had hoped she would have come back to me when Douglas was married now she is getting married herself so I must give up all thoughts of seeing her again, and Douglas well he seems to have upset all his plans they should have talked over their religion afairs long before the time

Appendix C **1948 April 27, Martha Brinn's letter pg3 sent to 606 Cassells St North Bay**

3

I don't like the ida of him living in the Flat by himself still he is old enough to know what he is doing. I am pleased Cliff is married give him my love and a big X hope he is looking after you & his daughter I am sure he is a proud father and I pray god will bless you both and the dear baby I am longing to see the snaps of her your mother tells me she got Cliffs dimple pity you are so far away from your home. I am here alone but I got lots of nice friends mind take care of yourself Good night- god bless you your Loving Granny
M Brinn

Appendix C   **1948 May 20, Grace Jones' letter pg1 sent to 606 Cassells St North Bay**

12 Prendergast St.
Llanelly.

Dear Dorothy + Cliff.

What a lovely surprize I had, having a letter from you; it was very sweet of you to write to me, and I do hope I shall hear from you again soon. So glad to know you like the woolly set, and that it fits little Judith. I only went by guess as regards the size, and after taking quite a while to reach you, I was beginning to think maybe it would be too small. Babies seem to grow so quickly don't they.

Aunty Phyllis told me all about Judith anne and she certainly

Appendix C   **1948 May 20, Grace Jones' letter pg2 sent to 606 Cassells St North Bay**

2

seems very proud of her too. I guess Cliff is thrilled too now he's a daddy??

I do hope you will write again Dorothy, tell me about yourselves. I'd love to hear from you. Has aunty been staying with you lately? I'm wondering if she's married yet. I haven't heard for a while, maybe she is rather busy though. There's always lots to do at these time. Well, what's it like in Canada these days. We have been enjoying some lovely sunshine here for the last two weeks, really hot tropical weather. We went to the beach quite a lot, Judith is very fond of the water.

Appendix c   **1948 May 20, Grace Jones' letter pg3 sent to 606 Cassells St North Bay**

3.

she's got quite a lovely tan now; the sun has been so strong. Anyway, the weather has now changed, it's bitterly cold again, and the rain has been falling. How long it's going to last I don't know. Once the rain starts in Wales it never knows when to stop. I expect Aunty has been telling you all about us here in England. We had a lovely summer while she was over, and I had a nice holiday at Grans while she was there. The last time I saw Aunty, I was only about six years old. It's a long time, but I'm still as fond of her as my mother tells me I was when I was

Appendix C   **1948 May 20, Grace Jones' letter pg4 sent to 606 Cassells St North Bay**

4.

Six:. I was sorry to see Len go back in a way; Well done. I'm afraid I haven't much to tell you in this letter, more news as we go along I expect. I've just been getting Judith back to school after the Whit holidays: am I glad too!, but she is fond of school, so there's no trouble about her going. So now I'll say cheerio to you both, write again soon won't you. My love to little Judith, + to you both.

Yours Sincerely
Grace.
x x x

Appendix C   **1948 June 6, Thomas Auld's letter pg1 to daughter Dorothy Hinton at 606 Cassells St, North Bay**

Auldsville Kingston
June 6 /48

Dear Dody

Poor little dear, haven't had a letter from home for so long, over a month was it, well that is too bad that is why I'm taking pity on you or maybe I'm inflicting myself on you However you will have to put up with it till I get through this time

I hear you are coming to Toronto on the 10 inst, well the chances are I will be there at that time also, if things don't (gang agley) which I hope they don't I had a bad leg all last week, it seems I hit my shin against something harder than the bone, and about a week after it got infected something like I had in my face last year, last Sunday I went to Dr Bennett and he advised me

Appendix C   **1948 June 6, Thomas Auld's letter pg2 to daughter Dorothy Hinton at 606 Cassells St, North Bay**

(2)

to put hot applications to it so I was in bed for a couple of days, it is a little sore yet but the pain is almost gone. I got my potatoes all in a week ago last Friday Gordon helped me for a day & a half. The ones I put in the last of April are up and I have some of them hoed but I still have 21 rows to hoe before I can get away at least I'll try to. Mrs Heagy wrote last week & said they were having their Reunion on the 12th of June so I'll have to be in Toronto before that as I have to go to Stratford first and see the crowd there, and as the Reunion is at Guelph this year it will be on my way back, and I want to stay at Cobourg a day or two. Perhaps Violet will be able to go with me to Guelph. I don't suppose you can go and Mabel can't get away this year.

Appendix C   **1948 June 6, Thomas Auld's letter pg3 to daughter Dorothy Hinton at 606 Cassells St, North Bay**

Rather a surprize Ma Hinton getting married was it, or did you know it was coming. Well according to what you say. He is to be congratulated. and I hope they will be happy

You were asking how I liked the tractor. I think it is just dandy it never thinks the day is long. and feed it. oil it + water it. it just goes on + on + does the work a lot quicker than old dobbin + look at the time I save, Well times do change don't they

Well I guess Judy is going to have an anniversary soon so I'm sending her a card and I suppose I'll be seeing you at Vi's sometime this week

Hoping Cliff + you + Judy are keeping well. Dad

Appendix C   **1949 January, Martha Brinn's airmail sent to 606 Cassells St North Bay**

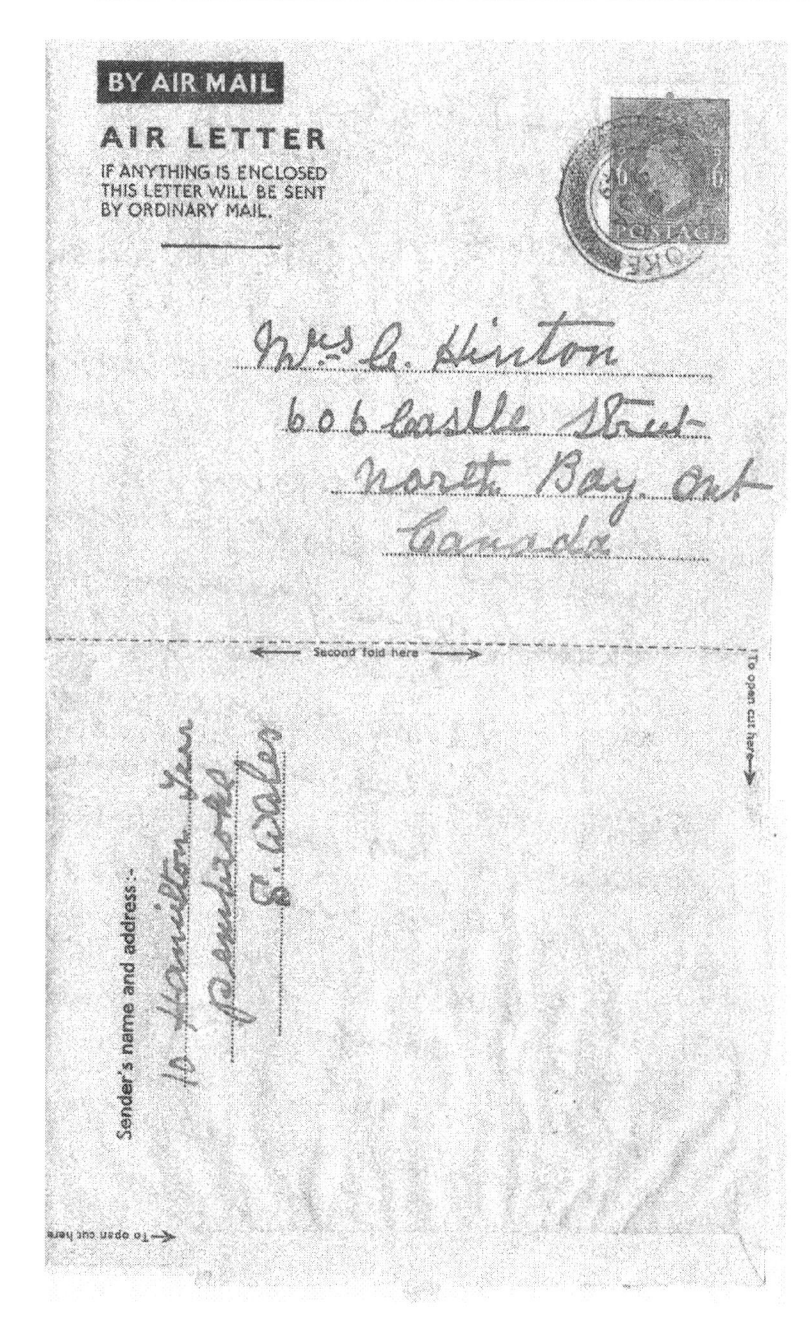

Mrs G. Hinton
606 Caslle Street
north Bay. Ont
Canada

Sender's name and address:-
10 Hamilton ten
Pembroke
S. Wales

Appendix C   **1949 January, Martha Brinn's airmail sent to 606 Cassells St North Bay**

10 Hamilton Terr
Pembroke. S. Wales

dear Dorothy
the lovely photo of baby Judith came xmas day how lovely of her she looks just the same as Cliff looked when he first went to Canada & just the age thank you for sending it to me all the friends say she is a lovely girl I am so pleased to know your mother will be with Cliff & baby while you are in Hospital Cliff will be quite a family man with 2 children, mind take care of yourself please to say I keep well

Appendix C   **1949 January, Martha Brinn's airmail sent to 606 Cassells St North Bay**

Madiline came home for Christmas she is so bright full of life she is in the Sand army. Margreat is nursing in Hospital in London Cliff will tell you about the girls. I'd loved to see baby & hear her trying to talk

I go back over the time when the 3 boys ware her age now they are all so far from me Thank you for the nice big box of choctales you are too good to me my dear I fee a shame to write to you. my eyes is realy bad it is a job to get new glasses so please excuse this badly written letter. thank Cliff for his letter he is a dear

Appendix C   **1949 January, Martha Brinn's airmail sent to 606 Cassells St North Bay**

Boy gives him a hug + for me. The weather is cold and such a lot of fog and rain. Hope dears you all spent a real happy Xmas did Father Christmas bring you all a lot of gifts will close trusting you are all well, good night. God bless you all
your loving Granny
M Brinn

+ + + + + + + + + +

Appendix C **1951 November 4, 22nd Ave, Pemberton Heights, North Vancouver BC Thomas Auld's letter pg1 to daughter Thelma at 1120 W**

Auldsville
R.R. 7 Kingston   Nov 4, 1951

Dear Thelma Alex + Ronnie

Now hang on to your hearts this may not happen again for another blue moon or until I have another spasm, in fact I did not intend to write you to night. I intended to write to Violet + we were just eating a little snack about 10.30 + Violet rang up to say that Ruth + her + the baby were coming to morrow night (it seems Bill is away for a week) so they could get away all night. So that ruled out a letter to Violet but I considered you might not take it amiss if I dropped you a line. According to Helen you must have heard I have been busy getting a house fixed for the Sudd's family. Well I started along about July 15th at the house I had a lot to do it I had let Burke put up a stair-way in it + then along in June when I was up at the reunion at Stratford + Toronto they had a falling out with Mary Margaret it wasn't Mary's fault. She was baby sitting for Jack + Isabel + Frankie + Elsie were keeping her company. Isabel had left 50 cts on the table for Mary I should say two 25 ct pieces. Well Frankie + Elsie picked up the money + told their parents that they got it for minding the children. Well you know what Helen Ois like in anything like that

(over)

Appendix C   **1951 November 4, 22nd Ave, Pemberton Heights, North Vancouver BC
Thomas Auld's letter pg2 to daughter Thelma at 1120 W**

(2)

She told them what had happened & she says you should have seen the way he carried on and he gave Frankie an awful licking and said they had better get out before they were accused of some thing else. Well of course I did'nt hear about it till I came home, and, in the meantime he had ripped up all his garden stuff packed it all in boxes & had it all ready to move. He got a house in Odessa. I think he is there yet but he was back trying to get rooms with Mrs Bertrim, in which he didn't succeed. Well he finally moved about the middle of July, and ever since then what with the potatoes and tearing the house apart I have been pretty busy. I tore out the stairway and then I took in the cement Porch on the east side & built the stairway right up the east side. I took out the dividing wall on the Porch side and put it all in the living room. I insulated all the new part & even insulated the whole of the roof. I had to put in about half a new floor upstairs & made one bedroom downstairs instead of two. Clifford had two weeks holidays and he helped me quite a lot. The result is you would hardly know it for the same house. Well I worked along at it till I had to get at my potatoes I think I got them out in two weeks time. I did not have so many this year but of course I did not put in as many

Appendix C   **1951 November 4, 22nd Ave, Pemberton Heights, North Vancouver BC
Thomas Auld's letter pg3 to daughter Thelma at 1120 W**

(3)

But they are twice the price they were last year so that helps a lot. Well I finally got the house so it was livable and about three weeks ago I started to tare down the Thomson cottage I had the Kitchen + sunparlor or the front part down & Violet happened to come down She wanted to buy the cottage & move it up just east of the barn. so I sold it to her. I have to finish taking it down I would have had it down last week but we had a snow storm Friday So I cant do anything till it clears up when Violet comes down she will likely be helping me to finish it up. She says (she) wants some place when she comes down that she can call her own, so that will be another house to build in the spring Cliff & Jody are going to build in the Spring also. So I don't think I'll be very idle next year. I am also getting a road built across the marsh on the west side of the railway. I want to put the whole of the back field in another Subdivision There are about 12 acres there and if I can sell the lots it will mean about 35 or 40 lots I had the surveyor look it over and he thought I had a good proposition of course the road across will cost one over a thousand dollars, but it seems to be the only way of making anything out of that back field

Appendix C   **1951 November 4, 22nd Ave, Pemberton Heights, North Vancouver BC
Thomas Auld's letter pg4 to daughter Thelma at 1120 W**

I suppose the girls keep you informed about the family news. Mabel was up to Grace's for a week before Dody left, Cliff has got a house in Oshawa for the winter, or perhaps until he gets his own built. I guess likely you know all that already. Well I finally lost my job at the light house they found out I was over 65 and of course that is the governments rule to retire employees, but why did'nt they fire me before they hired me I was over 64 then but of course there was a war on then and they couldn't get any one else who would take it no one in particular is taking my place they intend to run it from Prescott I'm not finding any fault. I am applying for the old age pension. I sent word to Mai Russell to try & get my birth certificate about two months ago. As I did'nt hear from them I applied to the Sun Life Ins Co for an affidavit of an Insurance I had taken out 61 year ago I got that yesterday so I'm all set now I think I have given you all my news or what have you Thank you Ronnie for writing to Graupa and when I get money enough I'll come & maybe stay longer than you want me to I wont have much to do after I get the house down I'm still building book cases I wish you were nearer so I could give you one   Dad & Graupa

I suppose you know we got in our oil furnace last year and the they told us the price so I'll have nothing to do and lots of time to do it in

Appendix C   **1951 November 4, 22nd Ave, Pemberton Heights, North Vancouver BC**
                         Thomas Auld's letter (added note) to daughter Thelma at 1120 W

> I notice where I told you about Burke building the stairway, it was not satisfactory it took up too much of the living room now the room at its widest is 16 ft and the front door now faces the south or the waterfront and it is 18 ft in length so it really looks nice

Appendix C   **1951 November 4, 22nd Ave, Pemberton Heights, North Vancouver BC**
                         Thomas Auld's letter (envelope) to daughter Thelma at 1120 W

> Mr & Mrs A. F. Burnard Jr.
> 1120 W — 22 Ave.
> Pemberton Heights
> North Vancouver
> B. C.

Postmark: Kingston, Ontario, 3 PM NOV 5 1951

Appendix C   **1957 March 1 letter Pg 1 from Edna Acton (Dodie's Kingston friend)**

March 1st. 1957
Kingston Ont.

Dodie dear,

It is very hard for me to write you this letter. I know there is very little I can say to make things easier, my heart is just aching for you. I was never so shocked in my life and I can't imagine what you must be feeling. I'm only sorry I can't be near enough to be of some help to you at this time.

It must be hard to understand why these things happen, knowing Cliff was not a careless man. I'm sure he would never want to leave you with such a responsibility. Yours is no easy task and if there is any way Joe and I can help you and the children please let us do that much for you. I know that is poor consolation at this time but we mean it from the bottom of our hearts my poor Dodie. Many people have asked about you and I'm sure they all send you deepest sympathy.

Please let us know what your intentions are and maybe we can help

264

Appendix C   **1957 March 1 letter Pg 2 from Edna Acton (Dodie's Kingston friend)**

May the Lord rest his soul and help you now when you need it so badly. Try and think of all the good things you two had and I'm sure you will have some awfully good memories. They are a far cry from what you had together, but you sure had a fine man. Some people never have one like him in all their lives. God bless him.

Please offer my sympathy to Cliff's mother, I'm sure like yourself her heart is heavy with sorrow.

Please write to us when you feel you can. Your children must be very sad, they have indeed suffered a loss early in their lives. They have a wonderful mother. Thank God.

God bless you Dodie and remember we are here to help all we can. Love and Our sincerest sympathy
Edna, Joe & family.

Appendix C   **1957 March 1 note from Helen Lush (Phyllis Wootton's stepdaughter)**

— Saturday — March 2/57

Dear Dorothy:-

My heart goes out to you today — How well I know what you are going through. I understand.

I didn't buy flowers — but wish you to use the enclosed for the children.

Love,
Helen Lush

Appendix C **1957 March 3 letter Pg 1 from Rose Mills (Daughter of Phyllis's friend)**

Box 262,
Fergus, Ont.,
Sunday, Mar 3

Dear Mrs. Hinton :—

Having known Cliff from the time he was 18 months old until young manhood, it was a great shock and sorrow to learn of his tragic accident.

It is so difficult to offer sympathy when your whole world is shattered,

Appendix C **1957 March 3 letter Pg 2 from Rose Mills (Daughter of Phyllis's friend)**

2.

but I do urge you to turn to Phyllis for comfort. She has suffered and lost so much. She has lost two sons — both suddenly, and the boys' father in a long, slow agony. Surely she will be able to help you from her wide experience and great faith.

You may recall she planned to visit us the last time she was in Preston, but your kiddies developed a contagious disease, so she thought it best not to come.

If she is in Preston now, I do hope she will come here

Appendix C **1957 March 3 letter Pg 3 from Rose Mills (Daughter of Phyllis's friend)**

3.

for a few days before returning home. We may be able to make some arrangement regarding transportation.

I understand you have 3 small children. They will wring your heart strings just now, but having to do the ordinary, everyday chores for them will help you hold on to your sanity, and in time, they will be a great comfort to you.

We are fortunate enough to have 3 girls — Linda, age 12, Maurine, age 7, Elizabeth, age 4.

I am writing to Phyllis, in care of yourself, in the

Appendix C   **1957 March 3 letter Pg 4 from Rose Mills (Daughter of Phyllis's friend)**

4.

hope she is staying with you for a while. If this is not so, would you be kind enough to send her letter on to her?

I would very much like to hear from you when you feel able to write.

As a tangible expression of my sympathy, you will find $5.00 enclosed. Use it in whatever way you think best.

Yours sincerely,

Rose (Slade) Mills

Appendix C   **1957 March 3 letter Pg 1 from Dodie's sister Thelma Burnard**

1120 W. 22nd St.,
North Vancouver, B.C.,
Mar. 3, 1957.

Darling Dodie,-

It is truly dreadful to be so far away at a time like this, but believe me dear, we have been right there beside you, both in our thoughts and our prayers.

You may remember when mother was so ill, she said that "life is just a test," and I can't help but feel that Cliff has passed his test somewhat sooner than most of us, for he was a perfect husband and daddy!

He has given you many glorious memories, and three darling little girls, who will

Appendix C   **1957 March 3 letter Pg 2 from Dodie's sister Thelma Burnard**

be great blessings to you. He has also given you a wonderful mother, who will be such a comfort to you, as, I'm sure, you will be to her. I was hoping that one of the girls might find time to drop us a note, and when you feel up to it, Dodie, we'd love to hear from you.

If there is anything at all that you would like us to do, you know you have only to ask it.

Will you give our love to Mrs. Wootton and tell her we have been thinking of her.

And now Darling, all our love to you and the girls and God Bless you all.

Al, Ron and Jim.

Appendix C   **1957 March 5 letter from Joan North, Calgary Alberta**

3419 - 31 St. S.W.
Calgary Alberta
March 1957

Dear Mrs. Hinton,

It was a great shock to us to learn of Cliff's passing and in such a very tragic manner. You have our deepest sympathy.

During Cliff's visit to Calgary last year, he was at our home, and one evening we went downtown for dinner and spent a long time talking. He told us about you and the children. You are all going to miss him terribly.

I hope you have relatives or close friends with you to help ease your sorrow. We are thinking of you.

Sincerely,

Joan North

Appendix C **1957 March 5 letter from Morris Wootton, (Phyllis's stepson)**

Tampa Florida
March 5/57

Dear Morily,

Our deepest sympathy goes out to you in this time of tragic loss. It is so hard to understand!

We have been so shocked since John gave us the news and we too have felt a keen sense of loss in Clifford's passing.

I'm sure that the comfort and sympathy and companionship of loving friends will be of great help to you at this time. We feel that your family needs you and the ever-presence of the Great Healer will all give you strength to carry on.

Love Morris & Grace.

Appendix C **1957 March letter Pg 1 from Pat Reid and family (Cliff's friend Alex Reid)**

634 Grierson St
Oshawa
Ontario

Dearest Dodie, Judie Susan, Deborough
I do hope this letter finds you all well. I wanted to write to you sooner but anything I could have said couldn't have helped such as a time like this, as you say there are so many things we do not understand and until something as Tragic as this happens none of us know how we could react to it. Cliff was so well liked & respected by his friends, etc & loved by those who were close to him. You, Mrs Woaten, the children have been very close in our thoughts & Prayers the Past weeks. I do hope it won't be to long before we see you all again & that you will

Appendix C   **1957 March letter Pg 2 from Pat Reid and family (Cliff's friend Alex Reid)**

be feeling better. Things want be the same for you Dodie, because we cannot live in the Past. You've got something no one can take away from you & that's the Happy Years you & Cliff had together. Now you have Yourself & your Health to think of so that you can continue to be the Best Mother in the World to 3 of the earliest well behaved little girls that you've been blessed with a very big challenge to any young woman. but we all know with out a doubt that you will make it.

I've never had to write a letter like this before Dodie I hope I've put the right things down I've just said what I feel & I do hope you will understand me.

I must go now & will write again soon
   All our Love
    Pat & Family

Appendix D
House Plans

24 Norway Ave, Toronto, Ontario, Canada   279
     Kate and Walter Hoad family, 1917-1962

The Auld Farm, Portsmouth, Kingston, Ontario, Canada   280
     Mary and Thomas Auld family, 1917-2000

28 Glengrove Ave, Toronto< Ontario, Canada   282
     Violet and Burwell Stephens, 1940-1963

Church St W, Colborne, Ontario, Canada   283
     Phyllis and Rev Frank Wootton, 1948-1970

33 Colborne St E, Oshawa, Ontario, Canada   284
     Dodie and Cliff Hinton family, 1951-1953

124 Laurel St, Preston, Ontario, Canada   286
     Dodie and Cliff Hinton family, 1953-1957

183 Blake St, Cobourg, Ontario, Canada   288
     Grace and Jack McNab family, 1920-2009

Author's note: During the winter of 2023 I was inspired to draw these house plans in remembrance of the spaces where I lived or visited with my father. I think my dad would have loved them!

Appendix D   **24 Norway Ave., Toronto**

This is the floor plan drawn as I remember it when there as a child in the late 1950s. Walter and Kate Hoad had owned the house since about 1916. It was the home where Cliff's family first lived when they emigrated to Canada. There were probably 3 bedrooms on the second floor. A kitchen plus bathroom addition was added at the rear of the first floor. After WWII Walter and Kate Hoad lived in rooms on the ground floor and rented out a second floor flat. The house was on a corner lot with a small yard, driveway and garage at the rear. *See* **Pg 8, 21, 27, 76**.

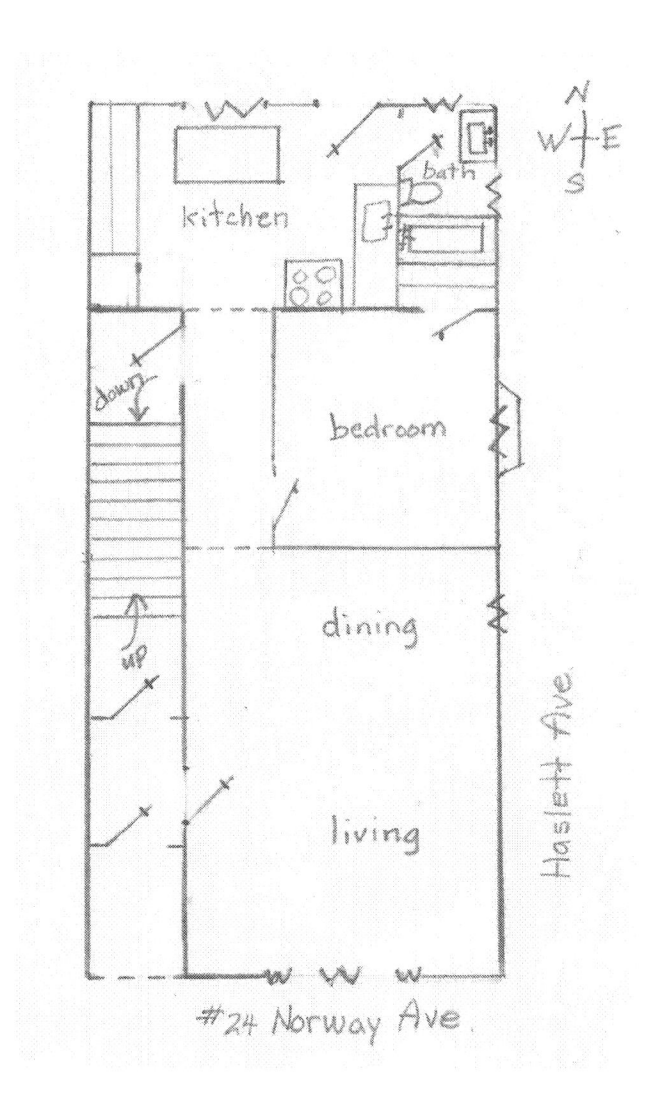

Appendix D   **The Auld Farm**

This page is from **Auld Forsythe Family History**, created for my cousin Mary Margaret in 2002 by her late husband Gord Smithson. In 1947 Grandpa Auld built a house for Mary Laturney's family across the laneway from the Auld residence. In 1951 he removed summer cottages at Front Road and remodelled the converted Icehouse for Isobel Sudds' family. See **Pg 105, 129, 141,145,155, 161, 176.**

The Auld Homestead In Its Early Years

Born of Scotch ancestors, Thomas Forrest Auld settled with his wife, the former Mary Moncur, about 1917 on a small acreage on the north side of Front Road *(renamed about 1952 as King Street West)* in Kingston Township, opposite the area known as Elevator Bay.

The 8.2 acre property, *(severed from the Graham Family's farm, original owners of Lot 14),* provided a homestead environment for the Aulds to raise a family of ten children.

Thomas Auld worked the land, as well as the fields of adjoining landowners such as the Graham family who owned the adjacent property to the east. In addition to growing vegetables, Thomas Auld maintained a small herd of milking cows enabling him to establish a small dairy business known as the Auld Dairy. The sale of bottled milk in the nearby community provided additional income to meet the financial requirements of raising a growing family.

When his wife Mary died on Mar 12 1939, the wake was held at their King Street West residence, with interment being held at the Cataraqui Cemetery, Cataraqui, Ont.

A portion of the Auld property abutted the Little Cataraqui River, in the area near the old Front Road and it was here that a small community of residential and cottage structures were erected in the 1940's(?) Although the name *Auld Subdivision* was bestowed upon the development project, Thomas Auld did not really want his name associated with it at the time.

Property Illustration, first buildings – not to scale   GDS 01-14-2002

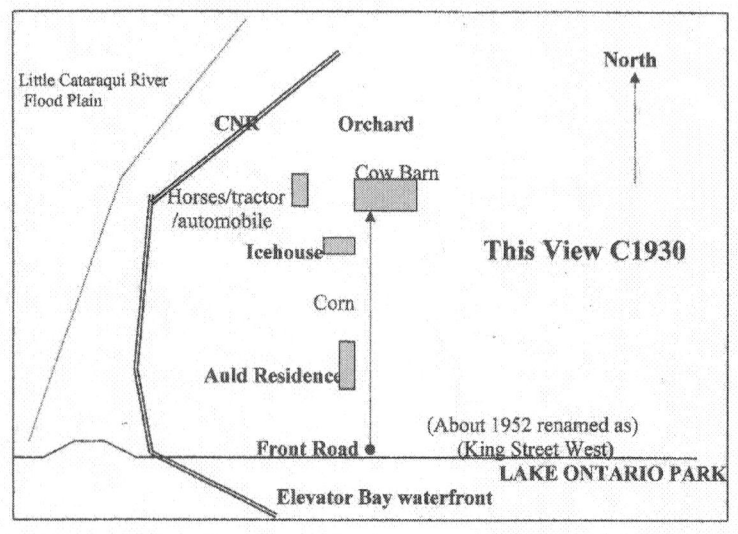

[Map showing: Little Cataraqui River Flood Plain, CNR, Orchard, Cow Barn, Horses/tractor/automobile, Icehouse, Corn, Auld Residence, Front Road (About 1952 renamed as King Street West), Elevator Bay waterfront, Lake Ontario Park. This View C1930. North arrow.]

Appendix D   **The Auld Farmhouse, Portsmouth, Kingston**

This is a floor plan drawn as I remember it when I often visited there in the 1950s and 60s. Mary and Thomas Auld had owned the "Rose cottage" farm property since 1917 when they moved there with their 9 children. Their 10th child, my mother Dorothy, was born in 1919 and was living there in 1946 when she met my father Clifford Hinton. *See **Pg 96***. I spent many summer weeks at the Auld Farm.

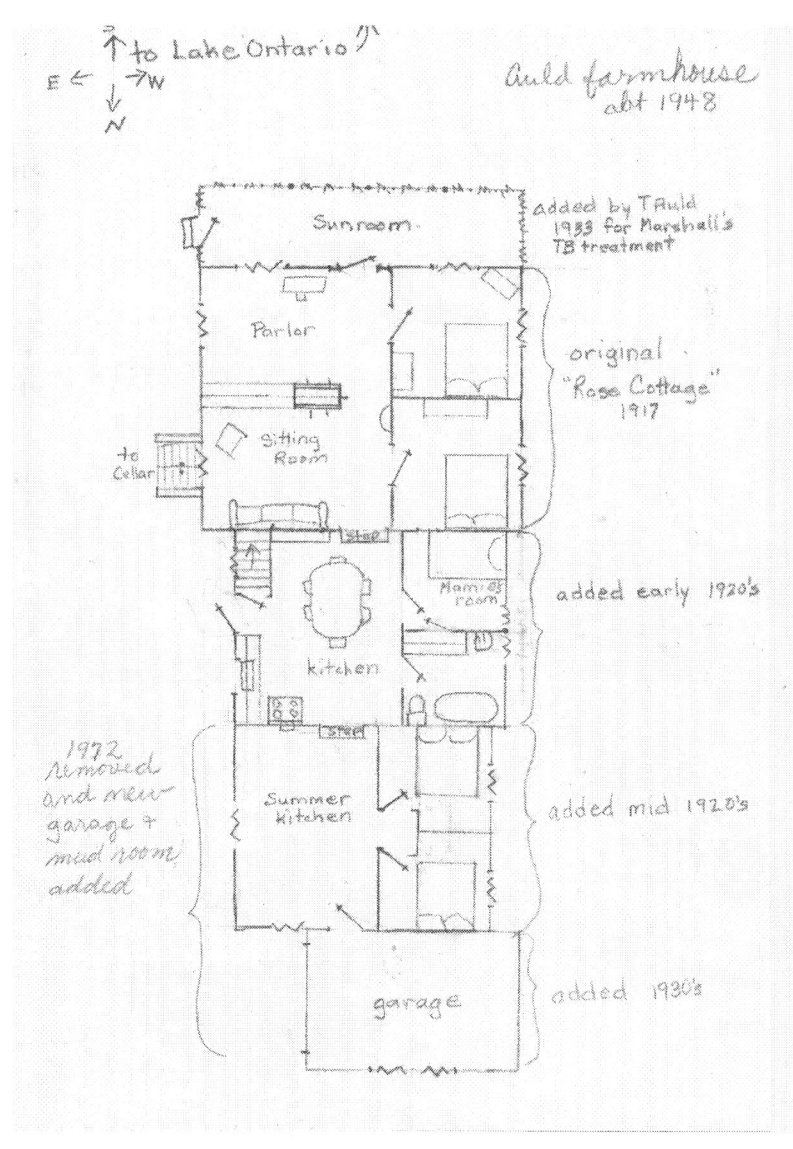

Appendix D   **28 Glengrove Ave., Toronto**

This is the floor plan drawn as I remember it when I visited there as a child in the 1950s. Burwell and Vi Stephens owned the 3-story house since the mid 1930s when they moved there with their son Bill and daughter Jean. Over the years they had various roomers including Betty Auld, Bill Dennison, and Jean's family in second floor rooms, as well as Bill's family in the third floor flat, not shown in the drawing. During the 1940s and 1950s we often visited. I remember sleeping in the front guest room and seeing lights from passing cars shine across the walls and ceiling. See *Pg 110, 117, 121, 139.*

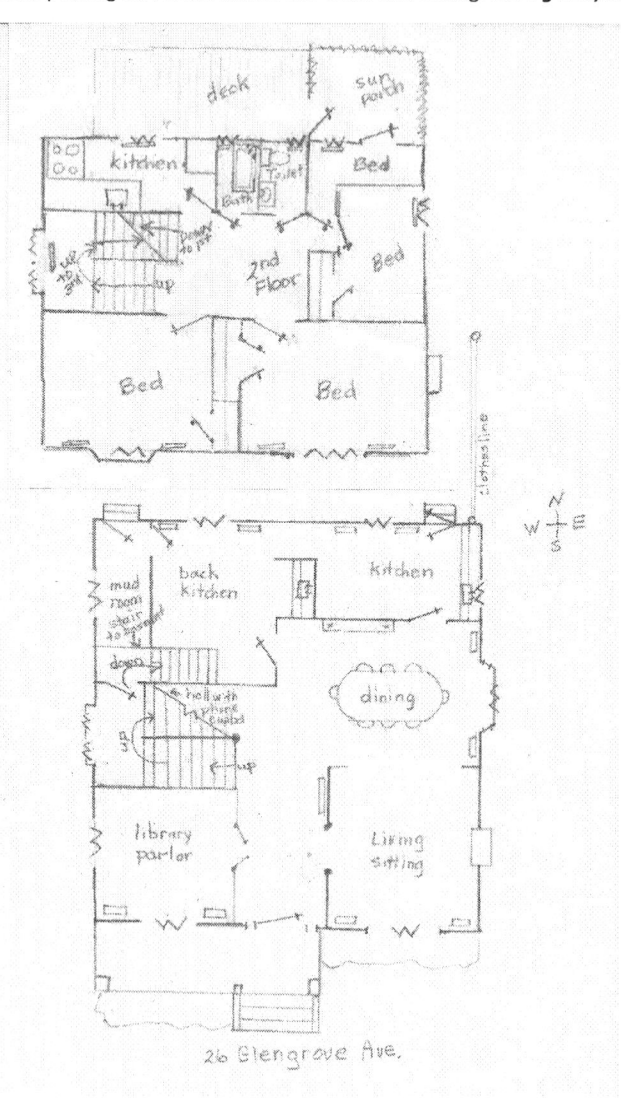

282

Appendix D   **Church St W, Colborne, the Wootton Home**

This is the floor plan drawn as I remember it when I visited there in the 1950s and 1960s. After Cliff's widowed mother Phyllis Hinton and Reverend Frank Wootton were married on 11 June 1948, they moved into this Church Street home. After Frank died 29 February 1952 Phyllis continued to live in the little two-bedroom cottage until about 1970 when she moved into Maple Court apartments for seniors in Colborne. *See **Pg 128, 168, 170, 175, 178.***

When I was about age 13, I took the bus to Colborne to stay with Grandma for a few days. I remember classical music on her radio and at night I could hear the quarter hour chiming of her clock in the hallway by the bathroom. We made 'fiddle diddles' in her kitchen, and I slept in her little spare bedroom. I remember her telling me that Rev Frank Wootton had written his sermons at his desk which I inherited after Phyllis died 25 October 1974. I also inherited her cedar chest, her pearl necklace, and a 'milliner' figurine which grandma said was a gift from her mother to celebrate the completion of her millinery apprenticeship. *See **Pg 8**.*

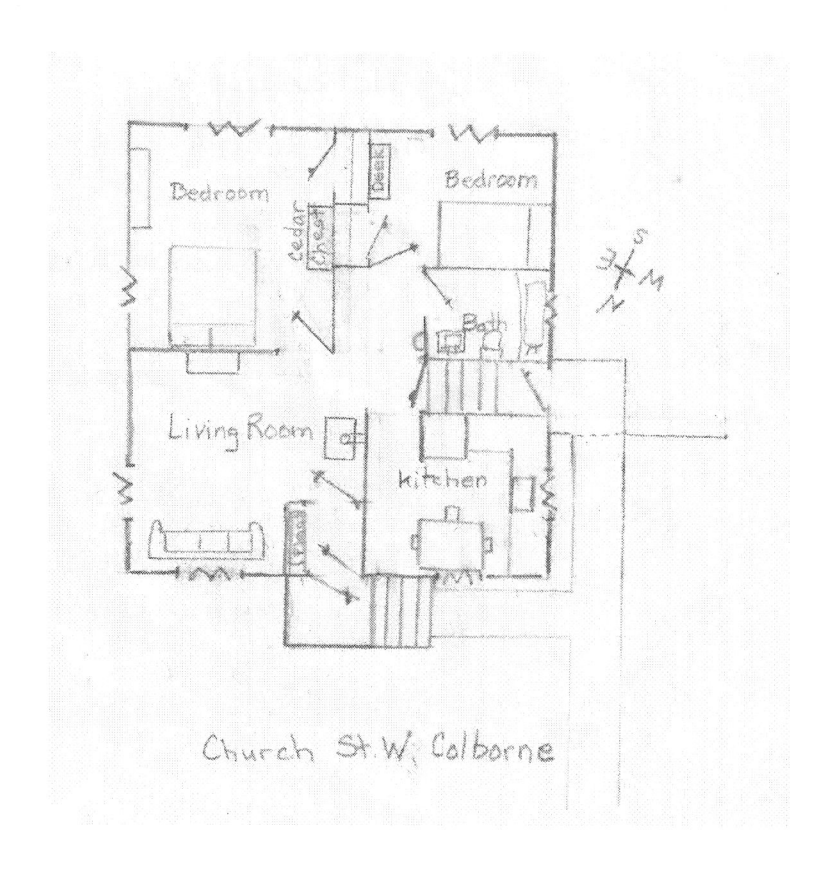

Appendix D   **338 Colborne St E, Oshawa**

This is the floor plan drawn as I remember it when we lived in this second floor flat from 1951 to 1953. My youngest sister Deborah Jane was born in Oshawa on 28 September 1952. She slept in a cot in Mom and Dad's bedroom. My sister Susan and I slept in the little bedroom over the stairwell. I went to afternoon kindergarten at Ritson Rd PS and brought home measles and mumps infections. I remember Mom keeping the blinds down in our little bedroom while we recuperated. Susan remembers our father putting her in the bathtub with her socks on. We both remember 'helping' mom in the kitchen. See **Pg 162-163.**

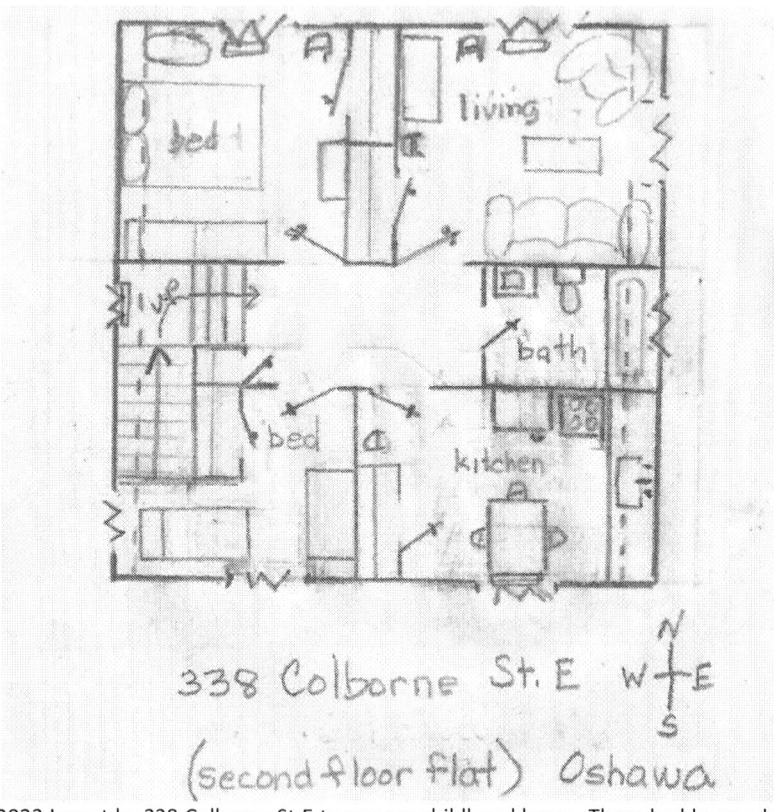

338 Colborne St. E
(second floor flat) Oshawa

In May of 2023 I went by 338 Colborne St E to see my childhood home. There had been a housefire that destroyed a first-floor addition at the back of the house. Renovations were underway for the first and second floor as well as a new addition at the rear. I was able to go inside to take some photos of the structure to inform my memory of the layout of the rooms. I'm including some of those photos on the next page for readers who might be interested.

Appendix D   **2023 Photos I Took at 338 Colborne St E., Oshawa**

The house was being renovated after a fire. The stairway to the second floor is as it was in 1952. Susan and Judy slept in a small bedroom over the front hall. It can be seen with the boarded window below left. Beyond that is the kitchen with a window on the same wall. The gambrel roof gave sloped walls on the east and west sides of the second story.

To left are photos of the upper hall directly into the bathroom with a boarded-up window over the tub and the kitchen with a sunny window at right. Left bottom photo is the upper hall with the larger bedroom to front left and the living room beyond to the left of the bathroom.

285

Appendix D   **124 Laurel St., Preston Ontario**

This is the floor plan drawn as I remember it when we lived in this house from 1953 to 1957. This was the first purchased house for Cliff and Dodie after their move from rentals in Toronto, North Bay and Oshawa. It had hardwood floors which needed waxing and polishing. I remember riding on the floor polisher, as extra weight, while my dad pushed it back and forth along the hardwood floors. The 3 Hinton sisters shared a bedroom on the second floor and the one bathroom was on the first floor. There was an extra storage closet in the upper hallway which is not shown in the drawing. Mom also had an extra chest there, where she stored her sewing projects. See **Pg 167-169, 171-175, 181-183**.

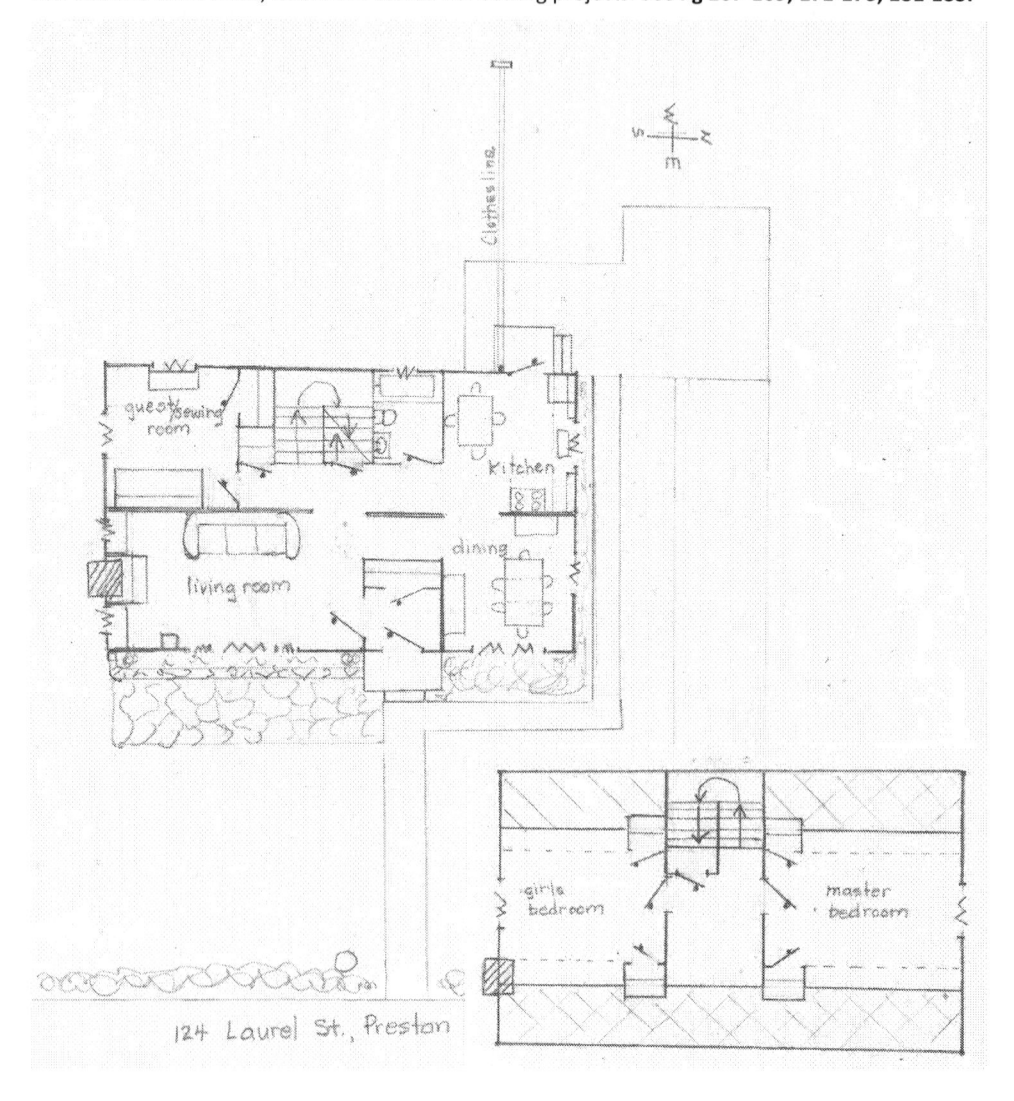

Appendix D   **2004 Photos Taken at 124 Laurel St., Preston Ontario**

These photos were taken in 2004 at 124 Laurel St in Cambridge Ontario (formerly Preston). My sister Susan and I think they were taken by Deborah when she took our mother Dodie and Aunt Betty to their great niece's Wedding in Kitchener. Heather Senior and Ben Samuel were married 7 August 2004, just 4 months before our mother died. Some time after we left 124 Laurel St in 1957, new owners had added the dormer at the front to expand the second story and a garage was built on the concrete pad.

Appendix D   **183 Blake St., Cobourg Ontario: the McNab home**

This is the floor plan drawn as I remember it when I visited my Aunt Grace and Uncle Jack McNab at their two-story house in Cobourg. Over the years, many family photos were taken in their beautiful gardens which could be enjoyed from the sunroom addition built to replace the storage shed after Uncle Jack died in 1964. After cousin Jean Grace McNab died in 1978, at age 53, her in-house hair salon was converted to a bathroom and Aunt Grace moved from her second-floor bedroom to the sunroom. *See **Pg 127.***

Cousin Agnes owned a cottage at Grafton Beach where she lived when home from her teaching position at Peterborough.

After retirement, Agnes moved to Grafton and then back to 183 Blake St in Cobourg to care for her aging mother Grace, who died in 1998 at age 99. Agnes died in 2009 at age 89.

Comparison with old photos and with similar houses on Blake St reveals that the front hall was originally an external front porch. There were 3 small bedrooms on a second floor over the front section of the house, accessed by a very narrow winding stairway.

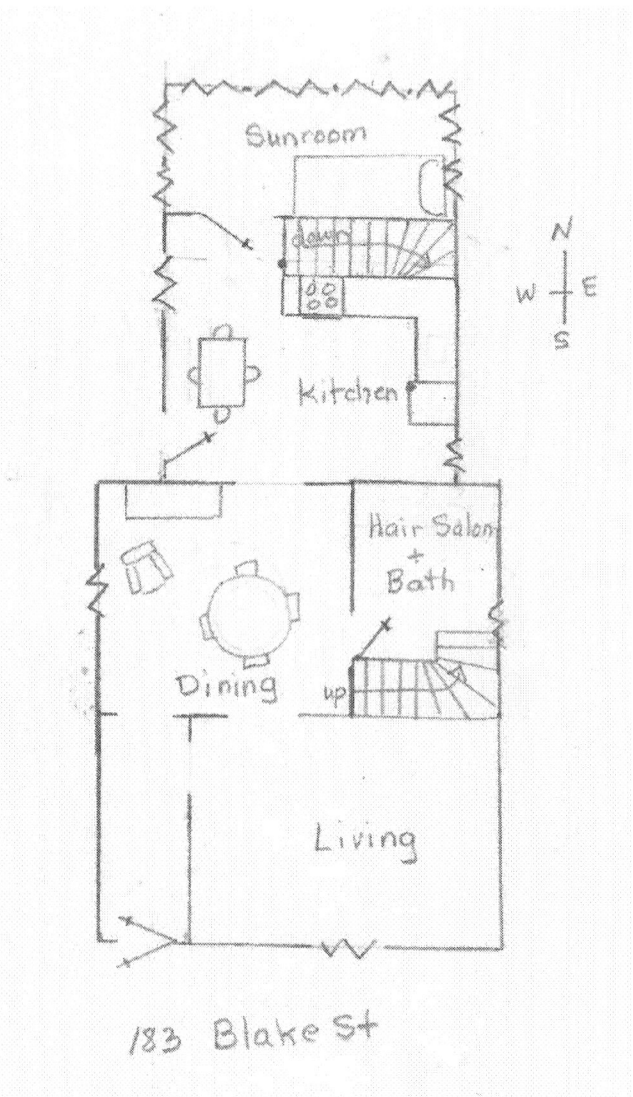

Appendix E
Ancestry Summary Reports

Clifford's Mother: Phyllis Hoad 1887-1974	291
Clifford's Father: Herbert Hugh Melville Hinton 1891-1939	294
Clifford Ley Herbert Hinton 1921-1957	296
Clifford's Daughter: Judith's Family	298
Clifford's Daughter: Susan's Family	299
Clifford's Daughter: Deborah's Family	300

Author's note: These are reports printed from the family tree which I have created in Ancestry. They are not complete nor completely accurate as there may be pieces of information yet to be discovered and family yet to be added.

Phyllis Hoad
1887-1974

BIRTH 13 MAR 1887 • St. Daniel's Hill, Pembroke, Wales
DEATH 25 OCT 1974 • Colborne, Northumberland, Ontario, Canada
paternal grandmother

Facts

Name
Phyllis Hoad

Name *(Alternate)*
Phyllis Davies

Gender
♀ Female

Age 0 — **Birth**
13 Mar 1887 • St. Daniel's Hill, Pembroke, Wales
Phyllis was born to Martha Davies, domestic servant, on 13 March 1887 at St Daniels Hill near Orange Gardens, Pembroke Wales. Her father's name was not listed. It is confidently decided by DNA cousin matches that her biological father was Walter John Hoad

Residence
3 Sep 1887 • East Molesley Surrey England
marriage of parents Martha Davies and Walter John Hoad

Age 4 — **Residence**
1891 • East Molesey, Surrey, England
Age: 4; Relation to Head of House: Daughter

Age 14 — **Residence**
1901 • Pembroke St Mary, Pembrokeshire, Wales
Relationship: Niece of John Davies 15 Mansel St., Orange Gardens, Pembroke

Age 24 — **Residence**
02 Apr 1911 • 6 Clifton Vale, Bristol, Gloucestershire, England
Marital Status: Single; Relation to Head of House: Visitor, employed as a Milliner, Phyllis lived with the Morris family.

Family

Parents

Walter John Hoad
1869–1896

Martha Davies
1860–1950

Siblings

Walter Alexander Hoad
1888–1962

Frederick Colling Hoad
1889–1944

Grace Hoad
1892–1903

Dorothy Mabel Hoad
1894–1896

Spouse and children

Herbert Hugh Melville Hinton
1891–1939

Douglas Melville Hinton
1918–2000

Hugh Frederick Hinton
1919–1944

Clifford Ley Herbert Hinton
1921–1957

Spouse

Frank Morrison (Morris) Wootton
1872–1952

Phyllis Hoad 1887-1974

Age 26 — Residence
1913 • Bristol, England
98 Victoria St., Bristol, England, HM Veale & Co Artists in photography Christmas wishes

Age 30 — Marriage
April 28 1917 • Wesleyan Chapel, Wesley Square, Pembroke, Pembrokeshire (2 media)
Herbert, Sergeant, Army Instructor, 4th Welsh Regiment, son of George Hinton (deceased); Phyllis, milliner, daughter of John Hoad (deceased); witnessed by John Brinn (step brother) and Frederick Colling Hoad (brother)

Herbert Hugh Melville Hinton
(1891-1939)

Age 31 — Residence
Aft. 19 May 1918 • Pembroke
Registration of 19 May 1918 birth of Douglas Melville Hinton at Pembroke Pembrokeshire Wales

Age 31 — Residence
30 Sep 1918 • 2 Hamilton Terrace, St Mary's Parish, Pembrokeshire, Wales
County of Pembroke address noted on absent voters list for husband Herbert Hugh Melville Hinton Sgt 4th Welsh #265806

Age 32 — Residence
Sep 1919 • 88 Grove Road Glamorgan, Wales
Clydach Polling District E. Clydach Ward

Age 32 — Residence
Aft. 14 Dec 1919 • Pontardawe, Glamorganshire, Wales registration after Dec birth of Hugh Frederick Hinton

Age 33 — Residence
Abt. May 1920 • 40 Kelvin Road Glamorgan Wales
Clydach Polling District E. Clydach Ward

Age 33 — Residence
Abt. Oct 1920 • 40 Kelvin Road Glamorgan, Wales
Clydach Polling District E. Clydach Ward

Age 33 — Residence
Aft. 11 Mar 1921 • Glamorgan, Wales
Registration of 11 March 1921 birth of Clifford Ley Herbert Hinton at Pontardawe Glamorganshire

Age 34 — Census
25 Apr 1921 • Clydach Parish, Glamorgan, Wales (2 media)
April 25th at 40 Kelvin Road, Clydach on Tawe, Glamorgan

Age 34 — Residence
Apr 1921 • 40 Kelvin Road Glamorgan, Wales
Clydach Polling District E. Parish of Rhyndwyclydach- Clydach Ward

Age 34 — Residence
Abt. May 1921 • 40 Kelvin Road Glamorgan, Wales
Clydach Polling District E. Parish of Rhyndwyclydach- Clydach Ward

Age 34 — Residence
Oct 1921 • 40 Kelvin Road Glamorgan Wales
Clydach Polling District E. Parish of Rhyndwyclydach- Clydach Ward

Age 35 — Residence
Mar 1922 • 40 Kelvin Road Glamorgan Wales
Clydach Polling District E. Parish of Rhyndwyclydach- Clydach Ward; the Hinton family may have already moved to Pembroke in preparation for their move to Canada; they applied in about February at Swansea when Clifford was 11 months old

Age 35 — Residence
Apr 1922 • 2 Hamilton Terrace, Pembroke, South Wales
Phyllis and her 3 sons are living with mother Martha and step father John Brinn while husband Melville Hinton has gone to Canada.

Age 35 — Departure
26 Jul 1922 • Swansea, Glamorgan, Wales

Age 35 — Departure
28 Jul 1922 • Liverpool, England

Age 35 — Arrival
4 Aug 1922 • Quebec, Canada
Age: 33

Age 44 — Residence
1931 • East Whitby, Ontario, Canada
Phyllis was married to Melville Hinton with children Douglas, Hugh and Clifford, living at 24 Jones Ave

Age 47 — Arrival
29 Jul 1934 • London, England
Phyllis took the train from Oshawa to Montreal and travelled by ship to London England

Age 47 — Departure
Oct 1934 • Liverpool, England

Phyllis Hoad 1887-1974

Age 56 — Address
1943 • Oshawa, Durham, Ontario, Canada
Edwards Apts, Quebec St., Oshawa (as noted on travel document for Douglas M Hinton, 1943 Sept 28)

Age 58 — Residence
14 may 1945 • 17 Quebec St., Oshawa Ont.
noted on son Douglas' passenger record

Age 59 — Arrival
14 Sep 1946 • Plymouth, England
Phyllis travelled by ship M.S. John Ericsson from New York to Plymouth to visit her mother Martha Brinn at 10 Hamilton Terrace, Pembroke, Wales

Age 60 — Departure
20 Oct 1947 • England
After visiting for over a year with family and friends in England and Wales, on October 20, 1947, Phyllis travelled on the SS Aquitania from Southampton, England to Halifax, Nova Scotia to go back to her home and family in Canada.

Age 61 — Marriage
11 Jun 1948 • Oshawa, Durham, Ontario, Canada

Frank Morrison (Morris) Wootton
(1872-1952)

Age 76 — Residence
1963 • Northumberland, Ontario, Canada
Marital Status: Widow Living on Church St in Colborne Ontario

Age 85 — Residence
1972 • Prince Edward; Hastings, Ontario, Canada
Marital Status: Widow, In 1970 Phyllis moved to Maple Court Apartments for Seniors in Colborne.

Age 87 — Death
25 Oct 1974 • Colborne, Northumberland, Ontario, Canada

Burial
Whitby, Durham Regional Municipality, Ontario, Canada
interment at Mount Lawn Cemetery, Whitby

⇘|ancestry

Herbert Hugh Melville Hinton
1891–1939
BIRTH 25 JUN 1891 • Peckham, London, England
DEATH 23 AUG 1939 • Oshawa, Ontario, Canada
paternal grandfather

Facts

Name
Herbert Hugh Melville Hinton

Name *(Alternate)*
Herbert Hugh Melville Stray

Gender
♂ Male

Age 0 — **Birth**
25 Jun 1891 • Peckham, London, England
Index of birth at Camberwell, London, England; name Herbert Hugh M Stray

Age 10 — **Residence**
1901 • St Pancras, London, England
Age: 8; Relation to Head of House: Son of Albert George Hinton employed as a cabman groom and living with his employer, cabman henry Brown. (error on census record, Melville should be 9 and Frederick 8)

Age 18 — **Military**
25 Feb 1910 • Dartmouth, Devon, England

Age 19 — **Residence**
02 Apr 1911 • Dartmouth, Devon, England
Age: 20; Marital Status: Single; Relation to Head of House: Ward room Officer To Steward

Age 23 — **Military**
1914–1920 • Scoveston, Pembrokeshire, Wales
4th Welsh Regiment during WWI

Family

Adopted father
Albert George Hinton
1872–1904

Biological mother
Edith Maude Murray
1871–1920

Additional parent relationships
Biological
Benjamin Charles Herbert Stray
1868–1908

Siblings
Frederick Hinton
1892–

Half siblings
George Percival Stray
1906–

Spouse and children
Phyllis Hoad
1887–1974

Douglas Melville Hinton
1918–2000

Hugh Frederick Hinton
1919–1944

Clifford Ley Herbert Hinton
1921–1957

Herbert Hugh Melville Hinton 1891-1939

Age 25 — Marriage
April 28 1917 • Wesleyan Chapel, Wesley Square, Pembroke, Pembrokeshire
Herbert, Sergeant, Army Instructor, 4th Welsh Regiment, son of George Hinton (deceased); Phyllis, milliner, daughter of John Hoad (deceased); witnessed by John Brinn (step brother) and Frederick Colling Hoad (brother)

Phyllis Hoad
(1887-1974)

Age 48 — Death
23 Aug 1939 • Oshawa, Ontario, Canada (2 media)
Melville died at home after being ill with cancer for over a year. his funeral was held at Northminster United Church officiated by Rev F Wootton. He was buried at Mount Lawn Cemetery in Whitby.

Age 27 — Residence
1918 • 2 Hamilton Terrace, St Mary's Parish, Pembrokeshire, Wales

Age 28 — Residence
Sep 1919 • 88 Grove Road Glamorgan, Wales

Age 28 — Military
1919 • England, Wales, Scotland, Ireland
record of military recognitions and medals

Age 29 — Residence
1920 • Clydach, Glamorgan, Wales
1920 spring and autumn records have Melville and Phyllis living at 40 Kelvin Rd while Melville works as an engine fitter at the Mond Nickel Works

Age 29 — Census
25 Apr 1921 • Clydach Parish, Glamorgan, Wales (2 media)
April 25th at 40 Kelvin Road, Clydach on Tawe, Glamorgan

Age 29 — Residence
Apr 1921 • Glamorgan, Wales
40 Kelvin Rd, Clydach

Age 30 — Departure
1 Apr 1922
Age: 30 Melville departed from Swansea to Liverpool across the Atlantic to Saint John New Brunswick.

Age 30 — Arrival
9 Apr 1922 • Saint John, New Brunswick, Canada
Age: 30, Melville took the CPR train from Saint John to Toronto to stay with his brother in law's family at 24 Norway Ave.

Age 40 — Residence
1931 • East Whitby, Ontario, Canada
Melville was head of household, married to Phyllis with sons Douglas, Hugh and Clifford. He was living at 24 Jones Ave, a 6 room single brick house. Melville worked as a line man at GM currently laid off and unemployed for 26 weeks.

⊰|ancestry

Clifford Ley Herbert Hinton
1921–1957

BIRTH 11 MAR 1921 • Clydach, Pontardawe, Glamorganshire, Wales
DEATH 27 FEB 1957 • Windsor, Essex, Ontario, Canada
father

Facts

Name
Clifford Ley Herbert Hinton

Gender
♂ Male

Age 0 — Birth
11 Mar 1921 • Clydach, Pontardawe, Glamorganshire, Wales
Clifford was born at 40 Kelvin Rd, Clydach on Tawe River, just south of Pontardawe. This area is 10 km north of Swansea, Wales and at the west area of the ancient county of Glamorganshire.

Age 1 — Departure
28 Jul 1922 • England
Clifford age 1, departed from Swansea to Liverpool and across the Atlantic to Quebec City and to Montreal Quebec with his mother Phyllis and brothers Douglas 4 and Hugh 2.

Age 1 — Arrival
Aug 1922 • Quebec, Canada
Age: 11 Months when the travel was arranged. Clifford would be 18 months old when he arrived at Montreal with his mother Phyllis and his brothers Douglas and Hugh. They took the CPR train from Montreal to join their father Melville at Toronto.

Age 2 — Residence
1923 • Toronto, Ontario, Canada
24 Norway Ave.; Clifford lived with his parents and brothers Doug 5 and Hugh 3 at his Uncle Walter Hoad's home with his Aunt Kate and cousins Roy 8 and Jack 1. the Hinton family soon moved to 18 Ripon Rd Toronto.

Family

Parents

Herbert Hugh Melville Hinton
1891–1939

Phyllis Hoad
1887–1974

Siblings

Douglas Melville Hinton
1918–2000

Hugh Frederick Hinton
1919–1944

Spouse and children

Dorothy Marguerite Auld
1919–2004

Judith Anne Hinton
1947–

Susan Elizabeth Hinton
1949–

Deborah Jane Hinton
1952–

Clifford Ley Herbert Hinton 1921-1957

Age 7 — Residence
1928 • Oshawa, Ontario, Canada
24 Jones Ave; Clifford's father Herbert H M worked as mechanic at General Motors

Age 10 — Residence
1931 • East Whitby, Ontario, Canada
Marital Status: Single; Relation to Head: Son

Age 16 — Residence
1937 • Oshawa, Ontario, Canada
101 Arlington Ave.; Cliff moved here with his family when his father was diagnosed with Cancer, Cliff left school to work as a clerk at General Motors.

Age 17 — Residence
1938 • Oshawa, Ontario, Canada
105 Arlington Ave.; for unknown reason Cliff's family moved from 101 to 105 Arlington Ave.

Age 21 — Military
20 Mar 1942 • Toronto, Ontario, Canada
Cliff applied for enlistment in the army; was appointed to serve as a private B-9203 in the No. 2 detachment of the RCOC/CA at Toronto until April 22, with No. 3 at Kingston until June 16, with No 2 at Camp Borden until June 16, 1943 when sent to UK

Age 24 — Military
10 Jan 1946 • Toronto, Ontario, Canada
Discharge order #1029 from service since enlisting 20 March 1942, B-9203 Private Royal Canadian Ordnance Corps. served United Kingdom, Continental Europe and Central Mediterranean Area

Age 25 — Marriage
10 Sep 1946 • Oshawa, Ontario, Canada
witnesses were Dorothy's sister Betty Auld and Cliff's friend Alex Reid of Oshawa

Dorothy Marguerite Auld
(1919–2004)

Age 28 — Address
1949 • North Bay, Ontario, Canada
606 Cassells St., Clifford and Dorothy lived here with daughters Judith 2 and infant Susan born 7 February

Age 30 — Address
1951 • Oshawa, Ontario, Canada
634 Grierson Ave, Clifford works as a regional sales manager for GM products. Clifford and Dorothy moved here from North Bay with their daughters Judith 4 and Susan 2.

Age 31 — Address
1952 • Oshawa, Ontario, Canada
338 Colborne St E upper 2 bed apartment with wife Dorothy and daughters Judith, Susan and infant Deborah born 28 September Clifford is a sales manager at General Motors

Age 32 — Address
1953 • Preston, Ontario, Canada
124 Laurel St, Preston, Clifford lives here with wife Dorothy and daughters Judith 6, Susan 4 and Deborah 1, Clifford works in sales at Kralinator

Age 35 — Death
27 Feb 1957 • Windsor, Essex, Ontario, Canada
Automobile accident, funeral at St Paul's United Church and interment at Park Lawn Cemetery, Preston.

Obituary for Clifford L HINTON
1 Mar 1957 • Kingston, Ontario, Canada

Clifford Ley Herbert Hinton
1 Mar 1957 • Kingston, Ontario, Canada
Notice on March 1 in the Kingston paper for Clifford's funeral at St Paul's United Church on Saturday March 2, 1957

Dodie and Cliff Hinton's daughter Judy with husband Joe and their offspring.

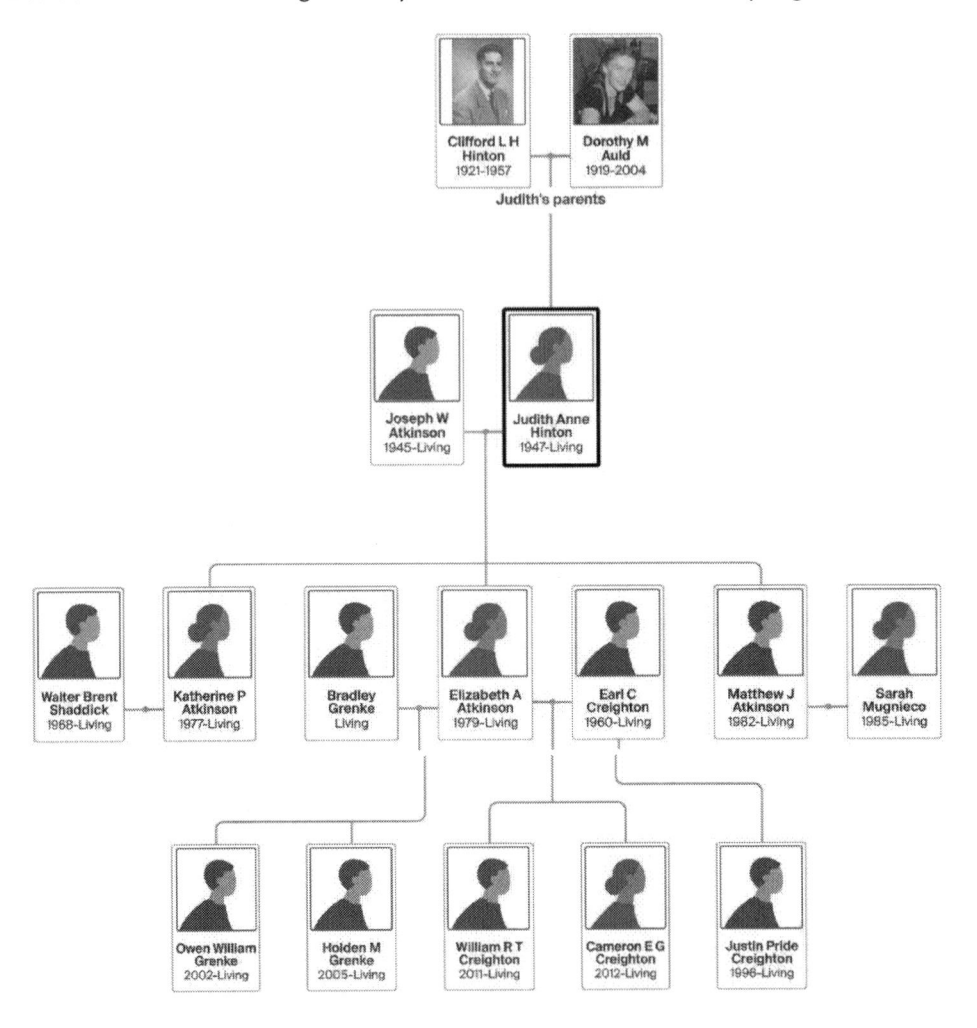

Clifford L H Hinton 1921-1957 — **Dorothy M Auld** 1919-2004
Judith's parents

Joseph W Atkinson 1945-Living — **Judith Anne Hinton** 1947-Living

- **Walter Brent Shaddick** 1968-Living
- **Katherine P Atkinson** 1977-Living
- **Bradley Grenke** Living
- **Elizabeth A Atkinson** 1979-Living
- **Earl C Creighton** 1960-Living
- **Matthew J Atkinson** 1982-Living
- **Sarah Mugnieco** 1985-Living

- **Owen William Grenke** 2002-Living
- **Holden M Grenke** 2005-Living
- **William R T Creighton** 2011-Living
- **Cameron E G Creighton** 2012-Living
- **Justin Pride Creighton** 1996-Living

Brent and Kate's daughter and 2 sons

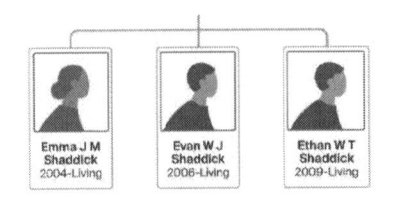

- **Emma J M Shaddick** 2004-Living
- **Evan W J Shaddick** 2006-Living
- **Ethan W T Shaddick** 2009-Living

Sarah and Matt's 2 daughters

- **Isabelle H Atkinson** 2012-Living
- **Alyssa M Atkinson** 2015-Living

Dodie and Cliff Hinton's daughter Susan with husband Scott and their offspring.

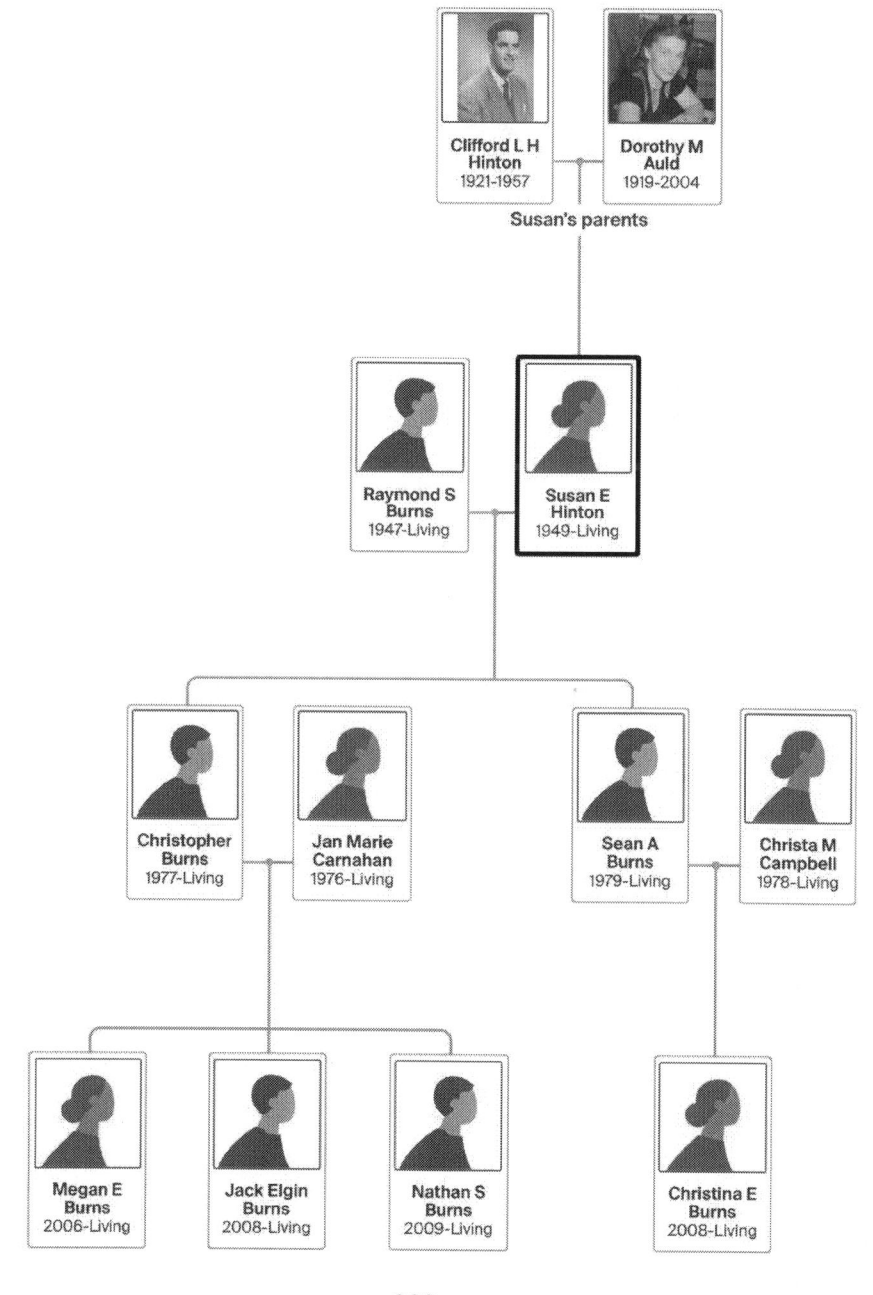

Clifford L H Hinton
1921-1957

Dorothy M Auld
1919-2004

Susan's parents

Raymond S Burns
1947-Living

Susan E Hinton
1949-Living

Christopher Burns
1977-Living

Jan Marie Carnahan
1976-Living

Sean A Burns
1979-Living

Christa M Campbell
1978-Living

Megan E Burns
2006-Living

Jack Elgin Burns
2008-Living

Nathan S Burns
2009-Living

Christina E Burns
2008-Living

Dodie and Cliff Hinton's daughter Deborah with first husband Cliff and their offspring. Deborah's second husband Bruce became her offspring's father and grandfather.

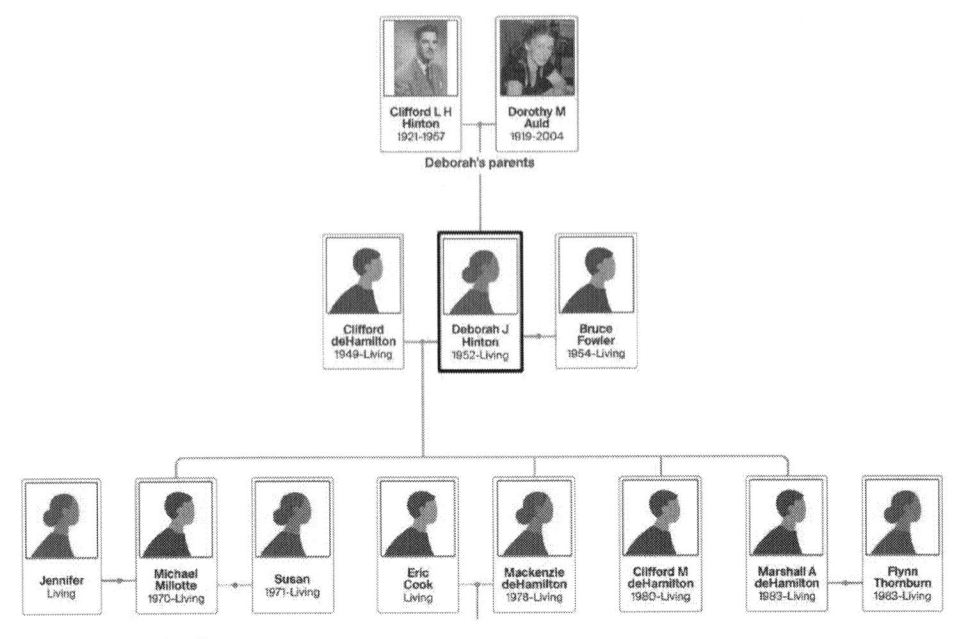

Deborah's parents

- Clifford L H Hinton (1921-1957)
- Dorothy M Auld (1919-2004)

Children:
- Clifford deHamilton (1949-Living)
- Deborah J Hinton (1952-Living)
- Bruce Fowler (1954-Living)

Grandchildren:
- Jennifer (Living)
- Michael Millotte (1970-Living)
- Susan (1971-Living)
- Eric Cook (Living)
- Mackenzie deHamilton (1978-Living)
- Clifford M deHamilton (1980-Living)
- Marshall A deHamilton (1983-Living)
- Flynn Thornburn (1983-Living)

Jennifer and Michael's son
- Jonathan Millotte (2016-Living)

Susan and Michael's 3 daughters
- Jazmin Millotte (2003-Living)
- Cameron Millotte (2005-Living)
- Brooke Millotte (2008-Living)

Eric and Mackenzie's 2 sons
- Mason Cook (2007-Living)
- Reed Cook (2010-Living)

Manufactured by Amazon.ca
Bolton, ON

35383677R00168